Engaging Imagination and Developing Creativity in Education

Engaging Imagination and Developing Creativity in Education

Edited by

Kieran Egan and Krystina Madej

Engaging Imagination and Developing Creativity in Education,
Edited by Kieran Egan and Krystina Madej

This book first published 2010

Cambridge Scholars Publishing

12 Back Chapman Street, Newcastle upon Tyne, NE6 2XX, UK

British Library Cataloguing in Publication Data
A catalogue record for this book is available from the British Library

ISBN (10): 1-4438-1763-5, ISBN (13): 978-1-4438-1763-9

CONTENTS

PREFACE

KIERAN EGAN

This series of essays has been collected expressly to showcase new ideas about stimulating and developing imagination and creativity in education. Clearly, many teachers already energetically engage students' imaginations and foster fascinating creative work, and there are many good programs available to teachers that can help them become more adept at attaining these desirable goals of education. But all surveys of schooling suggest that the average classroom is not in general wonderfully successful when it comes to stimulating imaginations and sparking creativity in children. Also one of the problems with many programs currently available to help achieve these aims is that they tend to see their role in either stand-alone activities or via arts subjects. What we want to emphasize through this book is that engaging imaginations and stimulating creativity is something that is properly done across the curriculum, in science and math no less than in history or language learning or the arts.

So a distinctive feature of our book and of the research group with which much of this work is connected is dedicated to showing how teachers may routinely engage students' imaginations in learning that alternate interior angles in a parallelogram are congruent or about the life cycle of eels or the way place value works in arithmetic or the industrial revolution or anything else. The Imaginative Education Research Group (www.ierg.net) is centred at Simon Fraser University in Canada, but it also has many affiliates around the world. The articles in this book aim to expose aspects of the IERG's work, and also extensions of it. We also want to provide understanding of the basic theory of imagination and creativity and their roles in learning and life. And we want to explore the many other arenas of learning in addition to the regular school classroom in which the imagination can enliven and stimulate both the work of the learner and of the teacher.

There is something about the normal conditions of public educational institutions that makes engaging imaginations seem a desirable frill, but a frill that can be attended to only after the hard work of controlling and directing the learning of twenty-five or more children. So, even though desirable, the difficulties of the primary tasks of control and basic instruction tend to leave little time for the imagination. What we are intent on showing is that engaging the imagination is not something to be attended to after the hard work of learning is completed, but is rather something that can make the tasks of control and basic instruction more stimulating to teacher and students. The imagination, we propose, is properly seen as one the great workhorses of learning, and a central workhorse at that, not a peripheral frill. The readings in this book are designed to expose various dimensions of this perspective on the uses of the imagination in teaching and learning and on stimulating creativity in students' own work.

Many of the most important issues that we deal with in education are matters of value and meaning, and these are areas where the dominant forms of educational research are powerless to help us. The value of engaging the imagination in learning is not something that has been enlightened by empirical research, and there is always a tendency to focus attention on those things we find easier to research. This is the phenomenon of looking on the sidewalk under the bright lamppost for the keys that were actually lost in the deep grass out of the light. But imagination and creativity are crucially important elements in education, and to continue to give them less attention that they merit is to persist in the folly of futile searching for keys under the lamppost. Through their work, the educators and researchers in this book provide a light that is directed at where we have misplaced some of the important keys to effective education.

In the first part of this book, authors explore and discuss different theories of development, imagination, and creativity. In the second part authors negotiate ideas concerning imagination and apply them to both broader social issues such as responsible citizenship and gender, and to a wide array of curriculum subjects, from the arts and literacy to mathematics.

Krystina Madej and I would like to thank all of the authors for their imaginative approaches and for allowing us to use their work, Stacey Makortoff for her organization skills, and Melanie Young and Peter Kovacs for their assistance with editing.

PART I

IMAGINATION AND CREATIVITY:
THEORIES AND DISCUSSIONS

THE TIES THAT BIND:
HOW IMAGINATION GRASPS THE WORLD

MARK FETTES

The Tools of Imagination

In a series of books beginning with *Educational Development* (1979), the Canadian educational philosopher Kieran Egan has argued that the modern individual imagination retraces, in its unfolding from birth to adulthood, a series of transformations rooted in the cultural history of our civilization (see especially Egan, 1988; 1990; 1997). The driving force behind this process, according to Egan, is the progressive acquisition of culturally embedded strategies of imaginative engagement with the world around us. Egan calls these cultural strategies "tools," following the Russian psychologist Vygotsky (Egan, 1997; Vygotsky, 1986). For both Vygotsky and Egan, such tools (for example, particular ways of using language) are first encountered in social use and gradually integrated into individual patterns of awareness and thought.

However, Egan's notion of "cognitive tools" only partially overlaps with the Vygotskian notion of "psychological tools." With his Marxist training, Vygotsky incorporated a firmly materialist conception of culture into his theory; a psychological tool for him was something particular and concrete – a gesture, a word, a drawing, a model, and so on. Egan uses the word to mean something much broader and more abstract: "binary opposites," "association with heroes," and "the search for general schemes" are among the key imaginative strategies he labels "cognitive tools" (e.g. in Egan, 2005). Egan's rationale for picking out these particular themes only makes sense in the context of his general thesis that the imagination develops through five "somewhat distinct" kinds of understanding, each characterized by particular sets of tools, or "toolkits" (1997; 2005). Throughout his work, Egan describes each "toolkit" on its own terms–the imaginative toolkit of oral language/Mythic understanding, for instance, being elaborated separately from that of written language/Romantic understanding, and separately again from the toolkit of disciplined abstract thought/Philosophic understanding.

In this brief essay I explore the notion that the imagination, as Egan describes it, may also usefully be viewed in terms of somewhat distinct "foundational capacities" which remain constant *across* kinds of understanding. The purpose of these capacities, their evolutionary function, is to help us "grasp" hidden forms of order and unrealized possibilities in the world. (This ancient metaphor of "grasping", which Brann, 1991, attributes to the Greek philosopher Zeno, still seems one of the best terms for alluding to what Egan calls the "reaching out" quality of imaginative thinking.) Foundational imaginative capacities, in this view, have developed in response to the most persistent and significant challenges of this kind faced by humans, and our cultures have learned to train and shape these capacities through a diverse range of language and behaviour.

One straightforward example would be an imaginative capacity for "grasping regularity"–that is, the ability to perceive new forms of order in the world, and indeed to impose them on a sometimes recalcitrant reality. Of course, probably all organisms need to be able to identify recurring or stable aspects of their environment, so imagination cannot be the only means of accomplishing this. But what imagination is supremely well suited for is coping with the unexpected, the rapidly changing, the unfamiliar. It is therefore plausible that, as the human imagination developed, it did so in part by inventing and assimilating cultural tools for quickly identifying regular patterns in new and unfamiliar settings. This means that, even today, we might expect to see the imagination drawn to pick up and use such tools–that this foundational capacity might be reflected in the "cognitive tools" identified by Egan in his various kinds of understanding.

What might be other candidates for foundational imaginative capacities? Although any categorization must probably be somewhat arbitrary, here I will focus on eight capacities that together seem to cover most of the tools identified by Egan (plus a few more). These include *grasping regularity*, as already outlined, and the following: *grasping detail*, that is, holding in one's imagination the individual richness of particular cases, situations, events, that makes them unique; *grasping composition*, or developing a sense of the invisible relationships that bind such details together into a greater whole; *grasping wholes* themselves, apprehending them as coherent entities with an identity sustained through time and space; *grasping possibility*, or developing an understanding of how such wholes may vary and change; *grasping struggle*, that is, gaining a sense of what drives and what hinders change, and how this plays itself out in myriad variations; *grasping indices* that help identify and characterize the possible limits of variation, change and struggle; and *grasping inconsistency*, or an appreciation for the ways in which the world does not always act as we imagine it will.

This is, of course, an abstract and perhaps overly cognitive way of putting things. It does not go into the emotional connections that seem so important to imagination and are properly emphasized by Egan; it leaves unexplored its aesthetic and expressive dimensions. But it does help us to see the imagination as an extension of fundamental adaptive capacities not unique to humans, and thereby to tie it more firmly to our embodied, biological, ecological identity. More immediately, it points to a way of thinking about imaginative development that is compatible with Egan's scheme, but that enriches it with new insights and possibilities.

The principal implication to be explored in this paper is that Egan's "cognitive tools" can be associated with one another not only "horizontally" (that is, within a particular kind of understanding), but also "vertically" (that is, in connection with a particular foundational imaginative capacity). This provides a useful way of probing Egan's description of each kind of understanding, asking whether each "toolkit" is truly comprehensive in the sense that it accounts for how these diverse functions of the imagination take up the affordances of oral, written or disciplinary language. (I follow Egan's recent practice, e.g. in Egan 2005, of focusing on the tools of Mythic, Romantic, and Philosophic understanding, leaving Somatic and Ironic understanding for exploration elsewhere.) In place of the catch-all term "cognitive tools," we might call these vertically linked cultural strategies "tools of imaginative engagement," or TIEs–a term that usefully echoes their contribution to "tying" together Egan's kinds of understanding.

In the space available, it is only possible to sketch what each set of TIEs may look like, without exploring the different cultural forms they may take or how they might be used in educational practice. Yet even this cursory introduction may suggest how Egan's theory may be linked to a variety of other efforts to understand and develop "imaginative education" (e.g. Blenkinsop, 2009; Jones et al., 2008; Leonard and Willis, 2008).

The TIEs of Substance

Of the eight imaginative capacities listed earlier, three might be thought of as grasping the substantive, stable nature of the world, its "thingness," three as grasping its emergent, shifting nature, its "becomingness," and two as spanning the divide. Rough as it is, this division offers a useful way of organizing the following exploration.

We might see an imaginative capacity for *grasping regularity* in what Egan describes as "the passionate drive to complete a set or to enlarge and organize, or constantly reorganize, a collection" (1997, 87)–a familiar passion in modern Western culture, and one that Egan situates firmly in the context of Romantic understanding. As he argues, collecting and organizing fits with other features of Romantic understanding–that is, horizontally, as part of the Romantic toolkit that develops as the imagination takes up the tools of popular literacy. The question that concerns us here is whether related drives exist in Mythic and Philosophic understanding, and the kinds of cultural tools or strategies they employ. Egan himself emphasizes the tensions between different kinds of understanding–their tendency to compete for imaginative space–and so we would expect these strategies, or TIEs, to be somewhat at odds with one another as well.

Thus, when Egan notes that "the Philosophic mind focuses on the connections between things, constructing theories, laws, ideologies, and metaphysical schemes to tie together the facts available to the student" (1997, 121), we may see this as a Philosophic TIE of systematization and generalization, linked vertically to the Romantic TIE of collecting and organizing. That is, both categories of activity respond to the same existential imperative, the urge to imaginatively grasp the regular, orderly nature of the world; yet they deploy different tools to that end, and thereby alter the end itself. As Egan observes, "When Philosophic understanding dominates the mind...Romantic knowledge...is often dismissed as irrelevant, pointless, a trivial pursuit. Romantic hobbies and collections lose their interest" (1997, 125). It is thus no easy matter to keep both sets of tools alive and well.

When we turn to Mythic understanding, however, we find nothing in Egan's description of this kind of understanding that stands out as an obvious counterpart to the Romantic passion for collecting, or the systematizing zeal of the Philosophic imagination. We must therefore ask ourselves what "grasping regularity" may look like when confined to the tools of oral language. Any imaginative strategy of this kind should still find echoes in our contemporary culture, which has not entirely abandoned its Mythic roots, as well as in the cultures of non-literate peoples. Some reflection suggests the activity of naming as a plausible candidate. One does not need familiarity with the story of Rumpelstiltskin to be aware of the power that names traditionally have in oral cultures. We still see echoes of this even in the most Philosophic realms, as when new and obscure species of plant or insect, or new comets or asteroids, are named after their discoverer. We might thus tentatively identify "naming and characterization" as a Mythic TIE for grasping regularity–enriching our picture of Mythic understanding in the process.

This produces our first set of three vertically linked TIEs. Proceeding further, we come to the capacity for *grasping detail*. At the Mythic level, this is clearly related to Egan's discussion of images in *The Educated Mind* (1997, 60-62): that is, the use of oral language to evoke vivid, affectively engaging mental images (not only visual, but aural, olfactory, and so on) is a distinctive kind of tool for imaginative development, one deployed in different ways by different cultures. As Egan argues, it is a tool of great educational power, albeit rarely used:

> When teaching about the earthworm, for instance, the instructor can augment the facts about its senses and structure by evoking for students images of what it would be like to slither and push through the soil, hesitantly exploring in one direction then another, looking for easier passages, contracting and expanding our sequence of muscles segment by segment, and sensing moisture, scents, grubs, or whatever...[I]t is not so much a matter of seeing the earthworm in terms of our senses as performing the imaginative act of recognizing earthwormness in ourselves. (1997, 61)

In the subsequent chapter on Romantic understanding, however, one looks in vain for a tool that might build on this capacity for holding vivid details in the mind. This is odd, in a way, because Egan emphasizes the "search for reality" that characterizes the Romantic imagination, as seen for instance in the need to provide a detailed life history of Superman in order to account for his extraordinary powers. In other Romantic tools, too, such as the urge to build and organize collections of things, one can see this same passion for detail: detail sought not merely to vividly evoke, but to identify unambiguously, to "pin down" in some mental map of the world. So let us remedy this omission by identifying "precise characterization" as a Romantic TIE– a means of grasping detail that calls on the resources of literate culture. To pick up on Egan's example: understanding earthworms using this TIE would adduce such details as the weight of castings produced by a single worm (up to ten pounds a year), the density of earthworms in arable soil (from about sixty up to several hundred per square metre), the value of the Canadian earthworm market ($10-20 million a year), and so on.

Regarded Philosophically, however, the Romantic grasp of reality is too focused on idiosyncratic particulars, too unsystematic, and hence constantly tending towards the trivial. The way the Philosophic imagination grasps details is by developing and applying standard descriptive criteria to case after case. In the "Earthworms" Wikipedia, for instance, one can read:

> Earthworms are also called megadriles (or big worms), as opposed to the microdriles (or small worms) in the families Tubificidae, Lumbriculidae, and Enchytraeidae, among others. The megadriles are characterized by having a multilayered clitellum (which is much more obvious than the single-layered one of the microdriles), a vascular system with true capillaries, and male pores behind the female pores. (accessed Jan. 23, 2009)

For most of us, who do not even have a particularly developed Romantic understanding of earthworms, this way of understanding them is not immediately accessible. But we can accept the importance of grasping detail to the Philosophic mind, and postulate a corresponding TIE that we might call "fine-grained analysis." Again, this is not a tool to be found in Egan's discussion of Philosophic understanding, which lays heavy emphasis on the role of theoretical generalization. Yet analytical detail provides depth and colour for theories in much the same way as images provide depth and colour for Mythic stories. Further, as we would expect, training in such analysis is a fundamental part of a good Philosophic (that is, disciplinary) education–though the means to this end are not always as imaginative as one might wish!

The next in the list is *grasping composition*, understood as a sense of the invisible relationships that bind many details together into a greater whole. This is clearly an aspect of the imagination that plays a vital role in music, literature, and the other arts. In Egan's account of Mythic understanding, we might see it implied by his discussion of rhyme, rhythm and narrative:

> Sacred stories were…recited to the tapping of a drum or strumming of a stringed instrument. Patterning sound helped to embed the tales in the mind of the hearers…. The larger trick is attaching the rhythms inherent in languages to the more general, peripatetic pattern of everyday life–hope and despair, fear and relief, oppression, resentment, and revolt, youth and age, the rising emotions of comedy and the pity and fear of tragedy, and so on. The elaboration of linguistic rhythms to match the patterns of our lives results in those larger forms we call narratives. (1997, 58-59)

There will be more to say about narrative towards the end of this chapter, but let us focus our present attention on the similarities between rhythm and pattern. Both refer to the way that elements of something hang or fit together. So we might focus our search for Romantic and Philosophic

TIEs for "grasping composition" on patterns of form and meaning that lend analogous coherence, beauty, and memorability to written or theoretical utterances. At the Romantic level, this TIE might involve both the appearance of text itself, as expressed, for instance, in the care lavished on medieval manuscripts, modern font design, and the art of calligraphy, along with the *deployment* of text to communicate meaning through form, as in concrete poetry, the art of sign making, and the huge range of devices used to represent information in visual form. At the Philosophic level, the corresponding TIE would involve patterns in how ideas and concepts are deployed to form greater wholes, which we might call arguments. In other words, grasping composition in Mythic understanding works primarily through the ear, in Romantic through the eye, and in Philosophic through what the Greeks called logic and rhetoric–the aesthetic shaping of language to reason and persuade.

What are we to call this series of TIEs? In more recent works, Egan refers to "the literate eye" as a tool of Romantic understanding (Egan, 2005). We might therefore call its Mythic equivalent "the prosodic ear" and its Philosophic counterpart "the noetic composer"–each a kind of metaphor for a range of related tools. There are, of course, forms of pattern recognition that fall outside this series of TIEs, which is specifically linked to Egan's emphasis on the role of language in imaginative development. Nonetheless, these ways of "grasping composition" seem deeply important for the development of imaginative understanding, challenging the tendency for the mind to become enmeshed in ever-turning treadmills of words and ideas.

Perhaps it is time to pause and take stock. We have identified the three sets of "tools of imaginative engagement" summarized in Table 1. In reality, of course, each TIE is not comprised of a single cultural tool but a whole set of tools or strategies for engaging imaginatively with the world. Presumably an important feature of imaginative education would be to expose learners to a wide variety of such strategies, some of which might be more engaging than others. The judgment of the teacher therefore remains central to the use of the TIEs: what is being elaborated here is not a single method but a palette of options.

Table 1. The TIEs of Substance

Tools for:	Mythic TIEs	Romantic TIEs	Philosophic TIEs
Grasping composition	The prosodic ear (rhyme, rhythm, and the music of spoken language)	The literate eye (design and display of text and visual information)	The noetic composer (organization of ideas and observations into greater wholes)
Grasping detail	Vivid imagery (not only visual, but involving all the senses)	Precise characterization (in ways that enhance a sense of objective reality)	Fine-grained analysis (in ways that make underlying forms of order more apparent)
Grasping regularity	Naming and characterizing	Collecting and organizing	Systematizing and generalizing

The TIEs of Process

If the emphasis in the first group of TIEs was on grasping the coherence and stability of the world, the emphasis in the second group is on change, variation, and unpredictability.

Let us begin with tools for *grasping possibility*, or developing an imaginative understanding of how particular features of the world may vary and change. We might see this as the domain of imaginative play, in particular–that is, play often seems to involve an exploration of possibilities, of "what ifs." So at the Mythic level we would look for the ways oral language is imaginatively used in play, and as teachers we would seek to establish settings for such play that would encourage the children to explore particular kinds of possibility. This is routinely done in many preschools and kindergartens, but as so often with the tools of Mythic understanding, the opportunities for play *related to the imaginative exploration of subject matter* seem to dwindle rapidly in regular classrooms. Games that involve making up stories, taking on roles, and generally engaging with each other in open-ended, emotionally meaningful ways, open the door to an expanded sense of what the world may hold.

A rather different kind of play appeals to the Romantic imagination. This is the kind of understanding that relishes formal games of all kinds: board and card games, strategy and chance games, solitaire and multiplayer games, and so on, along with dramatic and physical games constrained by formal rules. It is also a kind of understanding that builds elaborate virtual fantasy worlds governed by their own laws, traditions, and languages. Occasionally some small uses of this TIE may trickle into classrooms, as when students are asked to display their knowledge of a topic by designing a board game. Yet if one compares this to the fascination of many students with sophisticated online games, or even with trading card games such as *Magic*, it's clear that schools' uses of this tool are marginal by comparison.

How, then, does the Philosophic imagination explore possibility? One thinks immediately of Einstein and his famous "thought experiments" such as the one in which he imagines himself riding on a beam of light and asking himself how he might perceive the passage of time. But one might also think of how scientists sometimes expand the boundaries of knowledge through unorthodox real experiments, of how theoreticians in all fields benefit from tossing "blue-sky" ideas around, and how companies like Google encourage their employees to spend some of their time working on off-the-wall ideas. We might think of all these as instances of a single Philosophic TIE, summed up as hypothesis, experiment, and playing around with ideas.

Yet one cannot adequately grasp possibility without a sense of the forces that constrain variation and hinder change. A somewhat unsatisfactory term for this imaginative capacity is *grasping struggle*– understanding the world as formed through the interaction of opposing forces. Again, in the tradition inherited from the Greeks, we have the term "dialectics" to express one Philosophic version of this mode of thought, but the Philosophic TIE is broader, encompassing the struggle between contradiction, paradox, and the unruliness of data, on the one hand, and the quest for proof, consistency, and elegance on the other. T.H. Huxley summed up this TIE admirably when he referred to the "great tragedy of science: the slaying of a beautiful hypothesis by an ugly fact." The starkness of the metaphor aptly captures the importance of this sense of tension in the Philosophic imagination.

Where the Philosophic TIE helps the imagination grasp struggle as a conflict between opposing ideas, the Romantic TIE develops an understanding of struggle as a conflict between human agents (or human-like agency projected onto other aspects of the world). Egan draws attention to the increasing importance of revolt and idealism to children developing Romantic understanding: that is, they are increasingly drawn to stories that explain the development of ideas, technology, and so on as a rebellion against the constraints of tradition and authority. This is one aspect of a broader source of imaginative engagement in the struggle of opposing forces, often (though not necessarily) with one side seen as the hero, the other as the villain.

At the Mythic level, as always, the struggle is more abstract. Egan draws attention to the imaginative importance of binary opposites: "The most evident structural feature of children's stories or self-generated narratives is that the surface content very commonly rests on such underlying binary sets as security/fear, good/bad, brave/cowardly, love/hate, happy/sad, poor/rich, health/sickness, permitted/forbidden" (p. 40). As he points out, teaching history through such opposites would make it immediately meaningful to children, even if many of the ways in which adults understand history were not developed until later. What will Romantically be taken up as stories of heroic rebels and villainous rulers, or Philosophically as struggles of opposing ideologies and historical forces, begins Mythically as the conflict between weakness and strength, fairness and unfairness, good and evil.

This binary structuring plays a second and equally important role at the Mythic level, in terms of *grasping indices*–a term that refers to the way the imagination picks out exemplary cases to represent potentially unlimited variability. As Egan observes, "Organizing one's conceptual grasp on the physical world by initially forming binary structures–hot/cold, big/little, soft/hard, crooked/straight, sweet/sour–allows an initial orientation over a range of otherwise bewilderingly complex phenomena" (1997, 40). What is not emphasized here, however, is the extent to which each of these extremes is associated with particular experiences or images–the scalding tap/the freezing ice cube, the towering elephant/the miniature mouse, and so on. These become the imaginative indices against which new experiences and new information can be measured and seen in proportion.

An equivalent TIE is to be found in the Romantic fascination with the extremes and limits of reality, and particularly of human experience. Here is Egan again:

> By discovering the real limits of the world and of human experience, we form a context that enables us to establish some security and to establish proportionate meaning within it. Knowing about the biggest and smallest people allows us, on the one hand, to wonder at their extreme sizes, but, on the other, to be reassured about our own scale. Once we have some sense of context, we can begin to develop some sense of the proportionate meaning of things. (p. 85)

The imaginative strategy, in short, is the same as for the Mythic TIE; what has changed is the kind of understanding and the cultural tools it has available.

Evidently the Philosophic imagination faces an analogous challenge. For every general scheme it comes up with, there will be limits to its explanatory power; there will be anomalies to note, special cases to explain, and neighboring areas of knowledge to which it does not apply. Here, too, the Philosophic imagination grapples with this by focusing on canonical or paradigmatic examples–cases that perfectly illustrate the general scheme in action. Once these ideal cases are established, they can be used as a measure for the "fit" of other cases to the theory, perhaps leading to the identification of particularly problematic cases that establish the limits of the general scheme. The same binary structuring is at work here as well, establishing a continuum of explanation between valid and invalid, relevant and irrelevant, true and false. Table 2 summarizes the three sets of TIEs reviewed in this section.

Table 2. The TIEs of Process

Tools for:	Mythic TIEs	Romantic TIEs	Philosophic TIEs
Grasping possibility	Role-playing, invention of stories, and other forms of social play	Rule-defined games of all kinds, and the building of fantasy worlds	Hypothesis, experiment, and playing around with ideas
Grasping struggle	Tension and conflict between opposing binary qualities or concepts	Transgression, revolt, and conflict based on human values and beliefs	Contradiction, paradox, and the unruliness of data versus proof, consistency, and
Grasping limits	Binary contrasts and mediating concepts	Extremes and limits of reality	Paradigmatic cases, anomalies, and the limits of general schemes

The Integrative TIEs

The diverse TIEs reviewed so far are all means of getting an imaginative handle on the complexity of the world–on the ways in which it eludes direct and simple comprehension. Even so, they do not do away with our need to understand things as in some sense complete in themselves, even if we have no way of knowing everything that entails. This human capacity for *grasping wholes* is vitally important–so important that an entire branch of psychology, Gestalt psychology, was developed to try and understand it. But our purpose here is more modest: we simply want to know whether particular cultural tools or strategies exist to help us do this.

Egan, quoting evolutionary psychologist Merlin Donald, suggests that myth itself is one such tool–"the fundamental integrative mind tool" (1997, 35; citing Donald, 1991, 214-15). That is, particular kinds of narratives, structured upon the tensions and contrasts that most fundamentally shape human existence, enable us to hold together in our imaginations the vast range of elements in a complex reality. In particular, mythic narratives are capable of incorporating all of the Mythic TIEs we have considered so far: naming and characterizing, vivid imagery, the prosodic ear, and so on. One might even say that these imaginative components *define* mythic narratives, setting them apart from other kinds of stories or accounts. In this case, however, we might want to extend this category to include other oral genres such as songs, chants, and oratory that incorporate imaginative tools to a similar extent. A similar emphasis on the importance of speech genres for grasping wholes can be found in Bakhtin (1986).

We might therefore look for specific genres associated with Romantic and Philosophic understanding that offer analogous imaginative possibilities. In the case of the former, for instance, we might look for written genres that incorporate the TIEs of collecting and organizing, precise description, the literate eye, and so on, and that communicate a deeper message about the possibilities and limits of human agency. A quintessentially Romantic work of this kind is the Guinness Book of World Records, but so too are tales of real-life adventures, heroic biographies, historical triumphs and disasters, romances, mysteries, and family sagas, soap operas, gossip magazines, and a host of other genres. The wealth of possibilities in this area undoubtedly reflects the dominance of Romantic understanding in our culture, which has done much to eclipse the Mythic and has never awarded the Philosophic more than a marginal place.

It is scarcely surprising, therefore, that the range of imaginatively engaging Philosophic genres is underdeveloped in comparison to Romantic understanding. Theoretical statements and expositions, systematic taxonomies and methodologies, specialized monographs and case studies all certainly qualify, as perhaps do certain kinds of poetry, plays and novels in which a central purpose of the author is to work out the consequences of a general scheme or guiding principle. Such works can become definitive statements of a particular imaginative take on the world, to be pored over by scholars for decades, centuries or millennia. And it is surely their integrative quality above all, their ability to hold many elements in some kind of coherent relationship, that endows them with this timeless appeal.

Yet all kinds of understanding are flawed. The world does not always act as we imagine it will. Thinking back to the emergence of imagination in our early human ancestors, we can suppose the failures to have been more frequent than the successes–for every productive leap into the realm of possibility, there must be a multitude of fiascos. So it does not seem altogether surprising that we developed imaginative means of *grasping inconsistency*–of accommodating ourselves to the risks that imagination poses, indeed embracing them. When the imagination trips and falls on its face, we laugh.

Egan draws attention to the importance of humour in the context of Mythic understanding; he is particularly taken with its role in developing a reflexive awareness of language, through the use of puns and other forms of word play. We might expand this TIE to include all kinds of quirks in the tools of Mythic understanding: the incongruous image, the inappropriate name, the story that reverses expectations, and so on. The enjoyment that accompanies these violations of convention is surely one of the greatest spurs to the Mythic imagination, a reminder that invention and possibility are unlimited. And just as Egan proposes (1997, 65), we can extend this insight to subsequent kinds of understanding.

The inconsistencies that engage the Romantic imagination are of a more elaborate kind, just like the stories that develop this kind of understanding. The one-liner gives way to the humorous anecdote; the incongruous detail becomes the incongruous situation; jokes develop into comedy. To the Romantic mind, Mythic humour tends to be overly simplistic, too obvious and immediate to be really funny. The best humour comes from the gradual accumulation of inconsistencies, drawing the protagonists through inexorable logic into situations of greater and greater absurdity. Examples of Romantic humour abound in popular culture, of course, but they are almost wholly exiled from schools, where any uses of humour tend to be of the Mythic kind. One wonders about the consequences for the development of subsequent understandings.

Indeed, humour is not a trait most of us associate with the Philosophic imagination. Incisively serious at best, drearily ponderous at worst, Philosophic understanding does not come across as tolerant or appreciative of inconsistency. Yet the satirical writings of Swift, for example, or Pope, or Voltaire, display unambiguously Philosophic imaginations grappling with the hypocrisies and illusions of Enlightenment rationalism. Perhaps there is a tradition there that has become marginalized in the subsequent two centuries, and that needs reviving in the context of a holistic approach to imaginative development–a possibility that seems in keeping with Egan's championing of irony on other grounds (1997).

Table 3. The Integrative TIEs

Tools for:	Mythic TIEs	Romantic TIEs	Philosophic TIEs
Grasping wholes	Oral genres focused on fundamental tensions in human existence, including fables, myths, songs and chants, oratory	Written genres focused on human agency and the diversity of experience (too many to list)	Conceptual genres focused on general schemes, including theoretical statements, arguments and expositions, taxonomies and methodologies
Grasping inconsistency	Jokes, puns, and incongruities	Humorous stories and situational comedy	Irony and satire

With these two final sets of TIEs, summarized in Table 3, this preliminary theoretical reworking of Egan's notion of "cognitive tools" has come to an end. In no way exhaustive or definitive, it has nonetheless yielded a more extensive list of tools in each kind of understanding, along with an enhanced developmental sense of how each kind of understanding both builds on and competes with prior kinds. As a theoretical approach, it seems productive enough to warrant further exploration.

An important caveat about the scheme presented here, nonetheless, is that it is too neat. There is no particular reason for thinking that our imaginative grasp on the world can be corralled and explained so easily. The present exploration is only one sketch of the terrain. Other kinds of maps are surely needed.

Bibliography

Bakhtin, M. M. (1986). *Speech Genres and Other Late Essays*. (V. W. McGee, Trans.). Caryl Emerson and Michael Holquist (Eds.) Houston: University of Texas Press.

Blenkinsop, S. (2009). *The Imagination in Education: Extending the Boundaries in Theory and Practice*. Cambridge, UK: Cambridge Scholars Press.

Brann, E. T. H. (1991). *The World of the Imagination: Sum and Substance*. Savage MD: Rowman & Littlefield.

Egan, K. (2005). *An Imaginative Approach to Teaching.* San Francisco: Jossey-Bass.

—. (1997). *The Educated Mind: How Cognitive Tools Shape Our Understanding.* Chicago: University of Chicago Press.

—. (1990). *Romantic Understanding: The Development of Rationality and Imagination, Ages 8–15.* London: Routledge.

—. (1988). *Primary Understanding: Education in Early Childhood.* London: Routledge.

—. (1979). *Educational Development.* Oxford: Oxford University Press.

Jones, R. A., Clarkson, A., Congram, S. & Stratton, N. (2008). *Education and Imagination: Post-Jungian Perspectives.* London: Routledge.

Leonard, T., and Willis, P. (Eds.). (2008). *Pedagogies of the Imagination: Mythopoetic Curriculum in Educational Practice.* Berlin: Springer.

Vygotsky, L. (1986). *Thought and Language.* (A. Kozulin, Trans.). Cambridge, MA: MIT Press.

DIALECTIC EXPLICATION OF CREATIVITY

GADI ALEXANDER AND YAKIR SHOSHANI

Efforts to define and measure creativity by qualifying it with analytical and logical conditions have not proved to be very useful. In this paper we attempt to use a different method to crack the code of creativity, a method we call: dialectical explication. We see this type of explication as being more appropriate to cover a polysemic and fluid concept that is manifested in many fields and is driven by emotions and motivations and not only by cognitive processes. The first part of this paper reviews and criticizes several traditional approaches to study the nature of creativity, the most prominent being the psychometric and the biographical schools of research. The second part shows how an explanation based on the ability to locate different and even contradictory meanings on a flexible semantic space could help to capture the ill-defined nature of the concept. The paper includes implications of the different efforts to define creativity for the teacher and the educational system.

Introduction

When the words imagination and creativity are mentioned in public they tend to cast a kind of magic on their listeners. Their impression is especially evident when we use them as descriptors of an original and astonishing idea or product. In these instances we can wonder: "how come nobody thought about this great idea before?" or "how did this literary or artistic work manage to excite me so much?" However, while most people are able to distinguish between a creative product and a less original one, and can tell a real creator from a fake one, it seems much harder to agree on what creativity really means. We are even more perplexed when we have to measure the creative ability of certain people or select candidates on the basis of their creative potential.

What can be done to bridge the gap between our intuitive grasp of the term, the so-called folk theories about it, and the need to clarify its various meanings and communicate them to others? This need is especially acute for an educator selecting a working definition that will assist in the engagement of students in creative thinking. In this paper we will attempt to provide a partial solution to this problem, although the versatile and elusive nature of the concept seems to defy efforts to enclose it in one comprehensive definition covering all possible instances. Our efforts to catch creativity by its many horns and bridge the gap between an intuitive and scientific understanding of the concept will be based on a new method that we call *"dialectic explication."* The intricacies of this method and its potential advantages will be explained in the last part of this chapter.

To give the reader a preliminary idea of what we mean by dialectic explication we will say that it is based on the ability to encompass different meanings of a concept by locating them on an imaginary continuum between a number of binary opposites. Our main argument will be that since creativity tends to be a "fluid concept" (Hofstaeder 1993) the dialectic explication could be a possible method to account for that fluidity.

We will argue that as educators, we are asked from time to time to attend to the imagination and creative affordances of our students. Our job is *inter alia* to help them and ourselves, get rid of misconceptions and traditionalized understandings of these concepts. Some of these misconceptions unfortunately derive from efforts to define concepts too narrowly. We are all aware of tests that were designed to measure and capture polysemic meanings and do it by narrowing such meanings into a small number of factors or by using one simple operational definition.

A fair analysis of the traditional treatments of the terms imagination and creativity in psychology will reveal some of their contributions as well. The psychological studies that have been initiated by Guilford in 1950 have improved our ability to identify various types of creative abilities and locate them amongst other human faculties. Nevertheless, when we survey some of these efforts it will be clear that the desire to box such concepts in one concise working definition has widened the gap between lay understandings of such terms which leave many degrees of freedom and the more precise and restricted scholarly representations, particularly those suggested by the scientific community. Consequently, there is a need to redefine the concept and think about it in a fresh way.

Flaws in major trends which explore the nature of creativity

A. The psychometric approach

One course in the research on creativity taken by enthusiastic psychometricians defines the level of creativity on the basis of existing tests or by inventing new kinds of test items. These new tests reflect the frustration of psychologists like Guilford (1950) who felt that conventional IQ tests do not succeed to cover the myriad ways to reflect on things or solve problems. For example, most IQ tests and many of the examinations that we are currently using in schools assume that there is one right solution to every problem. In contrast, most creativity tests encourage the subject to think about as many answers to a given stimulus as one can. The well-known Torrance test (with items such as "list as many unusual uses for a paper clip") is but one popular example of such a test. However, the permission that is granted in these tests to free one's imagination can cause difficulties in grading the answers. Another problem regards the reliability and validity of many of the tests. This means, for example, that the ability to list many original and valuable answers in the test does not necessarily predict a later success to demonstrate creative behavior at work, or engage in creative problem solving in real life situations.

Creativity tests have been used for purposes ranging from the allocation of gifted students for special programs in education to the selection of candidates for demanding and challenging jobs. However, the success of these tests in helping to screen the best candidates is at best questionable. This is despite of the fact that the tasks on the tests require only the most common type of creativity, referred to by some British scholars as little "c" creativity (Craft, Jeffrey & Leibling, 2001). It seems that even this ordinary and more common type of creativity cannot be faithfully captured in a short pencil and paper assignment.

A main contribution of Guilford and the other psychometricians who followed his call to develop creativity test has been mainly in providing us with an assemblage of many measurable factors that are sub-skills of creativity. Among these factors are: the number of products that the subject can generate in a limited time (called fluency or ideation), the uniqueness of the product or response (its originality), the variance between several answers to the same question (flexibility), the ability to attach a different and new function to a familiar object (redefinition), etc. These measures have set the stage for several generations of creativity tests, which were developed by researchers like Torrance, Barron,

Mednick and others for the army, and helped to select creative workers for organizations and business companies.

In education, one can trace two common applications of these tests: allocating gifted students to special programs and evaluating the possible impacts of certain projects or educational practices, especially those labeled as constructivistic or alternative. However, it seems that educators of the gifted are generally more interested in intelligence tests and in convergent thinking than in divergent or creative thinking, and the ability to relate a specific educational treatment to improvements in creative thinking can be very limited.

Without devoting too much space to methodological issues, we can add that in most cases it would be a mistake to base an educational decision on a single score that a student got on a creativity test. The reason for the inability of the test to give an objective assessment of one's creative ability can be demonstrated by the problem of judging the degree of originality in the popular Torrance test. Should the scorer decide if the answer is really original by checking how much the subject's response deviates from a list of previous answers? Or should this be rather decided through inter-judge agreement? Both methods may not be sufficiently satisfactory. It is very easy to demonstrate that statistical rareness cannot be the only measure for one's originality, and agreement between different scorers runs the risk of arbitrariness and subjectivity. There is also the dilemma of what the scorer is supposed to do when a response looks unique but also appears bizarre and irrelevant? A decision to ignore or reject it can be controversial, since a response that seems to be irrelevant in the eyes of one judge may look like a springboard for impressive future elaborations and new discoveries by another.

These questions are of concern to educators as well. A teacher is often running the risk of ignoring a potential contribution of a student on the one hand or the opposite risk of being too quick to praise the originality of a student's response even when there's nothing creative in her thinking, on the other.

B. Learning about creativity from the biographies of great creators

A different school of research studied the lives of great discoverers scientists and artists in order to learn from their best contributions. Researchers like Barron, Simonton, Csikszentmihalyi, and their followers started an immense project of unveiling some of the secrets and processes that enabled these geniuses to come up with new ideas and inventions.

(See Sternberg (1999) for a coverage of some of their findings). The line of research that has been used by these scholars included interviews and documentation of the creative process of Nobel Prize winners and other acknowledged creators who excelled in their field of specialization. This line of research proved to be productive in many ways and managed to highlight crucial qualities of the creative process, at least as it has been experienced and reported by these geniuses. It yielded new concepts describing the nature of the commitment and perseverance that one needs to come up with something new and worthwhile. One of these researchers specified the term "flow" (Csikszentmihalyi 1990) for the energies and commitment that the creator needs to invest in the creative process. Another scholar came to the conclusion that an individual will not be able to succeed in pushing a new idea without the right amount of leadership skills and persuasion abilities that will yield the needed social support and acceptance (Simonton 1999).

Although we can learn a lot about the nature of the creative urge and the skills that are needed to develop an idea, materialize it, and share it with others, this line of study had several negative effects, especially in the eyes of educators who were eager to engage the creative potential of nearly every student and adult. The focus on best practices of an elite group of creators widened the gap between our intuitive concepts of ordinary types of creativity and the less common discoveries of exceptional men and women. From the point of view of the educator, such an elitist view of creativity can have many limitations and runs against the grain of a more democratic view of the potential role of imagination and creativity in everybody's life. It raises the question: how can a student who has not been lucky enough to be equipped with extraordinary talents benefit from the lessons learned from these exceptional creators?

A possible way to bridge the gap between the small creative acts of the regular person and the best practices of the geniuses is by looking at their example as a model that is partly transferable to other people and situations. This also means that the biographical research can help unveil some of the hidden and stated strategies of the big "c" creators that can scaffold specific acts in the classroom. For example, students can learn from these exceptional creators how to be sensitive to new problems, discover discrepancies in the information presented to them, or detect anomalies that are challenging certain familiar rules and conceptions that they have learned in the past.

Some specific work done on geniuses attempted to find common trends in their biographies. Gardner (1993), for example, pointed out similar key experiences in the lives of several great personalities that partly explain their great motivation and urge to think and act in uncommon ways. He has found, while comparing the life stories of several great people like Gandhi, Picasso, and Mozart, for example, that many exceptional contributions and crucial decisions of these creators and reformers followed a traumatic experience in their life. It could be either extreme poverty, presence in a war, or the death of a beloved parent. This does not imply, of course, that we have to wait for unfortunate events to be able to create. It fits, however, our romantic formula of people who are caught in a desperate situation and are sometimes saved by their ingenuity and by their problem solving skills. In the classroom, it may mean that the teacher should be able to present problems that can be conceptualized and worked upon by the students, or that she should be prepared to deal with authentic problems that emerge in the classroom. The effort to encourage students to practice their ingenuity and use their coping strategies can turn a frustrating situation to a challenge and possibly to a success story.

To sum up, biographical studies have enriched our awareness of the many faces of creativity. Without these studies it would be difficult, for instance, to realize the possible relationships between the ideas of the individual creator and the requirements of the domain in which she was making the contribution, be it architecture, physics, or painting. We could also make a mistake in ignoring the socio-cultural context of the contribution and the role of the professional community (the field) in accepting or rejecting it (Csikszentmihalyi 1990). We have also learned that although many of the creators have at first encountered resistance and had to defy misunderstanding and ignorance in their domain their acclaim had to meet the approval of their colleagues and that of experts in the field. Another benefit of the biographical studies stems from our ability to better comprehend the indirect and serendipitous way between a creative process and its unexpected consequences. These highly talented individuals were able to persevere and follow their curiosity and produce astonishing creations that have caused more than once a paradigmatic change in our thinking and provided the fuel to our progress.

However, thinking about the biographical research in a critical way can lead us to the sad conclusion that we are still not able to solve all the problems that are involved in grasping the meaning of creativity and that will guide us to how to start working with and on it in our classroom.

The first problem in relying on the evidence that these studies provide results from the limitations in the method of self-report which many of the researchers had been using. The reconstruction of the creative process from its inception is not always the most valid way to learn how things have originally started. One famous example of the fallacies of self-report is embedded in the famous dream of the German chemist Kekule, who is remembered as the scientist who revealed the structure of the molecule of Benzene. In his dream a snake was eating its own tale. According to this often-quoted story this specific image of the snake inspired his understanding that the structure of the Benzene molecule could not be forming a straight line but should rather be more similar to the ellipse that the snake formed in his dream. The truth about the link between the dream and the invention is evidently a little different. The dream was invented by Kekule to impress listeners in a talk given ten years after his original discovery. It was meant to be a story that would impress the other scientists and counteract the acceptance of a similar discovery made by a French scientist who challenged Kekule's priority (see Rothenberg 1995). This anecdote tells us that the reconstruction of the creative process is not always accurate and much PR and noise can accompany the recollection of the original inception of a discovery.

The second problem which qualifies our ability to gain from these biographical reports is that history never repeats itself in exactly the same manner. It follows that the apple falling on the head of a contemporary Newton would not have resulted with the same insights that it stirred in Newton's times (although the whole story is supposedly a legend). We should not forget that the impact of his discoveries had to do with the scientific context and dominant paradigms of his era and the beliefs that were shared in the scientific community from which he had to free his thoughts. The creative person often challenges the accumulated knowledge in his or her domain and the ideas of experts in the field by introducing new points of view and new paradigms.

Parkhurst tried to perfect a broad definition of creativity by pulling together elements from many previous definitions. This yielded the following comprehensive definition: "Creativity is the ability or the virtue that is presented when we face problems that were not solved in the past, when we offer solutions to problems that others suggested to solve in a different way, or when we develop products that seem (at least in the eyes of their creators) to be new and original" (Parkhurst 1999).

Although this more elaborated definition adds several new attributes to the conundrum, its main drawback is in conflating creativity with problem solving and thus failing to take into account instances in which human creativity could be expressed without having a particular problem in one's mind. In addition, it seems to be less applicable to artistic and non verbal types of creativity.

Several researchers would object to Parkhurst's definition since it fails to emphasize the place of a premeditated intention that precedes most decisions to create something that will be new and different. Another objection can derive from the camp of scholars and historians who believe that creative discoveries often emerge from accidents or blind coincidences. Although the evidence that they are bringing to prove their point may be convincing, accidents are not necessarily the best method to guide educational practice (unless you are Groucho Marx who had a rule of planning on accidents happening). This may be especially true in the current state of education when teachers are expected to be accountable for their students' achievements and when most educational systems aspire to deliver packaged knowledge in the least risky manner. Such an attitude will only rarely allow the door to be opened for chance or for deviations and improvisations fearing that the school will betray its main missions. This means that if we wish to empower others to use their creativity we cannot count on coincidence and miracles and will have to lean on a more pragmatic and controllable view of creativity. And it seems that the next theory that we are going to mention can move us in that direction.

Bereiter's description of a new type of creativity.

There seems to be no need to persuade the readers that people are asked to use more creative ways of thinking in many of their daily assignments. This requirement has turned in the last decades from a luxury to a necessity. We will not list here all the reasons for this historical change. However many scholars and economists have discussed the need to move from traditional ways of thinking and action to more innovative and original ones. This shift is perceived to be a precondition to allow individuals and groups to cope with a highly competitive global and postmodern world in which many past convictions and experiences are found to be irrelevant or invalid.

Carl Bereiter, attempts to address this challenge in a paper entitled "Educating toward new creativity." He advises us to think afresh about creativity in order to fit it to our rapidly changing world. His main point is that creativity cannot be seen anymore as being restricted to individual geniuses waiting for rare moments of inspiration. Creative ideas and products emerge today everywhere, to the point that it becomes hard to find their originator or keep a record of the time of their inception. Bereiter compares, for example, the older invention of penicillin with that of modern Viagra. The dramatic story of the discovery of penicillin portrays Alexander Flaming as a single hero and innovator who was sensitive enough to notice that the mould formation on the Streptococcus plates in his lab eliminated the growth of bacteria. His intuition has led him to the decision to isolate the penicillin and to see how it could fight certain illnesses. Different from this heroic discovery by one person having "a prepared mind," the success of Viagra is attributed to the work and to the surprises that were encountered by a whole group. Its effects were discovered accidentally by patients during the development of a new blood medication in Pfizer Pharmaceuticals. No single developer has been credited for this discovery. Bereiter uses this comparison to substantiate his point that the new type of creativity is not dependent anymore on heroic figures and on discoveries by exceptionally talented individuals. It should rather be looked at as a life long endeavor that requires intensive and persevering investment by many talented people who collaborate in teams. His view qualifies some of the claims of the researchers who conducted the biographical studies of exceptional geniuses. It transforms the responsibility and success in producing something new and valuable to a whole community collaborating on finding solutions to important problems and to members in the community who invest efforts in thinking afresh about familiar problems. Bereiter's view allows the educator, as well, to reduce the expectation that creativity will be only the business of a single talented student excelling on a creativity test or handing in a highly original class assignment. It should be rather redefined and seen as a product of the collaboration with others and the ability of a learning group to make the best use of a challenging and accepting learning environment. We replace here the former perception of creativity depending on inborn talents and unique success of an individual with a more democratic view that sees creative thinking as a way of living and as a task that is actively sought by a group of collaborating members.

Educators can take many things home from Bereiter's article. The measures that he links to the new type of creativity dictate a pedagogical strategy that is very different from the ones that were required for the old types of creativity. Berieter's conclusion seems to be in line with his other ideas about the development of knowledge communities in which students negotiate scientific ideas and concepts. His new conception of creativity helps bring it down to earth and makes it more accessible to both ordinary students and learning communities. If his diagnosis of creativity is correct–we should expect to find new ideas emerging from the work of collaborative groups. However, there are at least two main problems with his suggested scenario. The first is that it is based on a dichotomic view. Bereiter disregards the dimensions of the older types of creativity and sees them as obsolete and he presents both group thinking and collaborative cognitive processes as a kind of a panacea, or at least as representing the only way to be creative in the new reality.

Although the old elitist idea that has been discussed above–perceiving creativity as a gift of a small group of geniuses–had some problems with it, the alternative that Bereiter suggests seems to lean to the other extreme. He demystifies creativity, which may be fine. But it does not solve one of the main puzzles of creative thinking that has been dubbed as: "Where do ideas come from?" His hope that ideas will just pop up in task-oriented work groups or in regular classrooms ignores, among other factors, the potential counter influence of school norms, expectations, and past knowledge, that can counteract or abolish any type of possibility thinking.

One way to release us from the vicious circle in which critical thinking and existing knowledge produce in schools and in work places 'more of the same' and help students break the boundaries of the familiar and think about new and different possibilities, is by extending "the transitional space" in which ideas can be tried and played with. The psychologist W.C. Winnicott realized that in order to encourage the appearance of creative ideas one needs a "transitional space" in which the child will be able to experience new things. In this kind of space one can take risks and even fail or make mistakes without having to pay a price. This play with possible thinking scenarios often leads to new ideas. The realization that creativity needs a flexible experimentation space that allows students to free themselves from the limitations of existing knowledge could be the first move from an analytical type of definition of creativity to what we would like to call a "dialectic explication" of the term.

A dialectic explication of creativity

Our basic belief is that creativity, like many other human faculties involving feelings and emotions, cannot be defined analytically because of the limitation of our logical thinking. We would like to further explain this idea. Analytic definitions latently assume the validity of a so-called bivalent logic. This type of logic specifies necessary and sufficient conditions that are satisfied by the defined term. Each of these conditions has a binary nature: it may hold or may not. The logic expert would say that this rule latently satisfies the axiom of the "excluded middle." It means that when we are forced to select one of two contradicting options, there is no place for a third option or a middle way. However, propositions expressing our feeling and emotion do not have to necessarily satisfy the axiom of bivalent logic and can simultaneously imply one thing and its opposite. Thus, it may be possible to love someone and not love the same person at the same time. And the same may be true for the question "are you sad?" It may have more than two possible answers. This ill-defined state of affairs raises the question: how is it possible to define, or at least clearly explain, terms involving feelings and emotions? Such an explanation will be more ambiguous than definitions based on necessary and sufficient conditions.

In our effort to solve this problem and partly circumvent the complexity and elusiveness of creativity we would like to use an approach that allows fluidity by moving between oxymorons which coalesce opposite meanings. In referring to each pair of binary opposites the beholder will not be forced to decide where exactly to locate the meaning of the creative act on the continuum between the pairs. She will, rather, be left with the liberty to slide from one end of the continuum to the other and even locate herself at different and opposing points at the same time. Examples of axes of pairs of binary opposites that set the stage for a dialectic explication of creativity could be: creative potential vs. materialized creativity, nature vs. nurture, blind vs. intended creativity, combination of existing elements vs. creation (ex. Nihilum), "emotional cognition" vs. creativity as part of critical thinking, individual vs. collective creativity, human vs. machine-generated creativity. Some of these antonyms may look familiar to those acquainted with the literature on creativity and a few of them have been dealt with in the examples and discussion that preceded this section. They represent existing disputes among psychologists, or belong to the realm of philosophical thought. As indicated above, we see the novelty in our suggestion in not necessarily focusing on a specific pair of opposites but rather substituting analytical types of definition of creativity with a method of explication that is sensitive enough to its "fluid" and ill-defined nature.

In the last section of this paper we intend to relate two specific pairs of binary opposites in order to provide an example of what a dialectic explication of creativity could look like. The binary opposites that we will use here portray two valid "choices" or, in dialectic terms, a kind of thesis and antithesis between one way of defining creativity and another. Each has a validity of its own; the axis combining their poles or the possible synthesis should be seen as lying on a continuum rather than as a dividing line.

A. Creative potential vs. the materialization of creativity

One problem with the division between the creative potential that one has and its materialization is that the latter can be recognized only retroactively. We know that an idea is original and worthwhile only after it has been materialized in a product, in a scientific discovery, in a business initiation, a work of art, or some other type of innovation. This does not imply that the creative potential should not be recognized and acknowledged. Dartnal (2002), for example, finds that the preliminary stages of deliberation that lead to decisions on how to proceed in the creative process are not less important than the finished and polished product. Many educators judge the creative process in which a student is involved as being equally, or even more, valuable than the final literary or scientific work that is handed over. However, most educational institutions will concur with Martindale that creativity is dependent on the ability to elaborate a crude idea and turn it into a convincing product (Martindale 1990).

A crucial factor that can mediate the actual success or failure of the individual to learn something new or to generate something that looks original is the socio-cultural learning environment. Vygotsky's idea about the "zone of proximal development" and the socio-cultural tools that influence learning can pave the way to materialize some innate talents of the child. This implies that the ability to develop a raw idea and transform it into a finished product can only rarely be carried out by a single individual and is often a result of internalizing knowledge in the learning group. We can concur here with Bereiter's conviction that the ability to collaborate with other people in the search for creative ideas seems to be one of the best predictors of a possible success to produce a creative product.

A subcategory of the binary opposites of the creative potential versus its materialization in a product can be observed in another pair of binary opposites: nature and nurture. Children are born with many kinds of talents that they can cultivate and enrich. Nevertheless, although educators would like to believe that much depends on the quality of their teaching one cannot be blind to inborn differences between children that are partly inscribed in their personalities. Ignoring those talents and qualities will not be advisable, especially when they can be honed to kindle one's creativity.

It follows, that we should not underestimate the role of natural talents when we select candidates for special programs for the gifted or for activities that require specialized gifts such as an exceptional musical and artistic talent. This does not mean that we should exclude other less talented students from music lessons or from creative writing sessions or other creative opportunities. We believe that everybody is entitled to express herself in various domains and that in many cases a teacher can be surprised to encounter creative ideas in children that were not marked as gifted or talented in a specific domain. We should add that although these creative talents are usually specific we could also discover students who show a general capacity to be creative in very different situations. Some people seem to be able to think or express themselves in more creative ways than others. (This at least is the major supposition behind most creativity tests.) On the other hand, several inborn and natural virtues and thinking tendencies could sometimes hinder creativity. They could include a tendency to follow others and not lead the way or to be too critical in ways that could paralyze the creative thinking. Such a paralyzing criticism can be found even in children who are identified as gifted. In these cases the educator has to counter balance some of the critical tendencies that prevent these students from using their creative abilities and curiosity.

We realize that this model dictates complex and even conflicting assignments that require an ability on the part of the teacher to detect the creative spark in very different contexts. This complexity cannot, according to our belief, be resolved by the miracle of finding a simple recipe for creative education or a list of cookbook rules. However, if our definition of creativity becomes freed of the rules of bivalent logic, nature and nurture can be seen in many contexts as coalescing and not as requiring an either or decision of the educator. Our creative plans and strategies can be driven by both innate qualities and learned behaviors.

B. Blind versus intended creativity

The meaning of this pair of binary opposites can be enriched through the dispute between Spinoza and his opponents debating the importance of intention in explaining the works of God. Those adopting a Darwinian attitude will argue that ideas have their own process of evolution and what has been intended rarely matters. The best inventions and creative ideas according to this view appear as a result of lucky coincidences. Pasteur would not have discovered the relationship between sterilization and the prevention of illness had he not accidentally visited a hospital in which the death toll was extremely high and basic hygiene had not been kept. But an evolutionary or unpredictable course of events cannot only explain the initial act of revelation or discovery but also the transformation of discoveries and new tools from one use to a completely different one. Many great inventions were originally meant to serve very different purposes from those that they finally were used for. Newton, to give only one example, invented differential calculus not intending to create a new field of knowledge but to be able to calculate the "instantaneous velocity" that had not been acknowledged at his time. As strange as it may sound, he intended to use the calculations to solve Zenon's paradox about the Hare and the Turtle.

Maxwell, on the other hand, can demonstrate a case in which someone discovers a new phenomenon by coincidence. His insight on the possible interrelationship between electricity and magnetism resulted from a mathematical discovery; he noticed symmetry between the equations describing the corresponding processes in these two formally separated fields of study.

There are at least three groups of scholars who give different explanations to the serendipitous navigation of an idea from its emergence to its final application. One group is promoting the evolution of ideas agenda (Gruber 1999, Simonton 1999). These writers argue, following a Darwinistic evolutionary notion, that ideas, similarly to creatures in the world, are doomed to pass a natural selection process. They believe that the "survival of the fittest" approach lets only good ideas survive. A second group, represented by scholars such as Kanterovitch (1993) and Petrosky (1992), sees the process as hazardous and unpredictable. They remind us that Colombus started his journey with the intention to arrive in India but found himself instead in America. A third group sees the indirect connection between intentions and results as rooted in specific historical circumstances and the existence of a right or wrong Zeitgeist. Leonardo da Vinci's sketchbook, for example, shows how brilliant ideas are missed when the time is not ripe enough to accommodate them. He foresaw the submarine, the cannon, and even the helicopter in his drawings, but 400 years had to pass until some of his ideas turned into reality.

In applying the tension between blind coincidence and intention to the educational arena we have a responsibility not to discourage students from their efforts to carry out their original intentions and ambitions. They will have to realize that there are many possible roadblocks on the way to a new and workable invention. In this sense, ordinary people have a lot to learn from exemplar stories about great discoverers and scientists. It may be comforting for the students to realize that even these exceptionally talented people were only players in a world which Einstein described as one in which "God plays dice."

In conclusion, we hope that these two examples of a dialectic explication of creativity demonstrate how binary opposites can be used as markers of the coordinates on which different meanings of the term can be negotiated. Our main argument has been that it is not enough to replace the multidimensional and complex space in which creativity can be explored and made active with a fixed number of descriptors that obey the laws of bivalent logic. The either/or dichotomy of scientific explanation (is it original or is it not? Is the creative ability innate or learned?), is replaced in our method by an option to merge, mix and match different qualities of the concept in the same explication. We can enter the epoch of new creativity that is based on collaborative efforts but still provides a stage for individual students who have a unique way of looking at and explaining things.

The ill defined nature of creativity requires us to navigate in a terrain in which different options can be detected but moving in the direction of each of them while ignoring the others may be a wrong decision. In other words, we are asked to prepare the ground for new discoveries but allow surprises to happen. We have to reinforce and assure our students to make experiments with unforeseeable results but equip them as well to encounter frustration when they reach a dead end or when the experiment does not lead to the desired outcome. The plurality of points and manifestations in which creativity can be observed is the most typical characteristic of the dialectic meaning of creativity. This may be discouraging for some but present new options and possibility for others. According to this view the research on creativity and its possible application in the field of education and other related fields might emerge from an investigation into its boundaries and from the familiarity with the attributes of this subspace.

Bibliography

Bereiter, C. (2002). *Education and mind in the knowledge age.* Mahwah, NJ: Erlbaum.

Csikszentmihalyi, M. (1990). *Flow: The psychology of optimal experience.* New York: Harper & Row.

Craft, A., Jeffrey, B., & Leibling, M. (Eds.) (2001). *Creativity in education.* London: Continuum.

Dartnal, Terry. (2002). *Creativity, cognition and knowledge: An introduction.* Westport, Conn: Praeger.

Gruber, H., & Wallace, D. (1999). The case study method and evolving systems approach for understanding unique creative people at work. In Sternberg Robert (Ed.) *Handbook of creativity.* Cambridge Mass: Cambridge University Press.

Guilford, J. P. (1968). *Intelligence, creativity and their educational implications.* San Diego Ca: Robert R. Knapp.

Hofstadter, D. (1995). *Fluid concepts and creative analogies: computer models of the fundamental mechanism of thought.* New York: Basic Books.

Kantorovitch, A. (1993). *Scientific discovery, logic and tinkering.* New York: SUNY Press.

Martindale, C. (1990). *The clockwork muse.* New York: Basic Books.

Parkhurst, H. D. (1999). Confusion, lack of consensus, and the definition of creativity as a construct. *Journal of Creative Behavior,* 33(1) 1-21.

Petrosky, H. (1992). *The evolution of useful things.* New York: Vintage Books.

Rothenberg, A. (1995). Creative cognitive processes in Kekulé's discovery of the structure of the Benzene molecule. *The American Journal of Psychology* 108 (30) 119-138.

Simonton, D. K. (1999). *Origins of Genius : Darwinian perspectives on creativity.* Cambridge, UK: Oxford University Press.

Sternberg, R. (1999). *Handbook of creativity.* Cambridge, Mass: Cambridge University Press.

White, A. R. (1990). *The nature of imagination.* Oxford: Blackwell.

TEACHER AS THE IMAGINATIVE LEARNER: EGAN, SAITOU AND BAKHTIN

KIYOTAKA MIYAZAKI

Egan argued that teachers should engage emotionally with the teaching content when they teach it to children. In other words, teachers should be imaginative learners of the content they teach. This idea is one important aspect of Egan's thought on imaginative teaching. A similar idea was proposed by Kihaku Saitou, a Japanese elementary school teacher and the founder of Saitou pedagogy. He and his followers have developed the idea of Kyouzai-Kaishaku, or the interpretation of teaching, the teacher's activity to learn about teaching content. This paper examines how imaginative teachers learn about teaching content by analyzing some cases of Kyouzai-Kaishaku. The imaginative teachers who are carrying out the work of Kyouzai-Kaishaku can be compared to Bakhtin's "author" of the polyphonic novel.

The theory of imaginative education must explicate the characteristics of imaginative teachers and find out how they can become imaginative teachers. Though discoveries of useful cognitive tools and the development of curriculum packages are important to develop imaginative education, imaginative education finally depends on imaginative teachers who practice it. In Egan's theory of imaginative education, what is most relevant to the issue of the imaginative teacher is his assertion that the emotional engagement of the teacher is vital to the imaginative classroom (Egan, 2005). He says,

> The main point I make is that for this alternative approach to work in the classroom, the teacher's own emotional engagement with the content must become central. (Egan, 2005, p. 214)

Egan also argues that children are interested, excited, and understand the teaching content well only when the teachers themselves engage emotionally with the teaching content. He says:

> Teachers who do find that emotional engagement typically find themselves energized rather than drained by the end of the day. And their classes have

more children who are themselves imaginatively engaged. (Egan, 2005, p. 215)

Emotional engagement with teaching content means that teachers understand the content not only intellectually, but are also moved emotionally when they understand the content. This issue concerns how teachers learn knowledge about teaching content when they construct teaching materials for children. Egan means that teachers' learning is not just an accumulation of facts through logical understanding. It must be a process of getting interested in the knowledge while they acquire it. To make children learn imaginatively, teachers should also learn imaginatively.

However, it is not easy for many teachers to be imaginative learners. It is not easy for them to engage emotionally with the teaching content. Egan pointed out that teachers are skeptical that the kind of emotional engagement he is talking about is either possible or sensible (Egan, 2005). The situation is the same in Japan. Many teachers feel that it is not necessary for them to engage emotionally with the teaching content when they teach it to children. The difficulty lies in their feeling that the teaching material is too easy for them to get excited about, as the material is for children to learn. They think they know the teaching content very well. So, they do not feel it necessary to learn or get interested in it. They know it, so they can teach it to children. No problem.

In one sense, they are correct. As adults, teachers have already learned this knowledge during their studies. They already know 'the correct answers.' It is often difficult to engage emotionally with the knowledge they feel they already know. Still, it is necessary for teachers of imaginative education to engage emotionally with their teaching content. What can they do to do so? What, in the first place, does emotional engagement with content mean?

Kyouzai-Kaishaku and learning of teachers

One Japanese teaching practice will provide some suggestions on this issue. In Japanese traditional thought on teaching practice, teachers' learning about teaching material has been called Kyouzai-Kaishaku. Kyouzai means teaching material and Kaishaku means interpretation. This term is used to describe the process of learning the relevant knowledge of the teaching material and preparing it for the lesson. In Japan, textbooks are thinner than Western ones, and teachers are expected to construct rich lesson plans by their Kyouzai-Kaishaku . As the existence of this term shows, the issue of teacher learning has been traditionally thought of as important in Japanese education, and knowledge of the practice of Kyouzai-Kaishaku has been accumulated.

In particular, Kihaku Saitou's idea on Kyouzai-Kaishaku is relevant to Egan's idea of emotional engagement. Kihaku Saitou was a legendary practitioner in Japanese elementary education and the founder of Saitou pedagogy. His idea of teaching is very similar to Egan's (Miyazaki, 2006). According to him, the task of Kyouzai-Kaishaku is not just the accumulation of knowledge related to the teaching material, nor the acquisition of the correct answers to the problems of the teaching material. He says:

> First of all, a teacher should encounter and confront wholeheartedly with the teaching material in all its respects as one person. A teacher should wholeheartedly interact with the teaching material, analyze it, have questions of it, ask himself, discover something, and create something, as one person. Through these endeavors, he should accumulate new thinking, new logic, and new development. Only after the teacher has done such interpretative works on the teaching material and encountered with it, a lesson can have a definite direction, intention, and an explicit construction. It is because the teacher's knowledge about the teaching material stops being a collection of random pieces, but becomes a lively one, acquired by his own, sweaty efforts, only after such encounters. It is because the teacher can confront children with the lively knowledge which he acquired by being surprised by it, by doubting it, or by discovering it afresh. (Saitou, 1964, pp. 89-90. Translated from the Japanese by Miyazaki.)

Saitou's characterization of the task of Kyouzai-Kaishaku as the work of "one person" and his reference to surprise and doubt sounds very similar to Egan's emphasis on emotional engagement. As the task of Kyouzai-Kaishaku is done by a teacher as one person, it is not just a logical and intellectual work, but an emotion-laden one. His/her surprise and doubt in the process are some examples of emotional engagement.

Most remarkable in Saitou's characterization of Kyouzai-Kaishaku is his emphasis on discovery in the task. For successful Kyouzai-Kaishaku, the teacher should discover something new and interesting. The discovery makes possible the teacher's emotional engagement with the teaching material.

This assertion raises one question, though. As I noted earlier, teachers as adults have already learned the knowledge dealt within elementary education. There is nothing new for them. So, discovery in this context is not like that done by scientists in some advanced area of research. What teachers do is a re-discovery of something in the content they once learnt. This characteristic of teachers' discovery reminds us of one phrase Egan made when referring to Bertrand Russell (Egan, 1989). He says, "The educational achievement is not to make the strange seem familiar, but to make the familiar seem strange" (p. 47).

This educational principle holds true not only for children's learning but also, or more so, for teachers' learning of teaching content. In the context of teachers' learning, teaching content is familiar for the teachers in the sense that they have already learnt and know it well. Teachers should make the familiar knowledge strange. This is the process of discovery in the context of teachers' learning. Then, what does it mean to "make the known knowledge strange" in Kyouzai-Kaishaku?

Kyouzai-Kaishaku as the work of encountering with children and culture

Kihaku Saitou argued that there are three aspects in the work of Kyouzai-Kaishaku (Saitou, 1963). One is to have general knowledge of the content. In this aspect, teachers learn the correct answers in common-sense terms. Any adult can do it. The second one is the teacher's professional understanding. Here, teachers learn how each child in the classroom understands the teaching content and thinks about how to respond to his or her understanding. In other words, teachers understand the teaching content as children. In this aspect, teachers sometimes get excited by and discover something new in the children's understanding of the content. In those cases, teachers learn about the content from children. The third one is to learn from experts in specialized fields such as the arts and sciences. This is, on the one hand, to accumulate knowledge of the teaching content and to know "more correct" answers about problems in teaching content. On the other hand, learning from experts often stimulates learners to re-examine the "correct answers" they have accepted as commonsense. Such re-examination often tells us that the widely accepted answer is not the only correct one and there are other, possibly "correct" answers in addition to the accepted one. This third aspect is learning of the existence of multiple possibilities of the various interpretations of the teaching content. According to Saitou, these three aspects work together and interact with each other in the actual work of Kyouzai-Kaishaku.

The last two aspects of Saitou's Kyouzai-Kaishaku go beyond the correct understanding of the teaching material. They are the effort to generate understanding other than the one that is commonsensically correct. Understanding which is commonsensically correct is understanding which is familiar to teachers as adults. In this sense,

Kyouzai-Kaishaku involves the task of making the familiar strange for teachers as adults.

It should be noted here that in Kyouzai-Kaishaku the work of making the familiar strange is first done through encounters with other people. Second, it is done through encounters with children, and third, with the experts of any specialized field. Through such encountering with others, the familiar, commonsensical understanding of the teaching content is overcome.

The method of Kyouzai-Kaishaku

To see the process of making the familiar strange in Kyouzai-Kaishaku more concretely, let me analyze the method of Kyouzai-Kaishaku developed by Katsuhiko Sakuma. Katsuhiko Sakuma is a researcher of Social Studies education. He has developed with his colleagues in elementary schools the teaching method he called the "fieldwork method" based on Saitou pedagogy (Sakuma 2003). In this teaching method, children and a teacher collaboratively discover and explore a problem in their neighbourhood such as their town or a natural field. This is apparently the typical Social Studies lesson which Egan criticized. However, the emphasis is put on the discovery of the problem. Though the lesson starts by exploring some problem found nearby, the children and the teacher are encouraged to develop new problems in the course of exploring the first problem. The core activity in this method is to discover the problem, or the strange, in nearby, familiar areas.

The teacher's Kyouzai-Kaishaku thus takes the form of the field research done in advance of the children's work. In particular, the teacher meets many experts connected to the problem he/she and the children will explore and gets information about the problem from them. This kind of learning from the experts is very important to developing the "fieldwork method." Sakuma expands the definition of experts from Saitou's view. Experts here are not only scientists and artists, but, everyone who has useful knowledge with which to explore the problem. So, for example, old people in a town are the experts of the history of that town. In this learning from the experts, teachers get not only the correct answer to the problem but various different and sometimes opposing ideas. These different ideas are the material used to generate the binary opposition of the problem, stimulating dialogical discussion among children later in the classroom.

Example 1: What is a store?

To examine the process of Kyouzai-Kaishaku, two examples of Kyouzai-Kaishaku in Sakuma's fieldwork type of lesson are described here. One is the lesson done by Sakuma himself (Sakuma, 1992). As this is the demonstration done by the researcher for the teachers, it had a time limit of one hour and children didn't join the field activity in the lesson. However, the Kyouzai-Kaishaku he made for the lesson is typical and worthwhile of analysis.

The theme of the lesson was "what is a store?" Through exploration of this problem, a store, which is very familiar to children, became strange for them. Many issues were discovered around this problem. The lesson started with five photos that Sakuma presented to the children. These were photos of a vegetable shop, a barbershop, a launderette, vending machines, and a peddling woman. Among the five photos, a vegetable shop was a typical shop for the children. This is the commonsensically correct answer to the question. The other four photos deviated somehow from the typical definition of a shop. Comparison of these four photos with the vegetable shop generated four binary oppositions.

Children discussed if each of these four photos showed a shop. At first, the majority of the children said no to each of the four photos. As discussion progressed, they changed their minds. In discussion, children found out much new information about a shop. For example, they found out that there were many moving shops other than that of a peddler. Though such information acquisition was useful, more important was that they were stimulated to commit explorative activity. For example, they generated new questions about a shop such as, "is a taxi a shop?"

In the comments they wrote after the lesson, they didn't stop thinking. One child wrote:

> Before the lesson, I thought that it is not a shop if there is no shopkeeper. Now, I am not sure. I had thought that a launderette is not a shop, although it is inside a building and I pay money there. Now, I don't know. (Sakuma, 1992. Translated from the Japanese by Miyazaki.)

As this comment shows, the theme of the lesson, a shop, stimulated the children to think deeply. It was stimulating because a shop, which is very familiar and not stimulating, became strange for the children. And it was Sakuma's Kyouzai-Kaishaku that made a shop strange. How did Sakuma discover the strangeness of a shop, or how did he generate such a problem?

According to Sakuma (2006), his quest to design the lesson started from a vending machine. He happened to listen to someone asking if a vending machine was a shop. At that moment, he thought that a vending machine was not a shop, and he didn't think to develop a lesson around this theme. His mind changed a little later when he heard a shopkeeper say that a vending machine was a shop. He got really excited and believed that he could develop a lesson plan about a shop.

Sakuma began to engage with this problem emotionally. He realized it was a problem worth exploring in the classroom. The emotional engagement was caused by his encounter with thought different from his own. And that thought was from a shopkeeper, an expert of a shop.

He started to investigate "shops." He studied about shops in literature. He collected information on a shop, a vending machine, and other types of shops in dictionaries, in encyclopedias, in textbooks of economy and management, and so on. He also searched shops in telephone directories, to study what kind of shops there are, and what these shops are called.

Important to his investigation were interviews he conducted with various kinds of people. He interviewed scholars of economy and commercial law. He interviewed people whose jobs are connected to a shop. He went to the Ministry of Economy, Trade, and Industry to learn what the government thought of a "shop" and a vending machine. He also went to the mercantile section of the city he lived in, and the Chamber of Commerce and Industry. He asked every taxi driver whose taxi he took if they thought a taxi was a shop.

In these interviews, he received new information. For example, a vending machine sales manager told him that you need permission from a city's health center to set up a new vending machine with soft drinks in it and that the permission is the same as for a coffee shop. However, what became clear through these interviews was the fact that there was no clear-cut answer to the problem. A commercial law scholar told Sakuma that there was no definition of a shop in Japanese commercial law. An official from the Ministry of Economy, Trade, and Industry gave him no answer as to whether a vending machine was a shop. Officials of the mercantile section of the city and the Chamber of Commerce answered his question by saying that they did not know if a vending machine was a shop.

Furthermore, a group's answers were divided. Taxi drivers were divided into three groups concerning the question if a taxi is a shop. One group said yes. The second said no. The third said they could not answer.

Multiple understandings were generated in Sakuma about a shop through these interviews with the experts. The commonsensical understanding Sakuma first had about a shop was overcome through the encounters he had with experts. It is not that his initial understanding was rejected as false. Diverse understandings started to co-exist in Sakuma. He now knew that there were diverse understandings of a shop and each understanding had its basis. Based on this Kyouzai-Kaishaku, it became possible for Sakuma to present the problem of a shop in the form of binary opposites to children.

Example 2: Exploring the Onogawa agricultural water

The second example is a Social Studies lesson for 4th graders that used the fieldwork method (Yoshinari, 2005). It started with the exploration of the familiar, nearby river. New problems were discovered in solving the old ones. The lesson lasted for half the year. The fieldwork took the form of interviews with the people of the community, including children's family members. Though children and the teacher were committed to conducting fieldwork collaboratively, the teacher took the initiative when the exploration came to a dead end. The teacher conducted fieldwork in advance, solved difficult problems, and had the perspective to keep the lesson going. That was the Kyouzai-Kaishaku in this lesson.

The exploration began at a small stream running in front of the school that has the same name as the school. The first question was where the stream came from and went to. Children followed the path of the stream which was partly underground. They also interviewed the people of the area. It became clear that the stream came from and went into the same lake. So, new questions popped out. Children continued their investigations and discovered that the stream was not a natural one, but constructed about 70 years ago by the people of the area as the area's agricultural water.

New questions arose at this point. Children couldn't find out much information about the Onogawa agricultural water. The teacher conducted some fieldwork and found an old man who knew the circumstances of those days. He told them that there were major differences of opinion between the supporters and the opponents of the construction when the stream was constructed in 1939. It became clear that people of the area became mum on the topic because of the opposition of those days. The teacher started to think of having the children experience the opposition of opinions of their ancestors. To prepare for that, she visited a geographer who happened to study about the Onogawa agricultural water by himself and learnt that, geographically speaking, it was very difficult to construct a big reservoir in this area, and there were no means other than its construction for irrigating the area.

The teacher felt some hesitation for the children to share in the experience of the confrontation between two sides. Although the confrontation itself belonged to the distant past, it occurred in this area and some family members of the children participated in it. As the construction of the agricultural river had, after all, succeeded, the teacher felt that the opponents of the construction took the wrong side. If her feeling was correct, she thought, she could not organize the discussion between two sides, for she could not give the children who took the opponents' side enough support. The difficulty here was that the teacher could not understand the opponents' side. She knew they opposed the construction because there was a big risk of economic failure. But she understood them only intellectually. She could not understand them empathically.

Here again, the breakthrough was made by her encounter with others. The teacher met a daughter of the central supporter for constructing the Onogawa water and heard how she felt in those days. The daughter had high respect for her father, one of the driving forces for the construction. At the same time, she stated that she had a sad time in those days. She had to give up going onto high school because of the economic difficulties her family experienced in the construction of the river. Through this interview, the teacher understood empathetically how high the risk was for people in those days, and she realized that the opponents had a reasonable basis for their behavior.

Following this interview, she organized a one-hour lesson concluding the exploratory activities so far. In this lesson, children were asked to take either side of the confrontation and tell the reason why they agreed or disagreed with the construction of the river. The class split into two sides. However, children did not simply support one side. They showed some understanding of the side they did not support. The comments they made after the lesson showed that, for example:

> I disagreed. Because we will lose money if we fail. And we will get hurt in the construction work. ...I began to change my mind after the lesson, because I imagined what would happen if the water was not constructed. Nonetheless, I disagree. (Yoshinari, 2005, pp. 84-85. Translated from the Japanese by Miyazaki.)

In these two cases of Kyouzai-Kaishaku, encountering diverse ideas played an important role. In the first one, the teacher learned various understandings of a shop from many experts. He knew that there were other ideas than his own, familiar understanding of a shop. The diversity that was generated in the teacher's mind made possible the transformation of the familiar concept of a shop into an exciting intellectual challenge. In the second case, the teacher had to overcome her fixed idea that the construction of the agricultural river should be unconditionally supported.

This was made possible by engaging with others who personally knew how risky the construction was in those days. The teacher was enabled to understand the arguments of both sides. She could now organize the discussion among the children about the variety of opinions regarding the construction of the Onogawa water, and could provide sufficient information for the children to take either side in the debate.

Kyouzai-Kaishaku and Bakhtin's idea on polyphony

The work of Kyouzai-Kaishaku described so far can be analyzed with Bakhtin's concepts of voice and polyphony. Using Bakhtin's terms, the teacher who can learn imaginatively in Kyouzai-Kaishaku is comparable to Bakhtin's author of a polyphonic novel.

Bakhtin emphasized the importance of dialogue in the development of thinking and language usage. In this regard, his idea is relevant to theories of education and, in particular, to Vygotsky's theories (Holquist, 1990). It is also important for Egan and Saitou, in whose theories the concepts of opposition and dialogue play a central role. Bakhtin's idea on the polyphonic novel and the relationship between the author and the hero in the novel is suggestive in analyzing the work of Kyouzai-Kaishaku .

Bakhtin (1984) analyzed the novels of Dostoevsky and characterized them as polyphonic, compared to the monologic novel of Tolstoy. The key concepts of his analysis are the author and the hero. As it is the teacher's job to organize the classroom lesson, the teacher can be compared to an author. As Egan (2005) pointed out, the story is a powerful cognitive tool for the teacher, and he/she develops lessons as a story as an author develops a story. In the lesson itself, when the teacher is the author, the children are the heroes. However, there are other kinds of heroes in the classroom lesson, and they play an important role particularly in the preparation phase of the lesson.

They are thoughts, views, and interpretations about teaching content, which the teacher encounters in Kyouzai-Kaishaku. It sounds strange to characterize thought as a hero, for thought itself is not a character. However, it is reasonable to do so in the framework of Bakhtin's theory, for he defines hero as a point of view. He says:

> The hero interests Dostoevsky as a particular point of view of the world and on oneself, as the position enabling a person to interpret and evaluate his own self and his surrounding reality (Bakhtin, 1984, p. 47).

The teacher is the author and various views on teaching content are the heroes in the lesson as in the novel. Kyouzai-Kaishaku is the work of settling the relations between the author as the teacher and the heroes as various views on teaching content. And there are two types of relations between them. One is of the monologic novel, and the other is of the polyphonic novel.

Bakhtin characterized the monologic novel as the novel in which the author's voice controls all. The author of this kind of novel is the god who knows all:

> A second autonomous voice (alongside the author's voice) does not appear in Tolstoy's world; for that reason, there is no problem of linking voices, and no problem of a special positioning for the author's point of view. Tolstoy's discourse and his monologically naïve point of view permeate everywhere, into all corners of the world and the soul (Bakhtin, 1984, p. 56).

The teacher who thinks he/she already knows the teaching content is this type of author. Even when new information is accumulated, the information falls into the already-established framework of thought. Everything has already been explained in his/her knowledge structure, and there is no discovery. The teacher of this kind cannot generate real opposition of opinions in the classroom.

On the other hand, Bakhtin described the author of the polyphonic novel as the following:

> Thus, the new artistic position of the author with regard to the hero in Dostoevsky's polyphonic novel is a fully realized and thoroughly consistent dialogic position, one that affirms the independence, internal freedom, unfinalizability, and indeterminacy of the hero. For the author the hero is not "he and not "I" but a fully valid "thou", that is, another and other autonomous "I" ("thou art"). (Bakhtin, 1984, p. 63)

The teacher in Kyouzai-Kaishaku is always looking for new thoughts about teaching content. In the case of the fieldwork method, new thoughts are discovered in the teacher's encounter with others in the field. For the teacher, new thoughts are looked for not to accumulate knowledge, nor to confirm the "correct" knowledge he/she has already established. Rather, he/she is looking for new thoughts to relativize, to inquire anew into his/her already established thought. The teacher tries to find reasons to justify each new, diverse thought. As a consequence, many diverse thoughts co-exist in the teacher's mind. Each thought has not been integrated into a coherent knowledge system. It sustains its own right in the teacher's mind.

In this sense, new thought acts as a 'thou,' a partner in the dialogue for the teacher in Kyouzai-Kaishaku. As the teacher unceasingly looks for new thoughts, the dialogue never stops. From the endless confrontation of diverse thoughts in the teacher's mind, new, fresh problems arise. As diverse thoughts on teaching content co-exist in the teacher, he/she is enabled to present children with a lively binary opposition and to organize dialogic thought in children. The imaginative teacher is an author with many voices in his/her mind.

The research for this paper is supported by Grants-in-Aid for Scientific Research of JSPS #19530839.

Bibliography

Bakhtin, M. (1984). *Problems of Dostoevsky's Poetics*. (C. Emerson, Trans.). Minneapolis: University of Minnesota Press. (Original work published 1929).

Egan, K. (1986). *Teaching as Story Telling*. Chicago: Chicago University Press.

—. (2005). *An Imaginative Approach to Teaching*. San Francisco: Jossey-Bass.

Holquist, M. (1990). *Dialogism*. London: Routledge.

Miyazaki, K. (Ed.) (2005). *Sogo gakushu wa shikouryoku wo sodateru* [Integrated learning cultivates thinking ability]. Tokyo: Ikkei Shobou.

—. (2006). *Another Imaginative Approach to Teaching: A Japanese View.* Paper presented at the conference of Imaginary Education Research Group, Vancouver.

Saitou, K. (1963). *Jugyo* [The classroom lesson]. Tokyo: Kokudo-sha.

—. (1964). *Jugyo no tenkai* [Development of classroom lesson]. Tokyo: Kokudo-sha.

Sakuma, K. (1992). *Shakai-ka nazotoki yuzaburi itsutsu no jugyo* [Five stimulating lessons in social studies]. Tokyo: Gakuji Shuppan.

—. (2003). *Fiirudo-waaku de hirogaru sogo-gakushu* [Integrated learning through fieldwork]. Tokyo: Ikkei Shobou.

—. (2006). Personal communication.

Yoshinari, R. (2005). *Onogawa-Yosui tanjou hiwa wo saguriateru* [Exploring the secret of the construction of the Onogawa agricultural water]. In K. Miyazaki (Ed.) *Sogo gakushu wa shikouryoku wo sodateru* [Integrated learning cultivates thinking ability] (pp. 58-93). Tokyo: Ikkei Shobou.

Identifying Legitimate Tools for Learning: CHAT and Authentic Learning

Colin Sommerville

Learning tools are important, if not essential, elements in learning environments, and have been the focus of much discourse. They have been described as devices that scaffold, organize and extend thinking processes, as tools that facilitate generalisable cognitive processes, and, in the case of graphing calculators, as model tools for, "building conceptual understanding of mathematical ideas" (Alagic & Palenz, 2006). Although educators and authors have enthusiastically endorsed *cognitive tools*, *learning tools,* and *teaching tools*, astute researchers (Iiyoshi, Hannafin and Wang, 2005) have pointed out that,

> Tremendous interest has been generated in student-centred learning environments and their associated tools, but little research and theory is available to guide or support [tool] design and use. (Iiyoshi, Hannafin & Wang, 2005, p.292-293)

Although researchers and authors "understand comparatively little about how tools are used by students...we continue to develop and refine specific features and make assumptions about their use and utility (Iiyoshi, Hannafin & Wang, 2005, p. 292-293).

In the current environment with its plethora of definitions for educational tools and relative paucity of conceptual understanding regarding the nature of educational tools, educators may find themselves in a quandary when trying to identify appropriate and beneficial tools for developing the intellect and thinking processes of students. Founded upon the theories of Vygotsky and Leont'ev, Cultural-Historical Activity Theory (CHAT) can provide educators and researchers with a powerful conceptual framework for understanding educational tools.

The development of higher psychological functions as a result of the mediating action of internalized psychological tools must be clearly understood in order to appreciate how educators can identify and employ learning tools to construct effective learning activities. Vygotsky believed that thinking is a mediated action: psychological activity involving the use of indirect methods for accomplishing a mental objective by making use of tools. A simple example of tool use to complete an objective is the use of a calculator to find the sum of a list of numbers. The difference between using a calculator and the kinds of tools Vygotsky identified is that he was concerned with mental activity involving *psychological tools*. Vygotsky (1978) believed that higher psychological functions are a result of uniquely human, artificially created stimuli that are the genesis and mold of complex mental behaviour. Vygotsky was adamant in his writings that, "use of artificial means, the transition to mediated activity, fundamentally changes all psychological operations..." (Vygotsky, 1978 p. 55). He introduced a model depicting the change from a simple stimulus-response line to a triangle that indicates the use of a mediator or mediated act to complete the operation. In describing the use of the mediator, Vygotsky points out that,

> The simple stimulus-response process is replaced by a complex, mediated act.... In this new process the direct impulse to react is inhibited, and an auxiliary stimulus that facilitates the completion of the operation by indirect means is incorporated. (Vygotsky, 1978, p.40).

The use of mediators in psychological activity does not simply result in faster cognition or enable a person to connect thinking to the objective world, but results in qualitatively different modes of psychological activity because the psychological process itself has been altered. In Vygotsky's words, the, "system of signs restructures the whole psychological process and...reconstructs [the process]...on a totally new basis" (Vygotsky, 1978, p. 35). The acquisition of mediators results in a qualitative transformation of the higher psychological processes. The psychological mediator has an effect not on the environment but on the individual's mental activity. From this perspective it becomes clear that without an adequate mediator available for an individual to use, it may be extremely difficult if not impossible for an individual to accomplish an objective. Thus, there may be more than one adequate mediator for any given psychological function, and one mediator may be superior to another in some ways and inferior in others. The logical conclusion from this perspective and one critical to understanding the relationship between mediation and mental development is that an individual's higher psychological functions may be developed by the purposeful introduction of appropriate mediators.

Internalization, mediation, and the *Soroban*

As a demonstration, we will examine the use of two tools for performing mathematical computations; the calculator and the abacus. In North America, use of a calculator is considered to be a useful skill to acquire in elementary school. In British Columbia, many school districts such as Maple Ridge and Langley include a calculator in the list of recommended school supplies for students entering grade four. Students are taught how to use the calculator as a tool to complete basic arithmetic problems and to complete computations in various subjects. While the calculator is a very convenient apparatus for completing mathematical problems, it is not a legitimate learning tool because it does not act as a mediator that has impact on the inner psychological processes associated with mathematical operations. Often teachers in Canada bemoan the fact that if students do not have a calculator many of them are incapable of completing basic arithmetical calculations. In contrast to this situation, in Japan many children attend evening classes to learn how to use the abacus (called "soroban" in Japanese). Students are not permitted to use calculators in elementary or middle school however they are permitted to use the soroban. Learning to use the soroban is initially a time consuming activity that begins with students learning to represent numbers by positioning wooden beads in the appropriate positions on the soroban. From there, they learn how to manipulate the beads to perform basic addition and subtraction, and then move on to do multiplication and division as well. While the calculator and the soroban are outwardly similar in that they are both used to perform computations, there is a profound difference in the psychological activity of the students. Using the calculator, children learn the correct order in which to use the numbers to represent a formula, using the soroban, students are learning how to symbolically represent numbers as arrangements of beads.

The impact of the soroban on students' mental activity supports Vygotsky's argument that mediation alters higher psychological functions, including the imagination, because in the absence of a real soroban Japanese students can perform complex arithmetic by creating a mental image of a soroban and imagining changes in the pattern of the beads in order to complete the task. This is a mediated action because the students are not physically counting beads, but are converting numbers into patterns, manipulating the patterns on the mental soroban, and then converting the pattern back into numbers. Because the students are relying on the image of a soroban, the tool has shaped the nature of the psychological processes involved in performing arithmetic calculations and transformed those higher psychological functions into a unique format. Younger students often perform these mental calculations while moving their fingers over the imaginary beads, so the mental calculation is done accompanied by external indications of the mediation involved in the mental activity.

Psychological tools and legitimate learning

While the majority of educators may be able to identify pedagogically unproductive tasks, they are often unable to define the essential elements of legitimate learning activities and the role these activities play in the intellectual development of the student. When educators do not have an adequate conceptual understanding of psychological tools they do not have the ability to intentionally and knowledgeably create legitimate learning activities that are necessary for real learning and development to occur. In addition, it is not generally understood that psychological tools must be acquired as a part of a legitimate learning activity.

An example is the subject of poetry. Poetry is often taught by having students identify poetic devices and read various types of poetry because teachers often lack the conceptual understanding that knowledge of poetic devices, while necessary for poetry, is not sufficient for these processes to develop: the components that constitute poetry-making are not being appropriated as functional units of poetic activity. These instructional strategies may enable students to identify certain poetic devices and certain styles of poems, but leave them incapable of engaging in poetry-making. The result is students observing poetry rather than becoming agents in a poetry-making activity, which may in fact serve to impede their ability to develop poetic sensitivity because students have developed an understanding of the goal of poetry as only a search for and identification of poetic devices.

When incorporated into a legitimate learning activity as something necessary for completing an action, the study of poetry results in the development and conscious application of poetic thought processes by pupils. From a pedagogical point of view, in the interaction between the object and the subject, the object becomes reflected in the psyche of the subject and determines the nature of the mental activities occurring in the subject's psyche that are then used to produce and reflect on a poetic product. This dynamic relationship between external objects and internal conditions that results in the production of new objects, establishes an upward spiral of development best described as a co-evolution of subject with object through the qualitative development of mediators specific to the activity.

When creating curricula, it is important to understand the critical relationship between the object of the learning activity and the activity of learning itself as the nature of the object has a direct influence on the nature of the constituents of activity and therefore the nature of the acquisition of psychological tools. Directing his comments specifically at education, Leont'ev stated that the inability to understand the nature of learning and activity often results in educators creating lessons which contain inherent incompatibilities between the subject and the object of instruction, for the instruction of the teacher, "decidedly does not correspond with how the activity of the pupils develops under the influence of the...[content] material itself" (Leont'ev, 1978, p. 161).

Because conscious human behavior is an "instrumented" activity (Leont'ev 1978, p. 59), internalization of operations has a major influence on the development of psychological processes that are reflected in the psyche of the individual. The similarity between Leont'ev's description of operations and Vygotsky's psychological tools is not simply coincidence, for Leont'ev referred to operations as the "tools of action" (Leont'ev, 1978, p. 164). In this light, the selection of an explicit assignment or task results in the establishment of a set of operations necessary to realize that task. The result of this action is the development of mediated mental activities specific to the operations that have been carried out in a meaningful manner and that have been developed and internalized not as discrete units, but as part of a system of activity.

In regard to language development, researchers have argued that through the mediation afforded by language,

> The action has been transformed into a mental phenomenon and has become a chain of images and concepts... So as a result of subsequent levels of abstraction (materialized-verbal-mental) the action has attained a new form: it has become "pure" thought. This form, as Gal'perin (1989b) argued, represents a qualitatively new level of psychological functioning.... (Haenan, 2001)

By engaging in legitimate activities, students are exposed to the psychological tools which compose the actions of the activity. The internalization of these psychological tools results in qualitative improvements in their ability to participate in that activity.

True internalization of mediators in poetry means that the subject may engage in poetic modes of thought without a specific prompt or stimulus and without the intention of producing a concrete work of poetry because the individual is aware of certain affordances that this particular mode of thought may provide as a means of accomplishing some mental task. Although this theoretical perspective has direct applicability to educational contexts, it has been largely overlooked by educational theorists. It has, on the other hand, been adopted by engineers working on issues involving ergonomics who have realized that,

> Tools emerge as a socio-cultural phenomenon that encodes particular types of operations, implicitly imposing constraints and prescriptions, that in turn socially determine practical actions and mental operations, transcending individual psychological features (Bedny, Seglin & Meister, 2000, p. 170).

Because of the dynamic nature of activity and of the tools employed, learning systems researchers and designers who do not adequately understand learning tools have found themselves perplexed by the fact that "[l]earners tend to 'co-opt' or reappropriate tools, i.e. use them differently from (the purpose) presumed in their design and development" (Iiyoshi, Hannafin & Wang, 2005, p.292).

A Japanese Language Arts Unit Plan

The example of CHAT used in a cross-cultural context to examine a middle-school Language Arts lesson, specifically a lesson that incorporates traditional Japanese puppetry, shows how psychological tools can be embedded in practical learning activities. In this lesson plan the intention is to incorporate the traditional art of *bunraku* puppetry into a unit on traditional Japanese culture and language. One portion of the grade eight text book invites students to, "imagine the lives and thoughts of the people from the things they have handed down" (Kokugo 2, 2004, p. 158). The intent of the unit is to introduce the students to *"The Tale of Heike and Genji,"* followed by an assignment to produce a short bunraku play that reflects the lives and thoughts of people living during that period of Japanese history.

Bunraku is a form of puppetry developed in Japan that has no equivalent in western culture. The puppets are mechanically elaborate and often require two or three operators. Traditional stories are complex, lengthy, targeted at adult audiences, and often recount traditional fairy tales, folk stories and romantic historical tales. In a typical western classroom this activity would be considered a fun and engaging hook for a unit on Language Arts or Social Studies, or it could be used to preserve and transmit traditional culture to the next generation of Japanese students. CHAT can identify more complex psychological processes occurring and can present more powerful reasons for the effectiveness of this particular curriculum.

The key to understanding the role of mediators in a learning activity is what Vygotsky (1978) referred to as the "method of double stimulation" in which, "Two sets of stimuli are presented to the subject, one set as objects of his activity, the other as signs that can serve to organize that activity" (Vygotsky, 1986, pg. 103).

In the case of bunraku, the children are expected to perform a play for their classmates. The cultural artifact which mediates the performance is the traditional puppetry which has its own set of requirements that shape and organize the activity. The task set before the students is to develop an understanding of how to use the puppet to produce a successful and effective performance that portrays the issues and concerns of the people of the Heian era. Essential to the learning is the use of the puppets is an implicit requirement for the completion of the activity, and not as an end in itself. The activity is a collective one: interaction with adult experts, teachers, and more knowledgeable peers recruited from the school bunraku club play an important role in helping the students learn how to manipulate the puppets so they can convey emotions and actions that match the dialogue and narration of the play they are writing.

The puppets as objects place certain constraints on the activity, among which is the requirement that the students must conform as much as possible to the standards and conventions of traditional bunraku puppetry. The presence of these constraints is an important aspect of the activity because the students must employ artistic and literary conventions during the play. The fact that the students are not just writing a play, but are engaged in producing a *bunraku play* is a factor that is easy to overlook. The role of artifacts in defining the operations that may be employed in an activity has been neglected by many researchers, and, "the importance of 'cultural artefacts and representations as carriers of meaning' has been insufficiently recognized to date" (Daniels, 2001, p. 74). The bunraku puppets are essential because they require the children to use traditional expressions, proverbs, and language learned in the Language Arts classroom while manipulating the puppets. This use of artistic and traditional linguistic expression functions as another mediator for developing in depth an awareness of and familiarity with essential cultural concepts related to value and belief systems, identities, relationships, and social issues. Beyond the value of the puppets as cultural artifacts, literature has been described as a vital psychological tool because,

> Devices discovered by literary analysis become models in a study of everyday language. Literature helps to identify those possibilities of

language and verbal thought that are obscured in the individual language. Literature thus becomes a toolbox for a study of individual psychology. (Kozulin, 1993)

The development of these understandings is not simply a matter of cultural transmission, although that is also occurring, but the acquisition of a particular set of psychological tools which can serve as mediators for further mental development. Concurrent with development related to language acquisition and use, the removal of the person as actor results in the play becoming a form of drama that occurs purely in the imagination and therefore on a higher level of abstraction than with human actors. With the use of puppets, the emphasis of the activity moves away from watching an actor and, instead shifts to the semantic realm: meaning-making becomes the focus of the activity. According to Vygotsky, a focus on meaning-making is vital in development:

> ...operating with the meaning of *things* leads to abstract thought...[and] the development of will, the ability to make conscious choices, occurs when the child operates with the meaning of *actions*. (Vygotsky, 1978, p. 101)

In the bunraku activity, the manner of the performance of the play and the manner in which it is received are products of the children's interaction with, and interpretation of, the original literature. The importance of meaning-making is founded upon the argument that literature, "serves as a tool that develops in its reader a cognitive capacity for...multidimensional comprehension" (Kozulin, 1998, p. 150). Other authors agree with Kozulin's assertion and argue that

> Literature can serve as a prototype for the most advanced forms of human psychological life and as a concrete psychological tool that mediates human experience.... The human being masters his or her own inner psychological processes with the help of symbolic tools-signs, symbols and texts. (Lindqvist, 2003, p. 250)

From this perspective, the incorporation of bunraku into the Language Arts unit plan has the potential to turn a simple "read, interpret, and respond" activity into a powerful means for developing higher psychological functions. There is also another benefit to this particular activity that is generally overlooked by most theorists who tend to focus on internalization and cognitive development: students are also producing an object. While the process of internalization is an important part of development of the higher psychological functions, it is also true that the reverse process of externalization is a part of the activity–without externalization, there can be no expansive cycle of activity. According to Wertsch, "when...external modes are instantiated, they are already characterized not only...by object meaning, but by meaning in the real sense of the word" (Wertsch, 1985, p. 102). Activity is not complete unless the internalization that results in conceptual thinking is expressed in a purposeful and meaningful manner that is employed in activity and produces some kind of change or modification of the original object. This change or modification imbues the object with a different set of real or perceived characteristics and promotes another round of internalization.

Because of all the traditional Japanese cultural elements attached to bunraku, it can not be dropped "as is" into a foreign classroom, but the use of puppets as a tool for creating a rich learning activity that engages and enhances the intellectual development of the students is a workable proposition for any teacher. The key to success however is that the instructor must understand and recognize the forces at work within the learning activity so that real learning and development occur.

A solid understanding of the nature of psychological tools can assist educators in identifying and selecting educational activities that have the greatest potential for promoting the development of conceptual thinking in students, and can help them assess curriculum and instruction in order to provide valuable educational strategies and activities that encourage legitimate learning activities.

Bibliography

Alagic, M. & Palenz, D. (2006). Teachers explore linear and exponential growth: spreadsheets as cognitive tools. *Journal of Technology and Teacher Education,* 14(3), 633-649.

Bedny, G., Seglin, D. & Meister, D. (2000). Activity theory: History, research and application. *Theoretical Issues in Ergonomic Science,* 1(2), 168-206.

Daniels, H. (2001). *Vygotsky and Pedagogy.* New York: Routledge-Falmer.

Haenan, J. (2001). Outlining the teaching-learning process: Piotr Gal'perin's contribution. *Learning and Instruction,* 11, 157-170.

Iiyoshi, T., Hannafin, M., & Wang, F. (2005). Cognitive tools and student-centered learning: rethinking tools, functions and applications. *Educational Media International,* 42(4), 281-296.

Kokugo 2. (Heisei 16 nen). Tokyo: Mitsumura Tosho Shappan Kabushikigais [Japanese 2. (2004). Tokyo: Mistumura Publishing Company.]

Kozulin, A. (1993). Literature as a psychological tool. *Educational Psychologist*, 28(3), 253-264.

—. (1998). *Psychological Tools: A Sociocultural Approach to Education.* Cambridge: Harvard University Press.

Leont'ev, A. (1978). *Activity, Consciousness, and Personality.* New Jersey: Prentice Hall.

Lindqvist, G. (2003). Vygotsky's theory of creativity. *Creativity Research Journal* 15 (2/3), 245-251.

Vygotsky, L. (1978). *Mind in Society: The Development of Higher Psychological Processes.* Cambridge: Harvard University Press.

—. (1986). *Thought and Language.* Cambridge: The MIT Press.

Wertsch, J. (Ed.). (1985). *Culture, Communication, and Cognition: Vygotskian Perspectives.* New York: Cambridge University Press.

—. (1985). *Vygotsky and the Social Formation of Mind.* Massachusetts: Harvard University Press.

TEXT AND IMAGE: FROM METAPHOR TO DREAM

CONCETTINA MANNA AND GIULIANO MINICHIELLO

Between text and image there is an obvious difference: the text presents certain meanings, and the image presents shapes. They are two forms of representation of objects that can also be distinguished structurally: the text is discursive and almost always linear in structure, while the image is a structure that is uniformly perceptible. As Eugène Delacroix says, when a picture is painted, a thought is not written. Nevertheless, a subterranean connection exists between text and image: a text conjures up images, just as a picture prompts thoughts. Through the analysis of some examples in this study, we will consider the problem of how verbal and non-verbal language draw upon a web of symbols, and significant proof of this is found in dreams and illusion.

Metaphor as image of sense[1]

The notion of imagination is characterized by obscurity and vagueness and a theoretical ambiguity. The complex nature of the function of imagination has been investigated by scholars of various disciplinary fields, from philosophy to the arts, from the physical sciences to psychology, from literature to neuroscience.

On this matter, Maurizio Ferraris suggests that we distinguish between imagination and fantasy, pointing out that if the first is connoted as a "retention of the absent," and therefore as the faculty to retain in our minds images of absent things, the second is the "re-elaboration" of these images.

According to this new theoretical elaboration, imagination probably tends to be more fallible than "retention" and incline more towards imagery than towards imagination (Ferraris, 1996, p. 7). From such a perspective, we also see the inventive nature of the function of imagination and thus its ability to generate or create new objects characterized by its specific and profound creative potential. As a consequence, the image passes over itself; it is not simply the mental representation of an absent object. Instead, it goes so far as to become the symbol of something and traces, or as Kant says, notes, something else, so that distinction, more than clarity, will be a result of the imagination and its fruits. That is to say, physical appearance remains part of logic, just as logic is not completely detached from physical appearance.

As Paul Ricoeur says, it is as if the imagination pushed reflection to its limit, leading it to the threshold at which concept comes into contact with the world of life and with the symbols that express it, thus releasing an infinite resource of sense. Imagination therefore becomes a heuristic force, capable of opening and unfolding new dimensions of reality, to the point of performing a role of mediation between the intellectual and the volitional sphere.

The problem of the relationship between the thinkable and the visible, and between the intelligible and the perceptible, leads us to the question regarding the profoundly cognitive and innovative and not solely "decorative" value of metaphor. On the one hand, metaphor takes on the shape of an ornament, an aesthetic device for referring to concepts which could also be expressed in denotational terms; on the other, the metaphoric image itself is interpreted as the original, most direct and concrete means of expression of thought.

Aristotle once wrote in Rhetoric that "metaphor teaches us and gives us knowledge by means of category" (Aristotle, III), anticipating a theme that is the object of discussion some centuries later, when, on the basis of theoretical suggestions offered by phenomenological studies on language, some paths of research have emerged. These tend to go beyond the traditional opposition between code and subject, or the literal and metaphor, and thus observe the relationships of reciprocal influence and reciprocal conditioning between the two aspects of language: of language, that is, as a literal system, objective and precise, and as a metaphoric creation, subjective and free, that extends the human ability to represent reality and to give it sense, generating new backdrops and new versions of the world. As Aldo Giorgio Gargani reminds us, every time a new backdrop and new scientific prospect are created, we find ourselves before a living metaphor and with it the explosion and opening of a new prospect of sense (Gargani, 1999). Along this theoretical itinerary, the metaphor as mere rhetorical stratagem comes to connote a spark of sense, bizarre preaching, and even an impertinent attribution, able to re-depict reality and discover hidden ontological dimensions of human experience, generating a new sense and understanding of the world through the outburst of imagination (Ricoeur, 1975).

In such a perspective, metaphoric language thus becomes the place where image is fully created both as a reproducer, in its perceptible aspect, and as a producer, in its semantic aspect. In its stricter sense, by assuming the role of privileged entry key in the process of re-depiction of reality, metaphoric image goes as far as to open and release ontological power, or rather the power to say, capable of opening new ways of living in the world, through a sort of suspension operated by pretence (Ricoeur, 1975). From these assertions, it is possible to grasp a heuristic force in the notion of imagination, which is capable of opening and unfolding new versions of reality and bringing pretence out of itself, allowing the discussion to be projected *ad extra*, into the world of routine.

The language mode that probably best expresses this passage from text to action is identified by Ricoeur as the story (Ricoeur, 1986): the redescription of the world, and in final jurisdiction, also the redescription and the search for and discovery of new dimensions of self. For this reason, from analysis of the link between metaphoric language and routine, the attention shifts towards a reflection on the specific theoretic knot that imposes a consideration not only of the question regarding the projection of self, but also of the special form of self-projection represented by narrative identity, the synthesis of history, and storytelling.

Ricoeur-inspired studies on the structural forms of metaphor reveal its unlimited resources of sense, as well as those of the story. They are positioned within a context of philosophical reflection that recognizes, in language, non-conceptual, and therefore symbolic, narrative, and metaphoric, the extraordinary ability to speak of subject and of reality in many ways, expressing the most diverse forms, not univocally definable (Ricoeur, 1975).

Ricoeur attributes a specific pre-narrative feature to human experience, by virtue of which it is possible to "speak about life as a story in its early stages, and so of life as an activity and a passion wanting to be told" (Ricoeur, 1994, p. 180), to the point of identifying precise time scales in the action itself. The pre-narrative quality of human experience leads us to consider the set of events in our lives as untold stories waiting to be told. In support of the notion of the potential story, Ricoeur uses both the case of the patient who confides fragments of removed events to his psychoanalyst so as to obtain a story that is more bearable and comprehensible from these, and the case of the judge, who in his intent to expose the guilty party, unravels the tangle of confusion in which the suspect is trapped.

Ricoeur believes that the examples he gives will lead us to see the individual as being "wrapped up" inside the stories that happen to him before any story is told.

The tangle therefore seems to be the pre-history of the story told, the beginning of which remains the narrator's choice. It is the pre-history of the story that links it to a wider sphere and provides it with a background. This background is made up of "the active entangling of all the stories experienced" (Ricoeur, 1994, p. 182).

In the Ricoeurian circle of narration and time scale, a path is created which causes life to take on the shape of "a story or series of potential stories that ask to be told. This story-telling does not artificially create a meaning to which life in itself would be strange, but rather clarifies and strengthens a meaning that it already possesses in a nutshell " (Jervolino, 1993, p. 143).

In the reflections regarding the narrative configuration of life which unfolds in a fabric of stories told and untold, we can see the central role of the subject implicated in the stories is connoted as a narrative identity, or as a synthesis of history and story and as an operator of meaning. The story that gives the images meaning obeys various rules and in particular the metaphor, or the ability that forms the focal point of imagination and creativity and which, as Kieran Egan writes, can be described as "...the heart of human intellectual inventiveness, creativity, and imagination" (Egan, 2005, p. 3).

Metaphor encourages us to think more, and this skill in development distinguishes it strongly from other tropes, which exhaust themselves in their simple, immediate expression. We therefore recognize metaphor as an authentic cognitive tool, a privileged function in the process of the construction of conscience, and even the ability of the subject to tell its story and redefine itself. The imaginative ability of metaphor, at the basis of Mythic understanding, provides an inexhaustible reserve of meaning, and thus becomes a basic tool for acquiring a huge collection of daily metaphoric projections through language (Egan, 1997).

Moreover, on this subject, Egan reminds us that metaphor "is one of our cognitive grappling tools; it enables us to see the worlds in multiple perspectives and to engage with the world flexibly. Metaphor is much more profoundly a feature of human sense-making than the largely ornamental and redundant poetic trope some have taken it to be" (Egan, 1997, p. 58).

The text of time, the time of text[2]

In *De anima* Aristotle states that the human psyche is caught between two complementary focuses, dream and perception, and that we dream constantly, even during the day, but we are unaware of this because the oneiric fire is prevaricated by the blinding glare of its perceptive counterpart.

This statement could be fully supported by Freud, who summons his old friend Aristotle to have him say that the dream is the psychic activity of the sleeper. The idea that we constantly dream, even during the day, is corollary with the Freudian theory, according to which there are two integrated regimes of psychic functioning: the primary and secondary process, which respectively govern the unconscious and the preconscious/conscience.

The active dynamics in the primary process are the condensing and shifting of affection and representations, which correspond in linguistic and textual terms to metaphor and synecdoche. It is precisely these that characterize oneiric work, that is the psychic assistance assigned to lead from the latent dream which provides unconscious meaning, to the manifest dream which distorts this meaning and gives it back in the form of an incomprehensible and absurd alien film. This distortion aims to safeguard the sleep state, vulnerable to the invasion of wishes, through the hallucination of their substitutive fulfillment, in the pattern of the sketch that follows. The fall into the sleep state causes the perceptive fire to implode, to the advantage of the oneiric, which downstream now has free reign thanks to the alteration of state that has taken place, and upstream, finds fuel provided by the persistence of residual memories that are resistant to sleep. To use classic Freudian metaphor, these are good entrepreneurs of sleep, but do not possess the capital to solicit oneiric conscience; such capital can only be provided by the connection with strong, forbidden desires and which would as such be confiscated, if prohibition were not revocable by twisting their meaning through the condensing/shifting of representations (Freud, 1940).

The result is almost always successful. It manages to break down censorial barriers and to solicit the oneiric conscience, though providing it with a product that is ultimately bizarre in appearance; no longer so if, with the use of good interpretational work, it is possible to retrace the path of oneiric work from a manifest meaning to a latent one.

The classic Freudian approach is the last stage in a thousand-year journey, going from East to West, from the oracles to the prophetic dreams of biblical tradition, passing on the belief, even in popular culture, that dreams conceal a coded language that comes from some alien power, and that is subject to various uses. The starting point of such an approach includes some implicit premises that deserve further consideration. The first is that the dream has an essentially economic meaning: it is there because it serves a purpose (to warn of danger, indicate a direction to take in life, resolve a problem, relieve libido, suggest lottery numbers, etc.). The second is that the subject of the dream is somehow identifiable: it is the "god" who visits the minds of men, particularly those of some (priests, prophets, etc.), or the soul of some dead ancestor, or, still, a combination of unconscious psychic impulses. The third is that the meaning of dreams–always ambiguous, needing to be deciphered–is accessed through analysis of their content.

We believe that all of these premises should be faced with an important question, yet they are almost always undervalued or mystified. The question is: what kind of knowledge do we have of dreams? The function attributed to dreams is directly dependent upon the answer that is given to this question. It is wrong, for example, to start from analysis of the content, because it would be like trying to understand what it is like to see through the analysis of what we see, while ignoring the role played by visual apparatus, and even not knowing that this visual apparatus exists. This is why it is impossible to go straight to an analysis of the content without considering the phenomenology of the dream beforehand. The pre-eminent intention in the following pages is to outline this phenomenology.

Even if we leave aside the meaning that Husserl gives to the term "phenomenon," it has to be said that phenomenon is what is displayed and what appears. Now, the "psyche" is a phenomenon to us, since we recognize its manifestations, though not its internal nature (whether soul or libido). Nevertheless, because it is a phenomenon, it is made up of facts and situations that are "realities" (not mere illusions); "reality" being everything that makes resistance and poses an obstacle for the mind. Psychic reality appears in a privileged form in dreams. It should be noted, incidentally, that the initial state of our life is the dream state: we awake from the dream; it is waking that happens and not the dream. We abandon the dream for wakefulness, not vice versa.

There are two great examples that illustrate this concept. The first is a pair of fragments by Heraclitus which say: "The sleeping are the creators of the things that happen in the world and help to produce them"; "The wide-awake belong to a unique and common world, while each of the sleeping retreats into a world of their own" (Colli, 1980, p. 95). The other example is the beginning of *Metamorphosis* by Franz Kafka: "Awaking one morning from restless night's sleep, Gregor Samsa found himself in his bed, transformed into an enormous insect" (Kafka, 1989, p. 57).

Both examples portray the passage from being asleep to being awake, from dream to consciousness; a passage that is likened to a sort of second birth. Within their dreams, the "sleepers" mentioned by Heraclitus are "the creators of the things that happen in the world and help to produce them." Nevertheless, they retreat into a "world of their own," while the "wide-awake" belong to "a unique and common world." Here, it would seem, we "awaken" when we pass over from the "world of our own" of the dream state to the "common world" of conscience (of Logos, we could say). In this way, reawakening is a metaphor of the moment in which we ascend to the dimension of intersubjectivity, of a social birth. In Kafka the passage is similar but symmetrically opposite: precisely because the protagonist of the story is lucidly aware of the horror of his family environment for the first time, he goes from the "worry" of his own dreams to the nightmare of his family relationship. Childhood lives in dream and falls into wakefulness, the oneiric spell disappears forever and we find ourselves immersed in the prosaic world and at the tribunal bar of everyday life.

The event of being awake, nevertheless, is not the transit from illusion to reality (Doniger, 1984 p. 35 ff.), because the dream, it has been said, is also real. The dream is an objective phenomenon: in it, images and events pass by rapidly to give way to others, which they then mix with. This abrupt passing-by has a connotation that poetry has always expressed in metaphors inspired by dream: oneiric images and events vanish and this happens independently of us. In dream we are objects to ourselves, the object is the aspect of our human life that appears within it: it is the object because it offers resistance to us and, above all, because we are unable to change it.

Moreover, the dreamer is not surprised if a figure or an event vanishes from his dream; he is not surprised enough to question himself. He does not even ask himself about the chaotic multiplicity of events. However, this is not why he ceases to grasp its sense. If he manages to be sufficiently astonished to pose himself questions, then he awakens. In dreams, we never escape passivity: we never perform a real action in which we overcome an obstacle or find the solution to an enigma presented to us. Even when this should happen, we witness the possible overcoming of a conflict. In this way we sometimes find the solution to a problem that tortures us while awake. However, this is not thinking, but rather finding, or witnessing a revelation or resolution.

We come, then, to the second fundamental characteristic, from a phenomenological point of view: in a dream we don't think properly and this is because, oddly, we don't have time to do so. María Zambrano gives an example in which she describes a recurrent dream: a road narrows and narrows until it finally disappears. It is possible that in this case somebody appears to accompany us. Instead, we never witness a dream in which the protagonist who sees the road close before him, after having asked himself why, thought about the problem, stopped to think, and manages to go beyond the road (Zambrano, 1986, p. 14).

In dreams there is no privileged or unique moment, separate from the others, in which we ask ourselves questions or take the decision to do something, a moment of pure activity which is thinking or wanting. Everything happens as if from the very first moment the dream had already taken place, or were a story that had already been written and to which nothing can be added and from which nothing can be taken away. In other words, in dreams there is an immobile period of time, like the time of text, in which the events take place like sketches on a canvas (Nancy, 2003, p. 121).

We cannot make use of dream-time just as we cannot make use of time of text. We are within time, but it is not available to us; we are spectators of a time without an owner. In front of a text, nevertheless, we can stop to reflect, to think, to say, for example, "Look, this has happened." We are awake and, at the same time, absorbed by a time that stands still; in order to free ourselves of it, we need to abstract ourselves from it; the movement of closing a book indicates a void; the text is there, and we have left it, the activity of thought, claims its own autonomy. In dreams it is impossible to abstract ourselves; the closure of the pages of the book is the exit from the dream, the entrance into the state of wakefulness; the consequence is the non-appearance in the dream of the instant, or the moment of suspension of the course of events and the onset of thinking and of wanting. The use of time, properly human time, arises from a void, from porosity in the passing of time. When we say, while we are awake, that "this has happened to me," we mean that a void has appeared, and after this something has happened, and after that, another void has appeared, which has caused a slip back into the past. It is the conscience that projects the events of our life into the past. If it weren't so, everything that has happened to us would be contemporaneous, and would always be incumbent upon us. Whether the dreams were good or bad, it would make no difference: life would be a nightmare.

The dream is compact, closed, and portrays what has been conceived previously, with an unknown finality and by an unknown author. It is therefore the manifestation of the psyche in its ambiguous nature, both real and unreal. The ambiguity is due to the lack of time (which is not the same as Freud's "absence of the category of time"), it is the way of appearing in the form of undifferentiated unity of what the conscience separates and opposes. Thought begins to defeat ambiguity because it creates the past. This is the act with which the conscience throws the present backwards, or even, the past which is still there, which has not gone away–like in obsessions, which are daydreams–and renders it definitively past.

In dreams, or at least in those in which an action is proposed, an image appears first of all. Clearly, the image of a dream is different from the images produced while awake, by the memory or by the imagination. It is present before it is perceived and comes, therefore, from the very depths of ourselves, independent of our faculties. This constitutes its reality, which is a special kind of reality: although it is already there when it is perceived, it has just arrived and addresses the dreamer, proposing something to him: it wishes to be intercepted and deciphered. This accentuates its dream nature in a way that reveals the very depths of dreams: their enigma.

While we are awake and during daily life, reality, since it is stable, seems indifferent. We do not feel it arise for us, and it is not even in front of us like a scene from a play. It does not indicate or arouse the feeling of its inherent finality in us. With our own will and our life plan, we create the finality or else we accept it as being fixed. In order that reality arouses its purpose, the dream has to penetrate the awakened conscience: what can be termed as the metaphoric representation of reality. When we feel that reality is something directed towards us, that it is only for us, a call of what is known as "destiny," life truly becomes a dream, as happens in a vocation or in love. The image of life is already present, but it now turns towards us, imposes itself, and disarms us. In this case, we live the happiest moments of our existence: vocation, love, and also the perception of beauty or the discovery of the cognitive process. From this point onwards, until such time as the tension is maintained, we live within a dream.

In short, if the psyche is the subject of human life, time is its environment. The particular temporality of the dream–original and founding temporality–tells us that dreams are not something to be eliminated from a person's life, a sediment or a residue of life. They are instant manifestations, with unity of sense, of the real history of the person, and the process that leads it to integrate or destroy itself. Instead of simply being analyzed, the dream has to be assimilated, thus commencing a real training course.

The moments when the dream is present in the conscience, indeed, are the person's creative moments, when something that obsesses him, an enigma, appears to him as a completed story, like a musical melody, without any interruptions; when elements which are far apart in terms of time and space form a unity of sense. Not even then is there (the) time, nor can the awake person stop this chain of events in which the elements that were previously swirling around confusedly now appear in mathematical order. They are scientific discoveries, artistically solved.

Research on time in dreams therefore becomes research on the multiplicity of times in which man has always lived. Three basic forms of human time can be distinguished:

- in dreams, the immobile, textual temporality of the initial psyche manifests: a lack of time available to be able to stop, estrange oneself, ask questions, think, or have the time for reflection and freedom;
- established time (earned, economic) of the conscience: present, past, future; measurable time; and
- state of illumination: the appearance of a unit of sense in which time, without disappearing, has been transcended by the unit in which the ending is already part of the beginning: the latter is non-transferable, since it is a creation and thought, like dreams

These three vital times define an evolution: the time of the psyche, of the conscience, and of the person. Three movements correspond to them: the movement that corresponds to the psyche is ambiguity. Ambiguity is a sign of a lack of time, the need for temporal extension, tension without movement. That of the conscience is the movement of intercepting and dissociating, of connecting and disconnecting, opening and closing, intentional movements. The movement regarding the person is winding, integrating, indefinitely open and therefore never without a centre.

The finality that attracts this form of knowledge to itself is perhaps the aspiration of a guide, rather than a confession, which psychoanalysis usually aims for: a guide to help man cross various times and relate to his various masks. Since the plurality of times responds to the incomplete unity of its being, and its many ways of being.

Therefore, man does not have to build his life so much as bring his incomplete birth to a conclusion; he must be born gradually along the path of his existence, lead the integration process of the person into his own being, to the point at which he reaches freedom and progressive knowledge of himself.

End notes

[1] By Concettina Manna.
[2] By Giuliano Minichiello.

Bibliography

Aristotle, *Rhetoric,* tr. it di A. Plebe, Bari 1973.

Colli, G. (1980), *La sapienza greca, vol. III: Eraclito.* Milan: Adelphi.

Doniger, W. (1984). *Dreams, Illusion and Other Realities.* Chicago: The University of Chicago Press.

Egan, K. (1986). *The Educated Mind. How Cognitive Tools Shape our Understanding.* Chicago: University of Chicago Press.

—. (2005). *An Imaginative Approach to Teaching.* San Francisco: Jossey Bass.

Ferraris, M. (1996). *L'immaginazione.* Bologna: Il Mulino.

Freud, S. (1940). Die Traumdeutung, in *Gesammelte Werke,* 3, London: Imago.

Gargani, A. G. (1999). *Il filtro creativo.* Roma-Bari: Laterza.

Jervolino, D. (1993). *Il cogito e l'ermeneutica. La questione del soggetto in Ricoeur.* Genova: Marietti.

Kafka, F. (1989). Die Verwandlung, in *Erzahlungen.* Frankfurt am Main: Fischer.

Nancy, J. L. (2003), *Au fond des images.* Paris: Galilée.

Ricoeur, P. (1975). *La Méthaphore vive.* Paris: Éditions du Seuil.

—. (1986). *Du texte à l'action. Essai d'herméneutique II.* Paris: Éditions du Seuil.

—. (1994). La vita: un racconto in cerca di un narratore (1984). In D. Jervolino (Ed.), *Filosofia e linguaggio.* Milan: Guerini & Associati.

Zambrano, M. (1986), *El sueño creador,* S. A.: Ediciones Turner.

PART II

IMAGINATION AND CREATIVITY: PUTTING IT IN PRACTICE

The Interface between the Arts and the Sciences

Kieran Egan and Rod McKellar

The general cultural bemusement that has surrounded our attempts to grasp the differences and similarities between the arts and the sciences has been echoed in educational struggles about the curriculum. This paper will attempt to show how focusing attention on the child's imagination can lead to greater creativity and innovation in both realms of human activity. By structuring science lessons using the characteristics of pupils' imaginations, we show how one might approach science topics in an imaginatively engaging way. The result can stimulate scientific understanding, imaginative stimulation, and arts activity. We argue that if a more innovative technological society is desired, built on better scientific understanding, then we would be wise to attend to stimulating and developing students' imaginations. The imagination is richly developed by the arts, but it can also be developed by the sciences.

Introduction

If we focus our attention on products that seem typically "arts" and those that seem typically "science"–say, a painting by Picasso or Rembrandt and Newton's laws of motion or Einstein's theories of relativity–we can classify them as different ends of a continuum of human creative activities. We may then also characterize them as products of significantly different forms of cognition. This, anyway, is how they have been generally perceived in the modern world. The problems of accounting for the differences and relationships between these activities and establishing their relative values for human social life have been a major source of conflict, bemusement, and anguish in the cultural history of the West since the development of modern science. The conflicts, bemusement, and anguish have been echoed in the educational world in battles over the curriculum and methods of teaching. In this paper we will explore the interface between the arts and the sciences in, as it were, the child's mind. Our aim is to show how we might evade some of the old and fruitless battles between those who have argued for a greater emphasis on "arts" or on "sciences" as proper constituents of a good education. Instead we will show how we might focus attention on the child's imagination in a way that should lead to greater creativity and innovation in both realms of human activity.

We won't be able to evade all those old battles, of course, but we think it is possible to reduce the "collateral damage" they have caused in education. Most people believe that arts and sciences represent complementary forms of human thinking, each properly enriching the other. But our cultural history, and its influence on our conceptions of what we should do to children in the name of education, have not managed to work out routine ways of achieving this desirable end.

We will begin with a brief account of the issues in cultural history that influenced the making of the modern school curriculum in the latter half of the nineteenth-century, and of the protagonists in the struggles that gave us the relationship between sciences and arts that exist in schools today, beginning with the ideas of Plato and Aristotle, and reaching a kind of nadir with the Cartesian framework. We will show also why the history of education during the twentieth century has seen a constant diminution in the role of the arts, and a failure to facilitate creative thinking and learning of the sciences. In the remainder of the paper we will focus on the imaginative life of the child, and show how we might better educate children in both arts and science. We will conclude by considering how children's imagination can be used in making fuller sense of science in their education.

Arts and sciences in cultural history

The arts seem to have been with us from the beginnings of significant human culture, and indeed we identify those beginnings with the first signs of artistic activity. A recognizable line of descent to the modern arts comes from cave paintings of Lascaux and Alta Mira from around 30,000 years ago, paintings that indicate that the arts have always played a central role in culture. But by the time of Plato, that role was in some ways problematic, if we are to believe Plato's characterization of poets as being in some sense dangerous people. For Plato, the arts, and imagination in general, were suspect because they did not represent the eternal Forms, but were imitations of imitations, linked too closely to the mundane world of experience and appearance. Real knowledge was not attainable through the misleading representations of the imagination. Ironically, even Plato was forced to draw upon the imagination in order to illustrate his ideas, for he uses the metaphoric imagery of the cave, and of the chariot pulled by the steeds of the passions, in order to make his point. Plato's distrust of the imagination, however, continues to inform our conceptualization of knowledge, helping to create a false dichotomy that encourages us to see the arts and sciences as two distinct parts of education.

Aristotle, in contrast, was more sanguine about the prospects for using the imagination as a source of knowledge in both the arts and sciences. He seems much more willing to accept the role of the imagination as a source of real knowledge, particularly in art. In the end, however, Aristotle separates the metaphoric power of imagination from the pursuit of knowledge, preferring to emphasize the more literal power of imagination to form mental pictures, a conception which Tierney claims "entrench(ed) the empiricist attachment to mental images and so help(ed) to seal imagination's fate as a capacity irrelevant to truth" (1994, p.135). For Aristotle, although the imagination is a necessary component of thinking, giving reason its material to work on in the form of images, it must be subordinate to reason itself, which working on the images, produces real knowledge. Aristotle has presented us with a more balanced conception of the imagination and its relationship to perception, memory, and epistemology than had Plato, but it is a conception that ultimately reduces the function of the imagination to a subsidiary role.

Modern science may be dated to July 15, 1662; at least, that's the day the Royal Society received its charter from King Charles II, and provides as good a marker as any for the transition to a clear acknowledgement of science as a central distinguishing feature of European civilization. The birth of modern science, of course, owes much to the work of Descartes, whose epistemology is often characterized as focusing only on those aspects of cognition that can be proven beyond doubt.

Some commentators, however, such as Clarke (1982), argue that the role of certainty has been misunderstood in Descartes' method, and that our notions of what Descartes meant by "certainty" may be too narrow, and that he was in fact more open to the value of the imagination than is usually acknowledged. From this perspective, one in which hypothesis is an important constituent of methodology, imagination has a greater role to play in the sciences than we usually accept. If this reading of Descartes is in fact correct, then the conception of the nature of science that we implicitly accept, one that characterizes the sciences as somehow based on "facts" may be overly constricting our approach in education.

The arts, in contrast, are often seen to thrive on metaphor, seeking truths beyond words, capturing the consciousness of myth and dream, exploring ambiguity, representing the complexities of things. The

Sciences, seemingly in contrast, seek to bring "within the bright circle of our recognition" unadorned accounts of the prosaic nature of things, expressed in a language that avoids metaphor as far as possible and that approaches wherever possible the plainness of mathematics, reducing the complexity of things to laws, seeking regularity behind apparent diversity. The assertiveness of some proponents of the triumphal sciences in the eighteenth-century led to claims that the methods of science alone could deliver truth. This in turn led to artists being equally assertive about their ability to deliver a different, and more profound, truth: "beauty is truth, truth beauty," as John Keats rather succinctly put it.

The continued tangle of these seemingly distinct human activities in the nineteenth-century, along with the continued "march of science" through what had been considered the inviolable realm of religion, bequeathed to the twentieth-century a set of troubled beliefs about the relationship between the arts and the sciences. Matters were made more anxious for the non-scientist by the harnessing of the nineteenth-century idea of progress to the relationship between arts and sciences, and seeing the sciences as the real engines of progress–as, prominently among many, Herbert Spencer suggested (1851). The former were conceived as merely the vague and misty precursors of a mature rationality: but all sense making "must start with metaphor and end with algebra, and perhaps without the metaphor there would never have been any algebra," as Max Black characterized the view (1962, p. 242.). The unhelpful "two cultures" battles of the mid-twentieth-century did little to encourage understanding on either side of what had become a deep divide. The arts and the sciences were still assumed to represent different approaches to making sense of the world, and even to represent different kinds of thinking, distinguished as metaphoric/theoretic, or narrative/paradigmatic, or poetic/logical, etc.

More recently, however, there has been increasing concern to recognize these distinctions as perhaps overstated, or excessively polarized. Emphasis is put, for example, on Einstein's working out many of his insights in terms of images first, and then engaging in "the uncongenial and difficult" business of translating his images into the symbols necessary to communicate the insights to others. Or Friedrich Kekulè's theory of chemical bonds and molecular structure–foundational to Pauling's and Watson and Crick's discoveries about the molecular structure of the genetic code–came from visualizations that played before his mind in a "reverie." Similarly, emphasis is put on the systematic inquiry required both to create the pigments of those paintings in Lascaux or Alta Mira and to represent the movements of the animals depicted. And many modern artists are looking to the novel tools developed in science to create new kinds of images, such as those of fractal geometry and chaos theory. That is, while it is proving difficult to overcome the bifurcation of human thinking that has been represented in these two great human enterprises, it is becoming increasingly recognized that they are interacting rather than discrete features of the mind. In terms of educational theory, one need only turn to the work of John Dewey, such as *Art as Experience* (1934), to see evidence of an attempt to overcome this false dichotomy. Dewey argues that in the beginnings of Greek culture, there was no separation between art and science, that both were known by the term *techne*. Dewey points to the role that aesthetics, particularly metaphor, played in the Greek cosmology:

> The reproduction of the order of natural changes and the perception of that order were at first close together, so close that no distinction existed between the arts and the sciences.... Philosophy was written in verse, and, under the influence of imaginative endeavor, the world became a cosmos. (p. 149)

The arts and sciences in the state schools of the late nineteenth century

These currents in the wider cultural world have impacted continually on education, affecting both the curriculum and fashions in instructional methods. The nineteenth-century intellectual battles between science and religion, and between science and the arts, had an impact on shaping the curriculum of the new and expanding state schools, largely because proponents in these battles saw the curriculum as one of the main prizes to be captured–to use a not wholly inappropriate metaphor. Thomas Huxley's and Matthew Arnold's were powerful voices on different sides of the divide; the former arguing for a modern, scientific component to education, and the latter arguing on behalf of "the best that has been thought and uttered in the world," when that best was largely assumed to have been thought and uttered in Greek and Latin. Huxley looked, as it were, outward, on expanding scientific understanding and giving pupils the tools to better control the world and become useful citizens. Arnold's educational focus was, as it were, within pupils, believing that close acquaintance with the greatest achievements of human cultural activity would transform their inner lives. Educational debates, as Carlyle noted, resulted in some tension between supporters of the older metaphysical and moral sciences and those of the newer natural and physical ones. The older universities were criticized for their narrow liberal education and they, in turn, defended their turf. "Never let us believe" (wrote Edward Copleston, provost of Oriel College, Oxford, in reply to a critical article in the Edinburgh Review)

> that the improvement of chemical arts, however much it may tend to the augmentation of national riches, can supersede the use of that intellectual laboratory, where the sages of Greece explored the hidden elements of which man consists. (Gay, 1997, p. 168)

In one of his essays that it still commonly referred to, Herbert Spencer asked, "What knowledge is of most worth?" This essay has been influential in two ways; first, his answer was that science was the most worthy kind of knowledge at every stage of education. This answer helped embolden those who eventually succeeded in increasing very significantly the science components of the curriculum, pushed by, prominently among others, Thomas Huxley in Britain and Charles Eliot in the U.S.A. But, second, the essay was even more influential because of the way it set up the question. Spencer began by asking what were the most important things in life, and then arguing for what best enabled the child to become equipped with the knowledge and skills to perform those most important things. He put them in a hierarchy of importance: self-preservation, securing the necessities of life, bringing up children, producing good citizens, and last "those miscellaneous activities which fill up the leisure part of life, devoted to the gratification of the tastes and feelings" (Spencer, 1928, p. 7).

Most people thought Spencer's curriculum, made up from the latest scientific knowledge relevant to each element of his hierarchy, was too extreme and exclusive an answer to his question. But his manner of posing and trying to answer the question was accepted as the right way to go about it; and is still generally assumed to be right, especially by politicians and other paymasters of the schools. One must make schooling, it has been generally assumed since Spencer's time, useful; the school is to be an agent in achieving the requirements centralized states' development needed from their citizens. The trouble, for the arts at least, is that this criterion yields a utilitarian conception of education. And the arts are not especially "useful." Under the influence of Spencer's principles, education in the twentieth-century saw an increase in curriculum time given to subjects that were supposed to be useful–for citizenship, national competitiveness, employment, economic competence, etc.–and a decrease in time given to the arts in general.

Legislation for an increasingly useful curriculum

Early in the twentieth century, after Spencer's reputation had dissipated almost entirely, due in part to his extreme racist and right-wing views, his educational ideas, paradoxically, began to be enshrined in the curricula of the British Isles and, even more so, in the U.S.A. Energetically supported by Thomas Huxley, the Devonshire Report of 1875 had laid a basis for increasing science education in schools by ensuring encouragement for increasing numbers of science teachers. In the British 1902 Education Act, while six hours instruction each week are recommended for the study of an ancient and a modern language, seven and a half hours are suggested for mathematics and science instruction, and language and literature studies are to take four and a half hours. In the U.S.A. the most influential document concerning the shape of the country's education system was the 1918 report of The Commission on the Reorganization of Secondary Education. The document was almost entirely Spencerian in tone and recommendations. Taking its cue directly from Spencer, it declared that the purpose of education was "to prepare for the duties of life." It enunciated a set of Cardinal Principles that were to serve as criteria for selecting the curriculum for American schools. They echo Spencer's set.

The Commission listed them as health, command of fundamental processes, worthy home membership, vocation, citizenship, worthy use of leisure, and ethical character. The curriculum was to be made up of the knowledge that would support these. Given the growing belief in the importance of science in establishing national competitiveness, it was clear that many of the Cardinal Principles might require instruction in science, but it was less easy to see how the arts were to be called to the business of preparing for vocation or health or citizenship. With the increasing influence of utilitarian principles on education, a species of science gained increasing space in the curriculum at the expense of the arts–not that the latter had ever taken a large place in the state schools' curricula.

In Britain the sense of the state's schools as instruments of the economy and social welfare led to the creation of the distinctive Central Schools in the 1930s as a result of the R.H. Tawney-influenced Hadow Report. This contains the interesting observation that "[m]any people feel ill at ease in an atmosphere of books and lessons," and schooling for such people should of course be designed to spare them this discomfort. Similarly in the U.S.A., the experience of the Depression led to calls for greater "relevance" in the curriculum; relevance to the needs of the economy and the vocational training of pupils being understood.

The story of the following sixty years or so to the present follows much the same plot. Whether in the U.S.A.'s 1940 report from the American Council of Education or the 1944 report on "Education for ALL Americans" or the British 1944 Education Act resulting from the Spens and Norwood Report, increasing emphasis was laid on the schools' role to produce practical competence for citizenship and adequate preparation for jobs. Refined academic training was a luxury for the few, and socialization activities were the pragmatic requirements for the many.

It is hard to find any influences on the curriculum since those times that make changes designed to increase the time and quality of teaching in the arts. There have been large scale attempts to increase the quality of teaching in the sciences, most notably the movement resulting from the U.S.A. Woods Hole conference, whose deliberations and recommendations were summed up in Jerome Bruner's *The Process of Education* (1960).

Utility and children's imaginations

The central concern of these movements has been with what were perceived as social goods, and much less with any serious concern with educating the emotions and aesthetic senses of the child. There is indeed much attention given to such topics as "creativity," in the sense of some kind of skill that generates innovations, and delivers exploitable new products to the marketplace. We certainly do not want to suggest that attention should not be given to individual creativity–as that slighting way of putting it might suggest–but it seems far from clear in most accounts how it is to be stimulated and how it is to fit into some coherent notion of education and schooling. It may be all very well in practice, as a recent Irish Prime Minister is reputed to have said on occasion, but will it work in theory? That is, while people may treasure the appearance of creative performance in arts or science, the absence of any theoretical context that might lead to its routine replication leaves its appearance to chance.

What we have seen is a general support for "creative products" but without any significant sense of the imaginative life of the pupil that must be the source of them. The history of educational legislation and the approaches to teaching both sciences and the arts have gone forward on the assumption that something about the arts, and their encouragement and the disciplined control of pupils' expressions, ought to stimulate "creativity" and new ways of seeing and describing the world. And, it is has been hoped, this "creativity" will somehow rub off on their work in the sciences. But because serious science study in the secondary schools requires a lot of time, the focus on the arts for pupils who go on to study science has tended to be largely restricted to their primary education. And the arts retain a significant foothold in primary education, the cynic might note, because the direction to the later curriculum that is given by vocational needs is not yet seen as clear or urgent, so relatively unserious things might be allowed to go on. We recognize that this is a foolhardy way to put it, but even so, we think it is important to recognize that arts activities appear to survive so relatively well in the earlier years only because the paymasters of schooling have little interest in what goes on then, as long as children are adequately trained in literacy and numeracy. Hostility to the "progressive" ideas that still largely dominate early education comes when even these relatively simple requirements are seen as being inadequately met. Then we get "back to basics" reactions.

The idea that the school is primarily an agent in preparing for employment, citizenship, and other social roles and responsibilities has been reflected in most of the legislated changes to the curricula of Western states throughout the twentieth-century. The idea that the school is an agent in transforming the inner life of the child by means of the arts has persisted, but it has been of diminishing influence. Utility, in Spencer's somewhat complex sense–not merely, as he put it, for stocking the larder or replenishing the till–has been the implicit principle that has driven changes to the curriculum.

The tough voices that have directed these changes have insisted that schools teach children useful things. Thus when some new utility is perceived, it pushes out a little further those activities that cannot be so easily justified on utilitarian grounds. So, with the advent of ubiquitous computer technology, the school is expected to provide familiarity with the variety of programs that the future working world might require. Money and time spent on computers and computer instruction has to come from somewhere, and it isn't going to be taken from other useful subjects, so it has most commonly elbowed the arts a little further aside.

So, the significant differences in perceived utility to future employment and social roles of the sciences on the one hand and the arts on the other has not encouraged significant interaction between the two in education. Also the assumptions that they represent different kinds of thinking–"paradigmatic v. narrative" to use Jerome Bruner's recent characterizations–has also not stimulated much in the way of systematic attempts to have them interact. Of course, in individual schools, with individual teachers here and there, various programs have been mounted. None has shown such obvious success and benefits that it has compelled realization on a larger scale in national curricula.

Developing arts abilities to teach sciences: an example in primary education

Despite the general separation of arts and sciences in education, pretty well everyone would agree that they should interact more and enrich each other more. But how that is to happen has been the sticking point. We will use the rest of this paper to suggest a direction in which we might move to bring this generally desired aim about.

Instead of focusing on the level of curriculum and programs, we want to focus first on the child's imagination. We will identify features of students' imaginations at different ages, as they may be seen typically in arts activities, and show how we might deploy them in teaching the sciences. We will list some characteristics of students' imaginations in the primary years, and later some characteristics common to secondary years. Having outlined these characteristics briefly, we will give examples of how one might use them to rethink how to imaginatively teach science in primary and secondary years.

Fantasy and binary oppositions

If we look at some of the activities that seem to engage young children's imaginations, we might identify the kinds of fantasy stories that seem universally to be enjoyed by children. What is it about these stories that engages and stimulates children's imaginations, what can they tell us about children's imaginations, and how can they suggest better ways of teaching science?

One evident feature of these stories is that they provide a surface narrative built on conflicts between good and bad, brave and cowardly, security and anxiety, rich and poor, big and little, and so on. They are built, one might dangerously observe, on basic binary oppositions. This is a dangerous observation because our cultural history has been troubled by a series of damaging oppositions of this kind. Most notoriously exposed and investigated in recent years is that which associates male and female with active and passive, and a series of similar oppositions. However we might regret the way certain oppositions have been used in our cultural history, there is no evading them as long as we use language–an argument developed and defended at length in Egan 1997, and explored further in practice in Egan 2005.

Abstract and affective

We might note a couple of things immediately about these oppositions: they are abstract and they are affective. A part of the damaging folklore of the education business, since Herbert Spencer enunciated the principle and Jean Piaget developed it, is that young children are concrete thinkers, and that knowledge should be presented to them in concrete forms. If one observes a child's engagement with stories built on abstract concepts, it is obvious that they must understand and use abstractions all the time. (Aristotle, in a moment of distraction perhaps, wrote that flies have four legs. Despite the easy evidence of anyone's eyes, the authority of Aristotle ensured that this "fact" was repeated in natural history texts for more than a thousand years. The young child as "concrete thinker" has been a fair competitor as patent nonsense widely accepted.)

These oppositions underlying fantasy stories are also powerfully affective. They are emotionally charged, and determine a level of meaning that involves significant emotional engagement.

Another feature of these stories is that they involve creatures which are half human and half animal–talking wolves, middle-class rabbits, domestic pigs, and so on. What is going on here? Why do children's imaginations respond universally to such creatures?

Consider how we gain conceptual mastery over something like the temperature continuum. We learn "hot" and "cold" first–"hot" simply means hotter than our body and "cold" means colder than our body. We then learn a concept like "warm" that we can locate between hot and cold, and we can learn other terms to refer to temperature based on those first opposites. When we apply this most effective means of gaining conceptual control over the phenomenal world–from big and little and hard and soft and wet and dry and so on and on–to *discrete* entities, like nature and culture, or human and animal or life and death, what do we get? We get mediating categories, such as ghosts–which are to life and death as warm is to hot and cold–mermaids (human/animal) and talking middle-class rabbits (nature/culture).

Stories

The final item we might note is that the form that so successfully deploys these characteristics is the story. What is a story? It is a narrative which ends, and whose end determines the affective meaning of the elements that make it up. If we say that she went into the rose garden, you do not know whether to feel glad or sorry. If we add that she went in to console her sad grandfather, you might, tentatively, begin to feel glad. But when you discover that she was consoling the grandfather because their plan to ship drugs to all the schoolyards of the city had been foiled and that she has worked out how the plan can be revived–then you should feel sorry that she came into the rose garden. A story is the only unit of language that can fix for us how to feel about the events that make it up. As children's conceptual grasp is powerfully affective, then, we will be sensible to explore how we might use some of the features of the story form in teaching.

Let me pause with just these items that indicate something briefly about children's imaginations–that they readily grasp oppositions, that they deal with the most abstract ideas we ever learn, that they deal with them in an effectively charged way, and that they find the story a hospitable and engaging form in which to do these things. One could add a number of other items, such as children's ready use of metaphor (greatly superior to adults'), of rhyme, rhythm, and meter, and of forming mental images from words. But the few items mentioned earlier will be sufficient for me to make our point about how understanding of the child's imagination might help us teach in such a way as to engage that imagination in learning science.

An example of imaginatively teaching a science topic

So the educational problem we want to address is how we can take these kinds of "arts" activities and use them to make science imaginatively engaging and meaningful in the same way that stories commonly are. If we can devise ways to do this, we might also be able to provide a stronger, utilitarian, justification for greater space in the curriculum for the development of these useful "arts" skills. And we will incidentally show how arts and science activities can more richly interact and benefit one another. In our local curriculum, one of the early science units of study is to teach children about the properties of the air. We will show how we can deploy the above characteristics in teaching the topic.

We will begin by asking what is emotionally engaging about the topic, and how might we catch that engagement in binary terms. If we were to take a chunk of air, such as fills a classroom, what have we got? The air is full of noises, of waves and particles, smells, living things, and decayed skin. So we will show children that the air is full of wonders with seemingly magical properties. In the contrast between its apparent emptiness and its actual fullness of wonders we can locate an affective charge that will provide us with our starting point.

And what binary opposites can we build our "story" on? The sense of what is emotionally important leads us fairly easily to the binary set empty/full; "empty" here carrying the affective sense of dull, without interest, an undifferentiated lack, an absence of content in the air, and "full" carrying affective associations with richness, variety, and magical plenitude.

We might begin teaching about properties of the air by switching on a radio in one corner of the room and listening for a moment to voices. Then, switching it off, the teacher can walk to another part of the classroom, change the channel and then switch it on again, listening for a few moments to music. How do the music and voices get into the radio? Where do they come from? A number of the children will likely have asked their parents such questions, and the teacher can begin by harvesting and clarifying the answers. Then the teacher might ask what does the air in the room look like to the radio that can only see radio waves? To the "eye" of the radio, the walls of the room are not very significant–it can "see" through them. Alternatively, if conditions make it easy, the teacher can darken the room and shine a powerful flashlight or allow in a beam of sunlight to gleam on the endless dust particles in the room. They seem to be constantly in drifting motion, and while they are usually invisible, they seem to fill the air. What are they made of? Well, sixty percent of the dust in a typical classroom is made up of decayed flakes of human skin. (We commune with each other more fundamentally than we sometimes realize.) In a few minutes, the empty air can be seen to be full of a huge variety of particles. In both cases we underline the contrast between the assumed emptiness of the air and its almost over-fullness with varied, complex, and wonderful things.

If the teacher thinks of the lesson or unit as more like telling a good story than conveying a body of information, then the need to focus on how to tell the story as crisply and vividly as possible comes to the fore, rather than trying to meet sets of knowledge, skills, and attitude objectives. If the story is told well, the knowledge, skills, attitudes, or whatever, will be learned in a more meaningful context. We should perhaps add that when we mention telling a story, this does not mean simply that the teacher will be unvaryingly talking at the students. Any of the range of practical activities involving students exploring and constructing that typifies the most progressive programs can be incorporated into the story. Trips to museums, interviewing people in the community, building models, etc., can all be tied into the developing story line. What makes the lesson or complex unit story-structured is not some fictional component but its narrative development of the central affective, abstract, binary concepts.

How, then, will we story-structure the rest of the lessons on The Properties of the Air? We can deal with a range of properties of the air following the pattern of the introductory teaching event. We can find ways to help the students form images of other entities that fill the air of the classroom, focusing on, say, microbial life, gases, sub-atomic particles from the sun and from outside our solar system, pollutants, pollens, and perhaps even an exploration of the history of the chunk of air currently in the classroom from earliest times to the present. As with any story, the conclusion has to resolve or satisfy something set up in the beginning.

The conclusion, then, is not simply where we stop because we have covered the required material; rather, it needs to have, like the ending of a good story, a quality such as James Joyce describes as an "epiphany." In the case of our lessons, that means revelation of something about the topic that takes one's understanding that bit further, showing some deeper meaning, perhaps a mystery, that cannot easily be conveyed in the body of the lessons. We recognize that this might seem to border on the exotic, but we think the attempt to recognize some deeper meaning for oneself and try to express it to children can punctuate what might otherwise be routine teaching with moments of rich intensity.

So how might we conclude our exploration of the air? In this case the empty/full binary concepts will have been quite close to the surface, if not explicit, through the unit. While the air seems empty because it is not solid like chairs and tables and other visible objects in the room, students will have been taught to see it as full of the drifting life of tiny organisms, of endless dust, of amazing particles not pausing in their vast, speedy journeys from space, of titanic forces, of a rich stew of gases, and so on. Ask the children to sit still and close their eyes and imagine themselves shrinking and shrinking, like Alice in Wonderland. And when they have become as small as a tiny mote, the teacher can help them to "see" the air in their classroom quite differently. The teacher might prepare a "guided discovery" tour around the huge viruses and bacteria, the swirling winds that carry the varied and multi-colored boulders of dust around, the particles flashing by, the waves of radiation from light sources, fly feces, heat from bodies, radio waves, etc. Or, alternatively, the children can describe what they can "see" after some preparation and rehearsal, or can build models of "their" property–bacteria, dust, gases, pollutants, etc. The point of such an exercise is to emphasize that this amazing wonderland of unfamiliar thronging objects, life-forms, and forces, is the very classroom they are sitting in; unlike Alice's, it is a real wonderland.

We have dealt here with a typical six-year old and how a normal classroom can easily accommodate to teaching in story forms. Many teachers, of course, deploy features of such teaching, but very few in our experience routinely teach science in such a fashion. What we have tried to suggest in describing the lessons on the properties of the air is ways of seeing teaching of science as not so obviously disconnected from teaching arts. It is not just that the arts will be integrated in teaching the lessons–the children would be involved in constructing images of giant pollens or dust motes, etc.–but that the kind of imaginative engagement with the wonders of reality is of an imaginative kind that cannot be easily distinguished as arts or science, but is clearly in significant ways, both.

Developing arts abilities to teach sciences: an example in secondary education

How can we identify characteristics of adolescents' imaginative lives? Well, we can look at the kinds of activities in which we may see adolescents imaginatively engaged, and try to make inferences from them. For the sake of brevity, we will list a set of such characteristics, giving brief justifications for the claim that they constitute forms of imaginative activity, and then will, again briefly, sketch an example of how we might use them to improve students' imaginative engagement in learning science.

The limits of reality and the extremes of experience

It has been a part of the folklore of education that if you want to teach adolescents' about reality you must begin with what they already know, with "where they are at." This is a principle that derives from a focus on students' logico-mathematical thinking. But if we also consider their imaginative lives, we see something quite different from what this principle leads us to expect.

The most casual observation of what engages adolescents' imaginations shows that materials that deal with the limits of reality and the extremes of experience are most engaging: the most courageous or cruelest acts, the most bizarre and strange natural phenomena, the most wonderful and terrible events. The *Guinness Book of Records* exploits this characteristic, most profitably for its publishers, as do TV shows, comics, films, books, and so on, that focus on the bizarre, the amazing, the extreme, the exotic.

Transcendence within reality–the heroic

Adolescents are relatively powerless but grow increasingly aware that the society that hems them in and constrains them is one of which they are becoming a part. A common imaginative response to the constraints on their lives, such as the rules of parents, of schools, of authorities of all kinds, is to associate with those who seem best able to transcend, to overcome, the constraints that most irk the pupil. So a pop-singer or basketball star might form the object of a "romantic association" because she or he might seem to embody the reckless disregard of conventions or the independence and strength the pupils lack or cannot express in their lives. The pupil associates with the confidence, self-reliance, persistence, ingenuity, strength, or whatever, of the heroic character and so shares the transcendence.

It is not so much the heroic character with which the pupil associates, but rather with the transcendent quality the character embodies. It is not so much that we need to find heroic characters all the time, Lion Kings or Florence Nightingales, but we can locate transcendent qualities, such as courage, compassion, persistence, energy, power, ingenuity, and so on, in almost anything in the world. It could be the tenacity of a weed on a rock face, the serene patience of a cat, or the endurance of standing stones in a gale; almost any feature of the world can be imbued with a transcendent quality if we conceive of it romantically. Associating with the transcendent involves the pupil in imaginatively inhabiting the object in some degree.

Image and concept

Bringing the imagination to the fore in thinking about education raises the question of the role of affective images in teaching. We have inherited ideas and practices of education that give pride of place to the disembedded concept and seem to have neglected or forgotten that the affective image is crucial in communicating meaning and significance. We are not suggesting that we need more visual illustration of materials, but rather that the teacher be more hospitable to the mental images evoked by any topic. In planning teaching, to draw a principle from this observation, we should dwell not just on the concepts that are important, but give at least equal time to reflecting on the images that are a part of it. It is the images that can vividly carry the concepts most richly to the pupils' understanding.

Humanizing knowledge

As any journalist knows, information can be made more engaging if given a "human interest" angle. That is, knowledge seen through, or by means of, human emotions, intentions, hopes, fears, and so on, is not only more directly comprehensible but is also more meaningful and engaging than if presented disembedded from its human source. Every teacher knows how the illustrative anecdote, particularly if it involves extremes of human endurance or foresight or ingenuity or compassion or suffering, grabs pupils' attention.

Our problem, in some degree, comes from thinking of the book as the perfect model of learning–you write the codes down and there they are years later, secure and reliable. But written codes are nothing like living knowledge. Whatever is learned by a human being is never unaltered by our hopes and fears, and by our imaginations. In emphasizing the difference between inert symbolic codes in books and living knowledge in human minds, attention is drawn to something significant, and often neglected, about teaching. The point is not to get the symbolic codes as they exist in books into the pupils' minds. We can of course do that. But the teaching task is properly to reconstitute the inert symbolic code into living human knowledge. Knowledge in our minds is a function of the organization of our living cells; it is not a digital code like computer data, stable and infinitely replicable.

A second example of imaginatively teaching a science topic

We will briefly sketch an example about the topic of eels. The set of characteristics of pupils' imaginations discussed above suggest we begin by identifying some transcendent quality in eels because it is this that will enable us to catch up the pupils' imaginations in the topic. How can we find some transcendent human quality in eels? Well, there are lots of ways. For example, they were one of the commonest fish in ancient Europe but no one had ever seen a pregnant eel. The greatest discoverer of details of eels' lifecycles was a Dane, Johannes Schmidt. His pursuit of eels led him to voyages that would shame Ulysses or Drake or Cook. So a transcendent quality on which we can build our lessons is the persistence, courage, and ingenuity required for scientific exploration. This is what we will use to evoke wonder in the pupils' minds.

We next need to begin organizing the knowledge we want students' to learn into a narrative structure. We could begin with the mystery of the absence of pregnant eels. Where did they come from? We can begin with a romantic image–of Schmidt on the deck of one of rusting boats hunting eel larvae. In the late nineteenth-century, odd larvae floating in the Mediterranean had been caught and allowed to grow in tanks, and, to general puzzlement, grew into elvers–little eels. Schmidt's epic voyages began by scouring the Mediterranean, and discovering that the closer to the Straits of Gibraltar he found samples, the smaller they were. So he concluded that they were coming in from the Atlantic. He then spent about twenty years sailing from the arctic to the Azores, from the Bahamas to the North Sea looking for smaller and smaller larvae. In the end he tracked them down, discovering that all the eels in the world breed in the Sargasso Sea, and then drift on the currents, finding their ways to the river systems that feed the Atlantic.

So we have our humanized base for the knowledge, exemplified in Schmidt's transcendent qualities of persistence, courage, and ingenuity. We can provide pupils with a number of topics of detailed knowledge they can exhaustively pursue–such as the various changes the larvae go through in their odysseys, typically changing sex a few times, or the Sargasso Sea itself, or the variety of forms of larvae, or the voyages of Schmidt, or the triggers that set them on their long journey back to the Sargasso sea to breed, etc. We might conclude such a set of lessons with what still remains mysterious about eels.

Conclusion

We have tried, by brief examples rather than by extended argument, to show how we can reconceive our approach to the curriculum, by thinking firstly in terms of the pupils' imaginations. Starting there, we find that science becomes an arena for imaginative engagement no less than arts. We find also that quite quickly, once pupils become engaged in a topic, the distinctions that loom quite large when we focus on the products of sciences and arts become largely obliterated. Making emotional engagements, transcendent qualities, and narratives and stories prominent in science teaching does not distract from the science. Rather it helps to put the science in contexts of human meaning that can make it engaging and much better understood by pupils.

A further implication of these examples and our general argument is that if we want more imaginative and creative scientists, then we need to attend to those activities that seem especially able to stimulate the imagination. The characteristics we have sketched above are among our prime tools for making sense of the world imaginatively, and they are tools that have traditionally, for good reasons, been central to the work of the arts. So, if we want a more innovative technological society, built on better scientific understanding, then we would be wise to attend to stimulating and developing pupils' imaginations, and this is best done by careful attention to the arts, throughout schooling.

Bibliography

Black, M. (1962). *Models and metaphors.* Ithaca, New York: Cornell University Press.

Bruner, J. (1960). *The process of education.* Cambridge: Harvard University Press.

Dewey, J. (1934). *Art as Experience.* New York: Berkeley Publishing Group.

Clarke, D. (1982). *Descartes' philosophy of science.* Manchester: Manchester University Press

Egan, K. (2005). *An Imaginative Approach to Teaching.* San Francisco: Jossey-Bass.

—. (1997). *The Educated Mind.* Chicago: University of Chicago Press.

Gay, H. (1997). "East End, West End: Science Education, Culture and Class in Mid-Victorian Britain." *Canadian Journal of History,* XXXII, 153-183.

Schouls, P. (2000). *Descartes and the Possibility of Science.* London: Cornell University Press.

Spencer, H. (1851). *Social statistics.* London: Chapman.

—. (1928). *Essays on education, etc.* Introduction by Charles W. Eliot. 1911. Reprint, London: Dent.

Tierney, N. (1994). *Imagination and Ethical Ideals.* New York: State University of New York Press.

IMAGINATION IN THE DEVELOPMENT OF SPEECH AND LITERACY

MICHAEL HERRIMAN

Introduction

My basic argument is that our view of how the child acquires a language and becomes literate is governed by constructs developed out of our own literate world-view. These may in no way relate to the phenomenon of language as perceived by the preliterate child. Before the age of 6, the child has no view of language at all. Luria attributes to Vygotsky (1962) the view that up to a certain age, children see the world as through a glass, the existence of which they are not aware. At the stage at which they become aware of the glass–in Cazden's (1976) terms, when it becomes opaque–their view of it is probably structured by their imagination more than anything else. At this stage, we begin to intervene in their lives through formal instruction and we replace their imaginative schemes of thought with our definitive categories of knowledge. I believe that we might need to revise our understanding of the task children face in making sense of language and becoming literate, and be wary of invoking adult literate concepts in our pedagogy. The children's world prior to this stage has been an oral one, and their acquaintance with literate forms is likely to have been through stories read to them, but even these are based on oral modes of story telling. In this paper then the oral/literate divide, particularly as described by Walter Ong and David Olson, is a key concept.

The idea for this paper came from a claim put forward in a book on the co-evolution of language and the brain, by Terrence Deacon. In it he claims that languages may have evolved into their particular structures as a consequence of the needs of children in learning them. His claim is that "Languages are under powerful selective pressure to fit a child's likely guesses" (p.109) and, "Human children appear pre-adapted to guess the rules of syntax correctly, precisely because languages evolve so as to embody in their syntax the most frequently guessed patterns. The brain has co-evolved with respect to language, but languages have done most of the adapting" (p.122).

In other words, language structures evolved adapting themselves to the learning strategies of children. Deacon believes languages to be so complex that children would defy the attempt to learn them unless they evolved in the way he claims.

At first I thought of this as a bold and extraordinary claim, and simply not tenable. It throws conventional views on their head. I've thought about it often since and in this paper I wish to take it up again. The reasons are twofold: first as a Darwinian claim, it makes sense; and secondly, thinking this way may allow us to get outside of the adult literate view and consider what the child might do in acquiring the language of the parents. In this paper I want to develop the second point. In thinking about and researching children's language we have assumed that children face the task of learning a language by bringing to it conceptions that conform to the adult linguist's description of language. I believe this view is a consequence of literate thinking and may not reflect in any way the imaginative activities of the child. Indeed the very activities of classifying and analyzing are likely the products of the literate mind; this is an argument that I will take up later. So I want to try to move from the adult literate view of the language by showing ways in which it may misconstrue the task the child faces, both in first acquiring language and then in becoming literate. I can't offer an alternative, but I want to deconstruct the adult view because I don't believe it's the conception the child has. I want to know how the child's imagination of language fits the task of acquiring it and then learning to represent it in an entirely artificial way by squiggles on paper.

I would like to claim that the acquisition of the first language, and what follows from it, might be the greatest feat of imagination and learning undertaken by humans. For this reason alone it needs more careful attention. I then want to see how literacy might be influenced by the way language is first acquired. I suppose I could say I'm thinking in the Kieran Egan (1997) paradigm, trying to get outside of the adult view of what is appropriate and suitable for the child.

The development of literacy is perhaps the central concern of formal and even informal education. But it is preceded by an earlier feat of learning that should first be considered in talking about literacy, that is the acquisition of the person's first language. Literacy then may also be a consequence of the development of a further skill related to language, usually referred to as metalinguistic awareness; a phenomenon that seems to occur normally around the ages of 6 or 7. Metalinguistic awareness is probably a consequence of the experience gained in acquisition of the first language. But because it occurs at the same time that the first intervention that we call education occurs, it is not clear whether it can develop further independently of education. This issue is contested in the literature: for one thing, bilingual children are likely to develop a reflectiveness in regard to language that might be called metalinguistic awareness. If we consider these as three stages, we see that the first, language acquisition, is independent of any instruction, and that metalinguistic awareness may arise out of it, (though it may be spurred by the beginning of schooling too) but the third, the development of literacy, normally takes place exclusively in schooled environments.[1] Yet I want to claim that literacy critically depends on a well-developed meta-awareness of language. I want also to reflect upon the background to the child's attainment of literacy to ask what role imagination might have, either as contributory, incidental, consequential or as cause.

What is literacy?

First I'll identify what I mean by literacy. This is necessary because the term has had its usage extended recently. If we take it beyond its original denotation, that is, as the ability to read and write, or more correctly as the ability to encode and decode a language from a spoken to a written form, we can see that there has been a general acceptance of literacy as encompassing any coded form of information or representation. Thus we have terms such as mathematical literacy, film literacy, and computer literacy, and at a further extension, cultural literacy. Used in this latter way, literacy has come to mean the realization or comprehension of a code that lies behind the surface representation of the thing. For example, computer literacy means not just that a person is able to use a computer for word processing, emailing, or web surfing, but more that he or she can understand the acronyms and what they stand for, and the general way in which software works, such that new applications can be easily understood. The association with literacy in the original sense is preserved by the fact that being computer literate involves comprehension of a significant body of terminology supported by a grammar that is quite distinct and derived from what were originally programming languages. Cultural literacy can be seen as a further extension of the decoding skill, in this case understanding the norms (which are like grammatical rules) of the culture in which one is living. These rules extend beyond what we think of as cultural norms, however. Cultural literacy usually refers to the ability to critique the existing culture and evaluate its underpinning ideologies. In this case there is often an implicit assumption that what is the officially sanctioned ideology masks underlying social divisions and supports what is sometimes called a false consciousness.

In this paper I will remain with the original denotation of literacy and talk about the process by which a person comes to be able to read and write. It must not be assumed that learning to read and write is a natural extension of language learning. Though it may depend upon the first having been accomplished, it almost certainly isn't. Since literacy builds on the structures that the child has acquired in coming to speak and comprehend language, I will now analyze the form of discourse we commonly use to talk about the way children learn their native language. Then I will discuss literacy and its connection with metalinguistic awareness.

First language acquisition

The acquisition of the first language is accomplished largely by schemes of learning that are often said to be natural, by this I mean that children do not need formal instruction in the process of acquiring their native tongue. We don't need Noam Chomsky or Shirley Brice-Heath to tell us that children exposed to what might be considered non-standard, reduced, or even minimal linguistic input will develop a normal facility for the production of the language of their parents.[2]

However, when we talk about this topic, we tend to assume that the situation we are familiar with, that is, one in which children are positively encouraged in their language development at home and in which parents are encouraged to monitor their progress in this respect, is the norm. In fact it probably is not. In most societies in the world the idea of early intervention in the language learning process is not usually evident, reflecting perhaps the recognition that it is not needed. Indeed we could go further to note that the concern for this kind of intervention is itself a product of our social constructions of childhood and nurturing. This may be a natural reaction to living in a meritocratic society in which educational achievement is perceived to be a necessary means of economic advancement, and thus an investment. In this sense, promoting the child is like a capital investment.

Our concern with early intervention is probably too a consequence of the recently emerging field of developmental and child psychology. As we come to believe we know more about the learning process we tend to wish to intervene to improve upon it. It's also a product of the great self-improvement culture that is encouraged by the popular media and publishers. Playing Mozart to the child in the womb is probably the extreme manifestation of this.

The first point to make about language acquisition is that much or even most of the acquisition process is not susceptible to our analysis, understanding, or intervention. It is often referred to as a mysterious process. Its development has more in common with biological development except that there is no obvious physical change (unless one includes the shaping of the muscles controlling the vocal apparatus or synaptic neural developments). In saying this, I don't mean to dismiss the vast realm of research into childhood language acquisition, but rather to accept that it is almost entirely inferential, based on speculation about the kinds of schema or rules that might be involved in the output we hear from the child. In some cases we can control the input and observe the consequent output in making these inferences. But we cannot ask the child about the rules we presume are involved in their processing of the input, mainly because they are not the objects of the child's attention or thought (if they can be said to be objects at all—which is an extravagant term anyway). As well, the child would not have the vocabulary to tell us what is going on even if he or she were aware of the process. Whatever the process, the mechanism is, or can be likened to, a black box. The input can be largely known (it's the language that the young child hears spoken) and the output can be heard in the child's own speech productions. What is certain is that the child does not only produce the language he or she hears, but also produces novel utterances. It is what happens between input and output that is the mysterious process. This process, whereby the child progresses from single-word, to 2- and 3-word utterances, to fully developed and largely grammatically accurate statements, hides what we believe to be the operation of a set of rules or schema that are themselves being constantly adapted and refined to both comprehend and produce language reflecting that of his/her speech community. That is, of course, the way we talk about the process. We infer rules or hypotheses (but rules and hypotheses are the invention of the literate mind, so can we legitimately impute them to children?). In making this claim about the literate mind I am drawing directly on Walter Ong's (1982) study *Orality and Literacy.*

We go further than this to think that the set of rules can be regarded as a grammar. (Michael Halliday, who may well have done the most imaginative study of early language, regards it as such in the study of his son "Nigel"). Halliday (1975) detects grammatical relationships underlying the first gestures and utterances of his son (in the first years of his life. Nigel formulated, modified, and adapted several sets of grammars). These grammars have come to be seen as sets of hypotheses about the interrelationship of the structure, meaning, and sound of the language heard by the child. But again, in the absence of any evidence, we must ask if there is any warrant for saying that anything like rule-based processes are occurring or that the child has any knowledge of structures. The best we can perhaps say is that we can observe a progressive development in the accuracy, sophistication, and length of the language produced. To say that there is a progression is not to imply that it is a smooth one. Present thinking suggests that acquiring the first language involves trial-and-error procedures. But again this notion is a consequence of literate thinking. Probably the best evidence for this comes from the work of Annette Karmiloff-Smith. From her research it may be inferred that children generate hypotheses about the structure and meaning of the language heard around them and modify these as their application of the hypotheses approaches the target. At first the hypotheses over-generalize the case (example: the application of the past tense ending, *ed,* to all verbs) but as they perceive the misunderstanding, in their failure to communicate, children appear to refine their hypotheses, applying them to more restricted data, also developing pluri-functional ideas about categories of sounds (the "s" suffix as it indicates possession and plurality, for example). But children are at no stage conscious of this hypothesizing or making of inferences, so again we must beware of attributing such literate constructs to them.

The way I have been describing language acquisition, suggests that the child is required only to learn the grammar of language to be able to comprehend and speak it. This might imply that knowing that there are words, that sounds make up words and that words apply to things, is somehow already there. Nothing could be further from the truth, for the following reason.

The adult literate conception of language

When we think of the language we speak, our objectification of it is alphabetical. We think of language in its written form and with its representative elements comprising letters, syllables, words, phrases, and sentences. In this way literacy tyrannizes our thinking. It is difficult to get outside of this view of language. It is further compounded by the dominance of an analytic way of thinking, which Ong sees as itself the product of literacy. The literate view of language is probably as far removed as imaginable from the child's conception of the phenomenon. In fact, up until about 5 or 6 most children have no conception of language.

Children who pay any attention to writing at all appear to regard it as a kind of accompaniment to speaking, like beating time. The matter of having to consciously learn it doesn't even arise.

The error in our thinking about language comes about because we assume that the phonemes, morphemes, and sentences of our language are real objects (after all we can see them on paper). We also think that grammar is a kind of blueprint or superstructure that exists independently of language. I want to claim that all of these supposed objectifications of language are in fact not real properties of language at all. We think that they are because of the way our literate mind thinks of language, as a written thing. Ong cites Derrida's (1976, p.14) point that "there is no linguistic sign before writing" (1988, p. 75). These objectifications are instead abstractions or composites of abstractions. They exist in a realm apart from language and are just convenient ways of thinking about it, occasioned by the invention of alphabetic literacy.

We talk about the phoneme for example, as the smallest separable unit of sound. This is a gross overstatement, for though we think of there being about 42 phonemes in English, we can by no means say what these are or how they are able to be represented in any word. They are almost certainly made up of smaller units of noise. When the sounds we identify as phonemes, for example, are a part of words, their phonic representation is changed by the values of the other phonemes in the word. This is not obvious to us because we apply our literate conception of phonemes to the word heard and the force of this allows us to believe we hear the phoneme as a separate object. This sounds strange so I should give an example.

If we think of the word *bag,* for example, our literate mind tells us that it is made up of three separate phonemes. If we look at a spectrograph of someone's pronunciation of this word it becomes apparent that it is not a sequence of the three separate phonemes in serial order. It's much more complicated because each phoneme contains phonic information about the others. If we then look at *bat*, it is not as if there is a common section up to the final phoneme, rather the shape of the spectrograph is different from the onset of sound. The phoneme is a rather feeble construct that the literate mind thinks it identifies in the language we use. In the language of speech, it bears very little relationship to an object we identify as a word in the written form, our alphabet. Yet when we teach children to read, we assume there's an almost exact correspondence between phonemes and alphabetic characters.[3] Then we can't understand why children can't perceive this relationship.[4]

If it is not enough to destroy our conception of the reality of one supposed basic unit of language (phonemes) we might consider words.

Words don't belong to the same class of linguistic objects as phonemes. Linguists prefer to use the term morpheme as it is more easily defined, but since we introduce children to literacy via the metalinguistic term *word*, I will discuss words here. If anything exists in language we might think it to be the word. I want to claim, to the contrary, that the word is a construct that a literate world-view imposes on speech.[5] We can certainly see words in writing, but mainly because we mark what we regard as words by a spatial separation. This is a relatively recent phenomenon in text, first implemented by Bede in the 8th century (on the authority of Saenger (1982)), but by no means widespread until more recently. It came into fashion as it were with the "invention" of silent reading. Even as late as the 18th century we find James Boswell commenting on Johnson's ability to read without pronouncing the words aloud. The first silent readers, one understands, found the technique difficult, as it required control of the natural inclination of the lips to move in conjunction with the line of text. Words then, may be seen as constructs to facilitate the representation of speech in a written form.

The key question is whether the word has any reality in speech. We can begin by recognizing that in speech there is no clear separation of elements that we can identify as words. In other words, words are not defined by pauses in speech. We probably think they are because we believe spaces between words in writing also serve to delimit the sound unit in speech. As I've noted already, spaces between segments of writing are there only to aid reading. We certainly don't speak in words. Natural pauses in a stream of speech usually don't occur at what in writing we would see as the boundary of each word. Typical speech groups a set of sounds into what we might recognize as phrases. Our segmentation of speech conforms more to emphasis and rhythm. In word recognition tasks with children we find that prior to learning to read and write, the child's view of a word does not conform to the literate notion of word. When we give a child a sentence and ask them to pick out the parts, they will usually identify its parts, if they do so at all, as conforming to larger segments of language, the language as they hear it. Nouns for example, are usually associated with adjectives or determiners, verbs with prepositions. Such groups are the reality (and probably the meaning units) for children.

There is a similar idea expressed in the notion that words stand for things; that they are like name-tags for things. Outside of proper names, it is doubtful if this view is tenable. What does the word cat stand for? Clearly I can produce a cat and say that the word means the animal. Though this might seem convincing it is quite misleading. The sound/cat/accords with a complex set of thoughts (in the mind) that is possibly unique for each person. For a hypo-allergenic adult cat may mean something different from its meaning for a child. Ong maintains that there is no one-to-one relationship between words and items in an extra-mental world. The strength of the claim is more obvious when we think about terms like *democracy*, or *the unconscious mind*. It would be more accurate, though still probably wrong, to think of what we hear (and what the child hears) are chunks of language (strings) that contain large complexes of meaning. In teaching literacy we provide constructs such as words to help the child perceive the structure of written text.

Words then are abstractions that we impose on speech to encode it into written forms. The idea becomes clearer if we think about inflections, derivations, and compounds. If *cat* is a word, what about *cats*, *cat's*, or *cats'*? What could we mean if we said they are related words or the same words with certain grammatical differences? In what way is *baking* different from *baked*. We can ask the same questions of derivations: in what way are *he* and *himself*, or *initial* and *initialize* different words. Compounds also emphasize the point. Is *hardware* one word or two? What about objectless compounds like *nevertheless* or *counterfactual*? It just does not make sense to talk this way. The literate mind has problems with this, so we should try to imagine how the non-literate mind conceives of them or how the child thinks of them. Do children think of words as tags to apply to things? If they do, it is the product of our ostensive behavior in teaching them the referents of words in the assumption that words are tags. Some words are like tags, but as I've said already, their reality defies our description or understanding. I think we must accept that we can't define words (and that defining is itself only a literate activity). This is because they are not real in the way the literate mind or the dictionary leads us to think of them.

Another interesting reflection on the word comes from looking at the conception of words in non-alphabet using societies. In Japan, where I teach, I sometimes make minor errors in pronouncing students' names, this is almost always when a name, to my thinking, sounds similar to another. To give an example: I might use the name Yoshihiro for Hiroyoshi or Masayasu for Yasumasa (all of these being common names). If I attempt to explain my error by apologizing and referring to the phonological similarity I perceive between the two sets of names, I am met by blank stares. My students think of names not in a phonetic sense at all. The two names I confused are to my students as unlike as the Kanji used to write the names. When I ask my Chinese friends to tell me what they think of when they think of a word, it is not its sound, but its pictorial representation. This, of course, is a product of the written representation of that language. Saenger (1991) notes (citing Tzeng and Hung, 1981) that Chinese readers have direct visual access to the meaning of characters without the mediation of either physical or mental phonic articulation. The issue I am exploring here ultimately gets down to the question of representation in the mental lexicon. We do not know how speech is represented in the mind so it is a lavish assumption to think its representation is verbal. Such representations present themselves as natural only because of the alphabetical/literate dominance in our thinking about language.

We can carry the analysis further to the level of grammar. Again there is a grave danger of thinking of grammar as that set of prescriptive rules governing the relationships into which words may enter. We think that way because, for at least 250 years, books of grammar have instructed in these rules. Of course, it only takes a moment to adjust our thoughts to the fact that these so-called rules are canons only for writing and formal speech (even in these activities they are often disregarded though). If we move to think about the grammar of speech, we are confronted by an almost impossible task, that is, if we wish to systematize it. But aside from lexicographic reasons, why should we? For both writing and speech, we need to escape the tyranny of this literate view and recognize that grammar is no less than the totality of ways in which speakers use a language to communicate (that is when they communicate successfully).

We need to go beyond a structural view of language (that which sees it as able to be categorized into what we call parts of speech–such a view has too many problems anyway) and look rather at the way in which words are distributed in language, that is, look at categories of groups of words that fill the same slots, have the same functions, or relate to similar meanings. It is not an objection to say that this approach will lead to chaos where words can mean anything. Language is quite consistent and self-corrective. Failure to communicate is enough to keep it within bounds of comprehension.

Fortunately we now have an additional tool by means of which we can look at the way in which people actually use language. This is the computer based corpus, in particular the corpora of spoken language. The corpora reveal in a refreshing way the fact that speakers often ignore canons of grammar in preference to sounding like their fellow speakers. The division is both formal vs. informal and speech vs. writing. There are numerous examples of this. Here are two cases:

Neither you nor I are able to go.   (informal and spoken)
Neither you nor I is able to go.   (formal and written)   and

Who's there? It's me. (informal and spoken)
Who's there? It is I. (formal and written)

The corpora of spoken language reveal that the way in which we use language conforms only very loosely to what we think of as grammar. We would save ourselves much pain by rejecting the idea of grammar as rules and opting instead for grammar as the totality of ways in which particular words or strings of words can be distributed in speech or writing and be comprehensible to native speakers of a language. We could of course make generalizations about these usages that might sound like rules, but they may only help us in agreeing about acceptable written forms. This idea of grammar as the totality of comprehensible strings of a given language echoes Chomsky's notion of relying on the intuitions of native speakers for grammatical acceptability.

What I have been doing so far is attempting to deconstruct our notions of language which are based on literate conceptions which in turn are taken back to reflect on spoken forms. To think of what children accomplish in acquiring their first language it is necessary to cast these literate conceptions aside.

If we can break away from our literate view of language (a very difficult act of imagination or will is required for this) and think clearly enough of what the child accomplishes in the acquisition of the first language, we may fairly conclude it to be the greatest feat of learning (either self-instructed or taught) that humans as a whole undertake. All subsequent learning, no matter how profound, is more a matter of persistence over a long period of time. (Here I think we can except a few examples of the acquisition of ideas or knowledge that mark one or another form of genius–for example, that displayed by mathematical genius. In this case, it is often reported that ideas come by inspiration, as if revealing relationships or connectedness between things that the person was not aware of.)

I want to claim that we would do much better to think about language acquisition as a product of imagination, and maybe its greatest achievement.

Kieran Egan has discussed in length the way in which children at what he calls the mythic stage develop ideas of binary opposition and base much of their thinking on abstractions. This capacity for abstract thinking, which he believes to be reinforced by the imaginative worlds they are introduced to by stories, may well lead to their success at acquiring language. Egan rejects the view of children moving necessarily from concrete to abstract thinking, a rejection well justified if we think of language acquisition (1997, ch.2). It seems clear that there are no concrete objects of language for children to work with in any case (as I have argued above). The child's abstractions might come only from his or her imaginative interaction with the world of language and its most expressive forms (in imaginative fiction). That these abstractions succeed in most cases, leads us back to consider Deacon's claim about the evolution of language. The only alternative might be the Chomsky/Pinker view that sees language growth on an analogy with organic growth.

My major concern, however, is that this initial and profound feat of the imagination is followed by a process of instruction in literacy that in general takes no advantage of the previous imaginative achievement of the child. In fact, we might say it is opposed to it in that it takes the task of learning away from the child and passes it into the hands of the literate teacher who proceeds with the view that he/she is teaching about real things. How much more effective might be the teacher who begins by trying to understand the imaginative processes by which the child had gained the language in the first place. I'll say more about this in my conclusion.

In talking about language acquisition above I have perhaps promoted the idea that the child has fully acquired language by the time schooling begins. Although this assumption is often made, it is erroneous. The research in language forms used by children indicates that the process continues, probably aided by schooling, until late teens and maybe even beyond. The point is that children by the age of six or seven have a good grasp of the oral modes of speech, because in general this is the milieu in which they've participated, and out of which their competence has developed. What continues to develop is usually called late-emerging syntax. It's an interesting development because as already suggested, it's probably related to the process of schooling, and also because it reflects the demands of a literate worldview. Here again I draw on Walter Ong who has identified amongst other things that mark literate from oral cultures, the following:

Oral	Literate
Additive	Subordinative
Aggregative	Analytic
Situational	Abstract
Empathetic	Objectively distanced

I would suggest that to discuss adequately the above characteristics of the literate culture, one needs language with syntax based on subordination, employing the conjunctions that signal analytic and abstractive mental processes; words such as *therefore, nonetheless, however, notwithstanding,* to cite just a few. It can also be identified by subordinate rather than just coordinate structures, indicating the consciousness of hypothetical states of affairs. The facility to use language in this way seems to be acquired only in the second decade of life.

Metalinguistic awareness

Now I'll speak about metalinguistic awareness because I believe it to be the key point of intervention in the development of literacy. At the time at which schooling usually begins (for most children around the ages of 5 to 7), which is after the initial stage of acquiring a language, something of almost equal a feat of learning occurs. This is the stage at which the child begins to become aware of language as an object, that is, to separate it from its referent. Prior to this it seems that children think of names, for example, as being an intrinsic part of the property of things. This is the transition I referred to above in speaking of Vygotsky's glass theory. The child becoming aware of language as a separate system detachable from objects is able to direct this reflection towards language itself. It refers to an awareness of language at the meta-level, which means being able to see language as a formal system and as separate from the world of events and objects it usually describes.

A simple example of metalinguistic awareness can be seen when a child recognizes that a word is an arbitrary complex of sounds not inherently related to its referent(s), or that we can actually talk about words and word properties. This stage can be recognized easily because it's that at which puns and word games suddenly become things of great interest. Words take on a magic power because they can be applied to anything that the child cares to imagine. The change is quite dramatic and can be illustrated by a typical response to a type of word-game in which the child agrees that we might call the sun the moon, and the moon the sun. Though children of different ages can agree to this rule, the 4-year old will subsequently deny that sun shines at night, whereas the 6-year old will readily affirm it.

Development of subsequent language skills and success at schooling both depend upon continued growth of metalinguistic awareness. Metalinguistic awareness may also enhance cognitive functioning via the means it provides of expressing thought and reflecting on its products.

In common with the early period of acquisition, which I have spoken about already, this stage gives evidence of a rich play of the imagination.

The child is freed from the domination of the word as a property of things. Thus he or she can use words indiscriminately or selectively to apply to anything. Rhyming first appears at this time and becomes a tool to extend relationships between things that are bound only by the breadth of the imagination. Children can escape into a private world, free of the chains of denotation previously binding them. It is as if their imaginative capacity, previously devoted to sorting out the world of language, can now be applied freely to creating worlds other than those bound by strictures of name as word property. Egan identifies metaphor in early childhood language activity. Certainly at this stage metaphor plays a prominent role in language. Metaphor represents perhaps the greatest liberation for children from the denotative world and may well fuel the development of hypothetical thinking in general, the entertainment of contrary to fact situations.

Early literacy

It is almost certainly no accident that most societies begin formal schooling at the age at which metalinguistic abilities start to emerge. Teachers have probably realized that this is the age at which children are optimally ready to learn to read and write. But it is only very recently that educators have become aware of the importance of metalinguistic awareness as the basis for teaching literacy. The largest problem in early education is the failure of up to 1/4 of students to conquer the challenge of reading. This is in stark contrast to their success in learning to speak. I won't go into that problem other than to suggest that reading is a complicated process requiring recognition of the print-encoding of morpho-phonemic and morpho-syntactic structures of speech. It is not simply a matter of the child being taught to associate a sound with a written word. It almost certainly involves a set of operations as complex as those the child implicitly brings to comprehending language in the first place. Reading probably has a reciprocal relationship with emerging metalinguistic abilities and in ideal situations the interaction may benefit the child for the rest of elementary school. In most school systems however there is no deliberate program that treats the child's language needs as an elaboration of the language that the child brings to school. The texts used for much of reading instruction are usually created rather than real, whereas the child who will have had any acquaintance with literacy via stories read to him, will have had access thereby to language of an oral and highly imaginative kind.

More critical though is the relatively slight attention given to language itself, outside of it being an incidental adjunct of learning to read. An important exception to this is found in Russia where (at least until recently) there has been recognition of the need for formal language study throughout schooling. This is a consequence of ideas drawn from the research of Vygotsky and his followers. A carefully planned program introduces children to an awareness of speech, its verbal componential nature and social purposes, and subsequently, to the nature and purposes of print into which speech can be encoded. Such a program which draws attention to linguistic strategies at the meta-level, will contribute to metalinguistic awareness and thus to literacy more generally.

Much of present practice in early schooling also is based on the view that language acquisition is fairly complete by the time children come to school. Thus literate activities focus only on reading, with much less attention given to further language development. In some parts of the English-speaking world this has become a political issue. Intervention in the language development of the child is seen as discriminatory towards the language of the home or community where such intervention favors a standard form or one different from that of the community. The child's acquisition of literacy can be dangerously threatened by the failure to solve this question sensitively. A clear understanding of the role of literacy in achieving the goals of formal education must be sought, and come to be divorced from the political considerations of ensuring that the language of the home is not diminished in its status.

Contrary to the formerly-held, but unchallenged assumption, that most language development was complete by the age of five or six, it is seen that more complex and subtle grammatical structures are not acquired until later in childhood. This mastery is not an accretional process, but rather proceeds by steps. Karmiloff-Smith also sees later language development as related to cognitive development. The later-mastered syntactic forms are precisely the linguistic forms which characterize academic text and the expression of argument forms in most subject matter of schooling, yet little explicit instruction is given that would aid the child in understanding the metalinguistic basis of the cognitive and linguistic task confronted in later years of schooling.

Later literacy

We should not consider that because certain levels of skill in reading and writing are accomplished, literacy is thereby established. It is far from the case. Contemporary schooling, especially in the higher grades, requires more than the basic decoding abilities associated with reading and writing for its completion. The successful student must be able to comprehend and use a formal code of written expression in several or many different disciplines. This code is seldom explicitly taught or commented on. Moreover, the attention paid to formal language instruction in high school is minimal; in most systems it is gradually reduced from about the third grade onwards. Additionally, forms of expression derived from the oral mode characterize much of the language found outside of the classroom, especially in the dominant media, but also in literature itself. The student thus will encounter two codes; one speech-based (the transactional language of the classroom), the other text-based (the language of instruction and the school text). For most students and many teachers this is a difference of which they are not sufficiently aware.

The languages of written text and spoken utterance

The question of the distinction between text and speech-based language is therefore important. The strongest claim for the autonomy of text has been made by David Olson (1987). Although this earlier view has been modified by the recognition that there are oral language structures, which perform functions analogous to those identified for formal text, the argument for the distinctiveness of formal text in terms of the structures it engages, still stands. It relies on recognizing the historical development of English prose during the 17th and 18th centuries, particularly in natural philosophy. Writers of the time developed an argumentative prose style based not on the English vernacular, but rather on the model of that language more familiar to scientific, legal, and metaphysical writings throughout Europe, namely Latin, which consequently formed the basis for the syntax and lexicon of formal prose.

This formal style of text has been preserved in English, although some simplification has occurred. Academic text has also preserved a Latin and Greek derived vocabulary that marks it distinctively. This vocabulary can be seen in the technical terminology of this paper for example. Students' access to formal text forms is critical because it is the means by which our society generates, structures, and justifies knowledge.

Formal features of English

An examination of the academic text style of contemporary disciplines shows the formal features of text that reflect its logical purposes, a characteristic which Olson refers to as its argumentative capacity. The style embodies logical devices that enable inference, deduction, hypothesis formation, concept formation, and the expression of existentiality, conjunction, opposition, and qualification by means of modals, conditionals, counterfactuals and quantifiers. Ong would see all of these as properties of a literate world-view. The important point is that they embody the kind of thought patterns that typify the literate demands of higher levels of schooling. These patterns should be available to all students, yet we must ask how many students are made aware of them explicitly. This may be a major omission in most education systems.

I have moved fairly rapidly from early literacy to speak more about the importance of later literacy in school. The emphasis on the latter was meant to show the importance of the child gaining the initial stages of literacy, just because the later demands of schooling depend so much on success in the earlier ones

Literacy as developed metalinguistic awareness

I've suggested that the formal text-based nature of much of school learning necessitates the child's proficiency in handling text forms and recognizing situations that require the formal mode for their expression. The meta-awareness implicit in the notion of metalinguistic awareness will allow this proficiency to develop, but it must still be asked what linguistic knowledge base is appropriate to the manipulation of various text forms.

Literacy has historically been associated with the notion of letters–in this case not simply the knowledge of alphabetic characters, but rather the ability to find the appropriate combinations of them to formulate unique and revealing means of expression. A meta-awareness of language will bring these forms to conscious attention, but additionally a set of structural descriptions is needed to talk about the forms. There is no reason why children in elementary school should not be taught a technical vocabulary to identify those linguistic objects that are the focus of their metalinguistic awareness at any particular stage of learning. In fact it is only when children come to use some metalinguistic vocabulary (e.g., "word," "letter," "sound," etc.) that they can analyze their metalinguistic knowledge. Knowledge of the names of parts of speech and linguistic structures (use of terms such as "phoneme," "morpheme," "phrase," etc.) will enable them to discuss syntactical and stylistic aspects of language as well as reflect on their own written work.

Acquaintance with metalinguistic vocabulary represents a more developed form of metalinguistic awareness. This is akin to the level of knowledge possessed by the bilingual person who at least has access to the different representation of the same or equivalent forms (at the syntactic or lexical level) in each language even if the vocabulary to represent it abstractly is not known.

Literacy then may be seen as developed metalinguistic awareness and although much of this awareness is natural, in that it is part of an awareness or knowledge drawn from ordinary language experience, there are very good reasons for adopting a specific program of teaching for its attainment. Knowledge of the structure and function of language may stand in the same relation to literacy that mathematics does to numeracy. It thus invites the same reasons for its teaching. The fact that many people never achieve the level of personal literacy that will allow them to succeed in study or careers or in some cases achieve a degree of personal satisfaction, suggests the need for a continued program of language teaching throughout schooling with an emphasis on metalinguistic awareness and its application to the language of formal text. That would require not simply a program of language use, but a program that encourages thought about language. The benefit of learning another language also cannot be overstated. This is well recognized in Canada of course.

Possession of developed metalinguistic awareness will not only benefit a person's ability to comprehend and produce the language of the text forms encountered in schools, but will have consequences for the language of speech, and cognition. Knowledge of the language of various text forms can be used to instruct the language of utterance and refine it in such a way as to increase its expressive power. Speech, being spontaneous and ephemeral, is less subject to the checks and rechecking that formal text is. The ability to analyze one's written language and refine or modify it may be applied to oral language at the level of thought. Rhetoric traditionally taught this skill.

Conclusion

In this paper I have tried to show that the two most important areas of learning a person acquires are commenced outside of any formal learning system. They are the product of the mental operations of a normal human in his/her linguistic environment. Their mysteriousness leads me to conclude that they are the outcome of highly imaginative analyses that children use to make sense of speech. As literate adults we assume that the child is performing these self-instructed tasks with a view of language that we base on our knowledge of the written form. I have tried to deconstruct this view by showing that this view is a product of the science of linguistics, which has created a reasonably convenient set of constructs for categorizing written forms, in our case alphabetic forms. Unfortunately we take these structures to be real objects, whereas they are constructs that on closer examination break down. To understand what a child is doing in learning a language we must suppress our literate view, in favor of thinking about the language of speech, because that is what the child is working with.

What I have attempted to do here, indirectly, is to ask you as reader to imagine the world of language as constructed by the child. It is asking you to use your imagination, to conceive of what the child has to do to decode first the noises that he/she hears and then later is forced to code into another form. This is a nearly impossible task of course because our minds are so fixed on the literate conception of language.

I wish to go further and suggest that any investigation into the development of literacy needs to consider the role of imagination. As Egan suggests, language acquisition probably takes place as an extension of the abstractive mind of the child. This mind is open to schemas that sort the world into a coherent whole for the child. These, it may be argued, are the output of the child's imagination. The child is dealing with what he or she perceives to be images, yet they successfully sort out the linguistic world for themselves. The question then remains, why do we so intrusively take over the child's literary world and try to shape it to external models of what we as adults assume to be the correct world-view.

On a more practical level, children should be introduced to literacy via the contexts with which they are most familiar in their oral world. These might be the world of imaginative literature, tales, rhymes, or folklore that Kieran Egan so closely associates with the mythic stage of development. Although I have concentrated on the importance of later literacy for academic achievement in schooling (which I have closely associated with what might be construed as analytic disciplines), I must stress that this focus must not preclude the close attention that should be given to imaginative literature throughout schooling, especially as it might be an antidote to the banality of theme and language in television.

End notes

[1] This is not to deny that many children are taught to read by anxious parents, or may even teach themselves.
[2] The exceptions might be those born with a major mental problem or others for whom a physical incapacity may prevent speech.

[3] The pronunciation of vowels in English, for example, is so varied regionally that if we assumed there to be just one standard representation for each phonemic vowel, English might be incomprehensible. The versatility of human aural comprehension is such that most listeners can readily adapt their comprehension to unheard dialects and vowel values.

[4] The correspondence is much more accessible for languages such as Spanish where the alphabetic characters have a relatively regular correspondence with the sounds they are meant to represent.

[5] The difficulty of identifying words is well recognized in lexicography. Most dictionaries consist of words identifies in writing, not in speech. The OED, for example, bases all its entries on literate references. The emergence of corpus-based studies of language has brought the word problem to the forefront. See Leech, et al. (2001)

Bibliography

Cazden, C.B. (1976). *Play with language and metalinguistic awareness: One dimension of language experience.* In J. S. Bruner et.al (Eds.) Play. New York; Penguin.

Deacon, T. W. (1998). *The Symbolic Species: The Co-evolution of Brain and Language.* New York; W. W. Norton.

Derrida, J. (1976). *Of Grammatology.* Trans. by Gayatri Chakratory Spivak. Baltimore and London; Johns Hopkins University Press.

Egan, K. (1997). *The Educated Mind: How Cognitive Tools Shape Our Understanding.* Chicago; University of Chicago Press.

Halliday, M. (1975). *Learning How to Mean: Explorations in the Development of Language.* (Explorations in Language Study Series). London: Arnold.

Karmiloff-Smith, A. (1992). *Beyond Modularity: A Developmental Perspective on Cognitive Science.* Cambridge MA; MIT Press.

Leech, G., Rayson, P. & Wilson A. (2001) *Word Frequencies in Spoken and Written English; Based on the British National Corpus.* London; Longman.

Ong, W. J. (1988) *Orality and Literacy: The Technologizing of the Word.* London; Routledge.

Seanger, P. (1982) *Silent Reading: Its impact on late medieval script and society.* Viator, 13, 367-414

Vygotsky, L.S. (1962) *Thought and Language.* Cambridge, MA; MIT Press.

INCLUSIVE CURRICULUM DESIGN THROUGH NARRATIVE AND IMAGINATIVE INTERACTIVE LEARNING ENVIRONMENTS

LISA GJEDDE

This chapter focuses on the role of narrative and imaginative interactive learning environments (Gjedde 2004) in the development of an inclusive curriculum. There is a dearth of interactive learning resources that can be used by older learners with severe learning challenges. The chapter describes a theoretical framework and design principles for the design of narrative interactive learning for special needs learners. It also presents the results of the user-oriented design process and the learning outcomes that have been observed through action-research carried out in a number of schools. Through the anchoring of a concrete topic in a frame narrative, it is possible to create a digital interactive learning environment, which offers an imaginative learning arena augmented with assistive technology for learners with severe learning challenges, as well as learners with a wide range of skills and abilities. This type of interactive learning environment that is based on a narrative and imaginative approach (Egan 1997) offers learning activities that are differentiated and supports learning for even severely challenged learners. It is based on the narrative construction of meaning–on symbolic, iconic and enactive (Bruner 1966) properties of the learning environment–that is of importance to the development of an inclusive curriculum.

Introduction

Stories are fundamental to human communications and understanding of a culture. As such they are valuable as tools for teaching and for creating a sense of cultural background and identity. We are enculturated through stories (Bruner 1986) as they provide tools to help us create meaning at both personal and global levels. Whyte (1981) tells us that the study of narrative involves: "reflection on the very nature of culture and possibly even on the nature of humanity itself."

This connection between narrative and the nature of humanity is a strong factor in learning, and connects narrative learning and imaginative education with its focus on meaningful learning activities. As Egan (1992) suggests, there is an important relationship between narrative capacity and imagination because narrative is "central to the general ability to make meaning out of experience."

Another important feature of story is the potential it has to help build community and share experience. Since a story can be understood and interpreted in different ways according to the person who perceives the story, it is central in any communication and teaching endeavor that reaches out to a heterogeneous group. Because of this it can be an important tool in inclusive education.

The Danish Education Act stipulates that pupils with multiple disabilities have the right to education in line with other pupils. One important tool in achieving this goal is technology enhanced learning (TEL) and assistive technology which supports a range of individual approaches and can provide opportunities for differentiation, which makes it an attractive option for use in special needs education. A complimentary approach that can scaffold the learning environment of the TEL is based on imaginative education, a holistic approach in which narrative learning is defined as a cognitive tool (Egan 1997).

Bruner suggests that "it is very likely the case that the most natural and the earliest way in which we organize our experience and our knowledge is in terms of the narrative form" (1986). The function of stories may exist before language in the development of the child, and the child may learn the language to express its stories. He also suggests (Bruner 1966) that there are three modes of representation in relation to learning and acquiring knowledge: Enactive (actions), Iconic (pictures) and Symbolic (words and numbers).

In working with children with multiple functional deficiencies who often have no verbal language, the perspective of story can add coherence, and can make it possible to engage the learners particularly when the story draws on actions, interactions and pictures, thus activating the Enactive and Iconic dimensions.

A complimentary perspective on learning is provided by Kieran Egan (1997) who suggests that there are five kinds of understanding that overlap, each involving sets of cognitive tools. Egan has been instrumental in developing theories of imaginative learning in a holistic approach that endeavors to involve the learner's heart as well as mind, and sees story as important in teaching and enabling meaning-making as fundamental to education.

The five kinds of understanding that Egan (1997) describes as overlapping are:

- somatic understanding which relates to the senses and the body,
- mythic understanding which relates to understanding through story form
- romantic understanding which relates to heroes and the limits of personal self in the world
- philosophic understanding which relates to laws, theories and the connection between the individual and the world, and
- ironic understanding which relates to a sense of self-reflection and awareness transcending the other forms of understanding.

Bruner's and Egan's complimentary theories of modes of representation and modes of understanding both focus on the construction of meaning by the learner and the acknowledgment that narrative is fundamental in this process.

Narrative as a tool for inclusive imaginative learning

Pupils with multiple deficiencies have a need for meaningful learning activities just as other pupils do, but due to their lack of verbal skills, they require a different approach to teaching. As they do not have the same motivation for going to school that a pupil with normal employment prospects might have, it is essential that they are presented with meaning making potentials in the learning environment they are offered.

A narrative and imaginative learning approach can help facilitate meaning making, and at the same time can challenge the usual teaching practices.

An underlying design principle which can be found in most interactive learning programs aimed at learners with functional disabilities is to avoid complexity by limiting the number of choices available in order to facilitate use by the target group. This, however, rarely allows for the involvement of the learners at a deeper level where processes of meaning making are involved. The affordances of most of these programs are for isolated actions, like clicking at yellow ducks moving across a screen, which does not engage the learner beyond the current action. Such programs designed for access by users with functional deficits may be appropriate from a computer interaction perspective, but not from the perspective of curriculum and age-relevant contents for individuals such as teen-agers who, in spite of physical challenges, may be going through processes of growing up and having to find their own identity.

A pilot project involving a special needs teacher using a multimedia program about the Vikings showed that even learners with severe functional deficiencies responded very well to a narrative and imaginative teaching approach.

As a result of the success of this pilot, a project was developed that aimed at producing a research-based design for narrative learning in a technology enhanced interactive learning environment. The project involved interaction designers, artists, and special needs teachers, with the aim of developing a narrative interactive learning environment with augmentative functions, such as scanning the screen, to make it possible to use with a switch or alternative IO for older learners with multiple functional disabilities. The program offers interaction through specially designed interfaces that a learner can use with assistive technology, and content representation relating to the Symbolic, Iconic and Enactive dimensions.

The Symbolic dimension is represented through the oral storytelling that underlies the Iconic dimension: the animated sequences and flash games. The Enactive dimension is represented through the interaction potentials which allow the learner to choose between different themes, activities, and games within the framework of the story.

The software anchors curriculum-relevant material about medieval life in a frame story. It tells one of the King Arthur stories with a high degree of complexity on a visual as well as linguistic level, and, within a narrative setting provides the learners with more choices than those usually offered this target group,

Narrative anchoring, situated learning and the creation of meaning

The program's overarching theme is medieval life. The intention was to give students an insight into a number of themes related to daily life in medieval times. These themes are anchored in a frame story from the King Arthur Cycle about Sir Gawain and Lady Ragnell. The hero, Sir Gawain, a knight from King Arthur's court, rides out to find the answer to a riddle about what women desire most. If he does not find the right answer to the riddle, King Arthur will have to die as a punishment for having killed one of the Forest King's deer. The solution to the riddle and the morale of the story is: that which women desire most of all is the right to decide for oneself.

This story was chosen because it conveyed themes of medieval adventure as well as universal themes–love, transformation, to be accepted as you are, and a desire for self-determination. Precisely these themes, not least the one on self-determination, may have great relevance for the intended group of students, who are often subject to others making choices for them.

The psychologist Jerome Bruner (1996) writes about the situatedness of meanings in relation to the culture in which they are created, and the need for "culture's symbol systems" to communicate:

> Although meanings are 'in the mind,' they have their origins and their significance in the culture in which they are created. It is their cultural situatedness of meanings that assures their negotiability, and ultimately their communicability. In this view learning and thinking are always situated in a cultural setting, and always dependent upon the utilization of cultural resources.

In this narrative program, the learners are offered a communication platform involving "culture's symbol systems" using stories and images that reflect a historical epoch, in this case the Medieval ages, which allows students to communicate using cultural artifacts and narrative. These carry meanings by themselves, but they also assume additional layers of meaning when they are engaged with by students who bring the context of their own history and personal preference.

In a classroom, teaching with the use of an interactive whiteboard, the program offers a shared cultural context for learning. We can hypothesize that the function of this interactive narrative learning environment is to provide the learners with the tools and artifacts that support their construction of meaning. Through the use of the artifacts of the program– the story animated and told by the storyteller, the games, and the videos– they participate in a shared cultural space where they can implicitly mediate aspects of their identity and personality that they would otherwise not be able to communicate.

Narrative, knowledge, and identity

Since many of the students with multiple disabilities cannot be expected to use the program without a personal assistant, a significant parameter in developing the program is the requirement for a complexity and relation to universal issues that would also make it interesting for the assistant to keep using it over a lengthy time period.

An important issue in designing the program is how it will support the student's experience and expression of identity. Identity is dynamic and socially embedded. In this context, identity has to do with the learner's expressions and actions in relation to interactivity and making choices.

The program makes it possible to participate in a variety of game-like activities during which the user can make choices in relation to his preferences that support the student's own experience of identity through the potentials for action that are offered, and the choices the student makes. The program provides activities connected to the themes of daily life in medieval times:

- Monastic life
- Medieval food
- Knighthood
- Dressing up
- Juggling and games
- Storytelling
- Music

In relation to these themes the students have the opportunity to choose to participate in activities and little games. In relation to the theme on knighthood they can, for instance, design their own shield's heraldic symbolism. In the theme on music, they can choose to compose medieval music by combining a number of medieval instruments, or they can conduct a choir that performs medieval music, and choose and add different voices.

The aesthetic dimension

A key parameter in the design of the learning environment is a coherent aesthetic expression that can support the thematic content of the Medieval ages as a historical period. Inspiration came from a range of medieval imagery and music and the animation of the frame narrative was based on pictures from illuminated Medieval manuscripts. The intention was to create a consistent user experience in a situated learning environment that is based on a pervasive narrative and provides access to embedded themes–all within one coherent visual universe.

A second parameter has been the balance between a simple and easy navigation structure, and complexity in both linguistic and visual expression. In an effort to find that balance, several prototypes were developed before the current content was determined. Its linguistic and conceptual complexity, which went beyond what would normally be offered to this target group, seems to have been challenging and stimulating to the pupils. The aim was that the experience should not be monotonous, that it should have several layers of content and expression so users could play again and again and still be able to find new things in it.

Figure 1. Sample screen image showing the style of the design, based on illuminated Medieval manuscripts.

Method

The project was developed in an iterative design process that involved teachers and learners from two special needs schools in Denmark which teach students with the most severe and pervasive functional impairments. Most of the learners had no language, and most of them had cognitive as well as physical deficits.

The point of departure for the development of the project was an explicit need for age and curriculum relevant learning materials for the older learners, aged 12-16, that was ICT-based, had configurable navigation, and had augmentative functions like scanning and switch. Most programs that can be used with scanning and switch are not curriculum relevant; the programs which are curriculum relevant do not mediate it in a way that makes it accessible to the target group in terms of navigation or the target-group's linguistic or communicative competences.

Augmented and assistive technology may offer learners with multiple functional deficits a new way of learning and communicating. By anchoring learning material in a narrative setting and using stories as a vehicle for learning, it is possible to create an interactive learning environment that affords inclusive and differentiated learning experiences.

The principles for the design have been developed involving users at several iterative stages of the development. Doing user-oriented development work with learners who do not have a verbal language calls for development of usability-methods that use symbol charts, speech-machines, and log-books kept by the teachers; teachers had usually developed a great insight into the learners non-verbal communications. The study involved the two major special needs schools in Denmark with 5 teachers and about 5 classes with a total of 30 pupils.

The method used was based on a design based action-research approach with an iterative design process, where principles have been tested in a classroom and student/teacher context. This approach is similar to the concept in *Design Experiments in Educational Research* (Cobb et al. 2003). In order to develop a set of parameters for the evaluation of this resource and the underlying approach, the research also focused on evaluating the use of the program by the target group with regards its implications for communication and construction of meaning and identity for the learners,. Since much of the contact with the learners with multiple functional deficits depends on the interpretation of non-verbal communication, this has been carried out in close co-operation with the teachers involved. A significant part of the data collected to clarify usability issues has been observations of the learners' use of the program, individually as well as in teams and in a classroom context. Since the learners, because of their disabilities, are often tired or not able to participate in the activities, the teachers had an important role in relation to the observation of the learners' interactions with the program. Typically the program was used for very long periods of time. For instance, just one single theme in the program, medieval music, was the focus point of several weeks of activity.

The teachers' observations, which have supplemented the researchers' video-observations, were written as journal-type entries on a daily base and supplemented with case-studies. The program went through several prototype-phases in an iterative process in which each proto-type was tested by the learners and teachers, and the results then led to changes, which were implemented.

The teachers were interviewed in connection with the class-room observations. A qualitative methodology was used (Gjedde & Ingemann 2008), in which some representative cases were chosen in order to investigate how the program may support communication, identity and the construction of meaning for the learners.

Testing the learning environment in the schools

The project was divided into a number of overlapping phases in a dynamic interaction between prototype development based on testing in schools, gathering empirical data, and developing the prototype further.

The program was tested within pedagogical scenarios that involved visiting Medieval Life Centers and trying out physical tasks like cooking, jousting and dressing up.

One of the teachers indicated in a qualitative interview that the program held the pupils' concentration better than could be expected: "The concentration has generally been good when we have worked with the program, which also indicates that it has attracted the pupils' interest. And …[since] the pupils made meaningful and intentional choices using the program, it can be inferred that there was learning happening using the program."

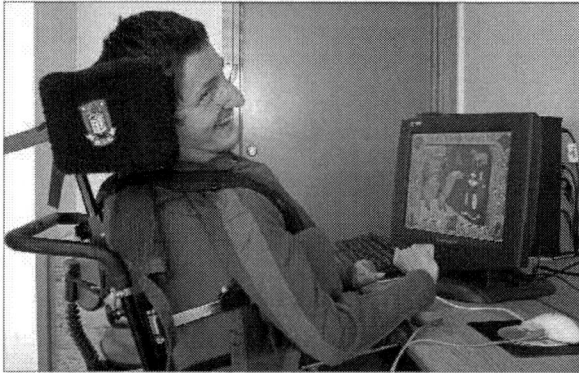

Figure 2. One of the pupils works with the program on his own

The frame story is told by a storyteller who uses different voices to express the different characters; these voices triggered reactions from the pupils. For instance, the forest king would shout with a deep voice and the pupils would respond to that. From the facial expressions of the pupils the teachers concluded that they enjoyed working with the program: "Certain sounds, images, music, games etc. prompted smiles, laughter and sounds of satisfaction from the students and increased involvement in the learning situation."

The approach to the design of the program, which uses multiple modalities like sound and pictures, is meant to create interest, concentration, and empathy and provide students with sufficient background on which to base choices.

Figure 3. Example of a menu in which the learners can choose to listen to different instruments or compose music; highlights and audio predictions guide choices.

The teachers observed that the story was understood at a general level, although there might be details that the students did not catch. When working with the frame story, they observed concentration even among students who otherwise were very restless, and found that the story succeeded in catching student's attention either with the intonation of the storytellers' voice, or with the flow of the story. Even learners' who had not developed any verbal language may have developed narrative competencies. This means that they may have an understanding of causality and canonical relationships, as well as a sense of schemas of the usual and the unusual.

Used on an individual basis the learners relate to the program relative to their personal preferences and history. While they are in the classroom context, where the program is used with a PC projector, it becomes a shared context for learning. Through making their choices in the program in the context of a group, the program becomes a tool for communication for learners with no verbal language and few opportunities to express themselves in complex ways.

Figure 4. As one of the navigational options the program can be set-up to use a touch-screen.

Perspectives of imaginative and narrative learning with interactive media

During testing of the narrative interactive learning program in the schools, some themes and issues emerged which relate both to a cognitive and a cultural psychological perspective. From a cognitive aspect, acquisition of knowledge is related to the way the narrative is organized and to the underlying internal structures. Research within the cognitive field has shown that content organized in narrative form may be easier to understand and remember (Mandler 1984). Major considerations in the development of interactive content have been to what extent one should use a canonical narrative text with conventional structure, and to what extent students could construct meaning out of a story that was multi-linear and diverted from traditional narrative structure (Gjedde, Robertson, et al 2008). The choice of the Heroic story of Sir Gawain and Lady Ragnell from the cycle of King Arthur in which the hero Sir Gawain rides out to solve a riddle and returns home and marries the transformed Lady Ragnell, provides a recognizable canonical structure of adventure. It is this framework of a linear traditional story that constitutes a frame story, and provides context and narrative momentum. Within this frame story, a series of stories are then presented as "meetings" with various individuals who Sir Gawain asks for help to solve the riddle, and each of whom represents a theme that could be explored interactively. This type of canonical narrative "works by triggering the conventional, tried, and tested narrative structures" (Bruner 1996), and the learner can be absolutely confident that the story unfolds as he would expect. A non-linear story-form is more unconventional and the same clear conception of how the story will unfold does not exist. For instance, the causal connections will be less apparent and may provide greater cognitive challenges for the learner as the content is not embedded in a predictable structure in relation to the construction of meaning.

In the design of the learning environment the intention was to develop the narrative content structure to provide narrative structures students are familiar with; the added multi-form narrative linearity then allows exploration of the content and interaction with the options in the game activities.

During the testing of the program we saw examples of students engaging immediately with the story and taking an interest in it, although due to their lack of spoken language we have been unable to enter into an explicit dialogue with them about it. Students were also able to participate in activities framed by the story and work on concepts related to it. In one type of activity offered within the context of the frame story, the learners could create their own story based on a canonical course of action and different characters they could choose. Teachers observed that intentionally creating a story was a favorite student activity. This goes beyond what would usually be expected from learners with no verbal language. Teachers also found that the students were motivated to listen to the stories and that their normal concentration threshold increased during the activity.

The cultural psychological perspective relates to the narrative as a situating context and views knowledge and learning as culturally conditioned (Bruner 1996, Vygotsky 1962). Egan (1997) describes it as a cognitive tool, or a tool for thinking. The narrative is also an artifact that helps to scaffold situated and collaborative learning processes.

This perspective was implemented in the teachers' didactic approach once they perceived the narrative program functioning as a communication platform. The choice making of the students came to the forefront in a classroom situation: it contributed to a social learning situation involving a group of learners among whom almost all learning otherwise happened one-to-one with the teacher. The teachers who brought a hermeneutic phenomenological approach to the learning situation were able to interpret aspects of the students' construction of identity and construction of meaning in the communication process. In a classroom where the program was shown on a large interactive whiteboard, the program also functioned as a communication platform because it provided a shared context allowing the learners to express themselves by making choices, and gave them an opportunity to be active through choice making. Students also had the opportunity to get involved in the shared space by observing the choices their peers made and reacting to the choices made, and reciprocally to be the focus of their peers' awareness. In a situation where verbal expression is not an option, the communication vocabulary then gets extended by the choices that are made, and these are related to narrative, mythic, and heroic dimensions of meaning. This can for instance be seen in the activities section of the program where the pupils can choose to dress up as characters related to the medieval universe, or to design a shield with heraldic symbolism, the meaning of which is made explicit in the voice-over. For instance, a pupil may choose to add symbols of courage or friendship to a shield that can then be printed and used as a prop in group activities.

One perspective of identity is that it is constructed and perceived in a social space: the program supports a classroom community where choices are made and individuals express themselves through these choices. Another perspective of identity is that it is developed and expressed through interaction with others, not just through behavior and gesture but also through artifacts such as clothing, colors, and props.

All of these perspectives have added to the development of the principles for the interactive narrative learning environment. These principles included both a narrative organization of the material using a narrative framework and the opportunities that the narrative gives for situated and cultural learning processes. In Jerome Bruner's (1996) writings on how meanings are situated in relation to the culture in which they are created, he points to the need for a cultural system of symbols in order to communicate. Further he points out how these meanings can be negotiated and identifies that learning is always situated within this cultural frame.

The underlying learning principles have been made explicit through collaboration between teachers and students. The way the program has been used in the classroom has also demonstrated its relevance in relation to identity formation and construction of meaning for the pupils.

Conclusion

Imagination and narrative as tools for learning, (Egan 1997) combined with assistive technology and an interactive learning environment, open new pathways for learning for learners with functional deficits. This new approach was developed in an iterative process involving the two major special needs schools in Denmark, and subsequently tested with groups of learners and teachers in the schools.

As the target group of learners with multiple functional disabilities includes very diverse abilities and disabilities, providing access to the normal curriculum for this target group is a challenging task. The employment of a user-oriented design approach involving severely challenged learners in the iterative process at the initial stages, led to the development of non-verbal methods for user response. Targeting the software at a larger group made it possible to use it in an inclusive educational setting because it was designed to have a high level of complexity combined with curriculum relevant content. Coupling this complexity and curriculum relevance with augmented navigation made the program viable for a much larger target group.

An integrated curriculum content with an augmented user interface that can be adjusted to meet the needs of the user afforded differentiation and allowed for very different interests, cognitive skills, and aesthetic and musical sensitivities.

The use of story as an anchoring and structuring device made the program accessible for a wide range of users as well, including both children and adult learners with disabilities like aphasia.

By using a classical story, the intention was to build a narrative framework for learning that would appeal to and motivate both learners and teachers, and build the interest and motivation to learn about aspects of life in Medieval times.

The role of the program in relation to the learners' construction of meaning and their expression of identity can be understood as a hermeneutic field, which primarily has been researched through the teachers' interpretation of the learners' choices and communicative actions.

The evaluation of the program, which was further validated by the feed-back from the teachers and special needs consultants, concluded that the design principles involved provided an augmented narrative learning resource with a high level of complexity which is offering new learning potentials to the target group of older learners with multiple functional disabilities.

An independent body, representing experts in the field, rated the usability for the target group and found it to be good, and the complexity of choices to be an activating factor.

The program serves as a framework offering new possibilities for learning scenarios for the target group, as it can both enable the individual learner to have independent activities and also serve as a didactic frame around thematic activities in the classroom.

After the initial testing the program has been localized into English and has been used for inclusive education with dyslexic children as well as with adults with multiple disabilities in the UK.

As such it is also an example of how to design an imaginative learning environment that can function in an inclusive learning situation.

The narrative framework, the use of activities and games, the videos, and the level of the program in relation to the curriculum, make it potentially a useful tool for inclusive education, as many different types of learners can use it at their own level. The range of differentiation and pedagogical scenarios for this use has to be explored in more depth with additional research.

Acknowledgements

This research has been sponsored by the Danish Ministry of Education, through the ITMF-program. The software has been developed in collaboration with Kirkebækskolen and other special needs schools in Denmark. More information on the project and software can be found at www.storiez.net.

Bibliography

Bruner, J. (1966). *Toward a Theory of Instruction*. Cambridge, MA: Harvard University Press.

—. (1986). *Actual Minds, Possible Worlds*. Cambridge, MA: Harvard University Press.

—. (1997). *The Culture of Education*. Cambridge, MA: Harvard University Press.

Cobb. P, Confrey. J, diSessa. A, Lehrer. R, & Schauble. L. (2003). Design Experiments in Educational Research. *Educational Researcher*. 32(1)

Egan, K. (1992). *Imagination in Teaching and Learning*. Chicago: University of Chicago Press.

—. (1986). *Teaching as Storytelling*. Chicago: University of Chicago Press.

—. (1997). *The Educated Mind*. Chicago: University of Chicago Press.

Gjedde, L. (2004). Designing for Learning in Narrative Multimedia Environments. In S. Mishra, & R. C. Sharma R.C. (Eds.), *Interactive Multimedia in Education and Training* (pp. 101-111). Hershey, PA: Idea Group Publishing.

—. (2004). *Et narrativt augmenteret læringsrum for elever med multiple funktionsnedsættelser* DPU, Copenhagen.

Gjedde, L, Ingemann, B. (2008). *Researching Experiences.* Newcastle upon Tyne: Cambridge Scholars Publishing.

Robertson, J., Gjedde, L., Aylett, R., Luckin, R., & Brna, P. (2008). Inside Stories–a Narrative Journey. London: Lulu.com

Whyte, H. (1981). The value of narrativity in the representation of reality. In Mitchell, W. (Ed.), *On narrative* (pp. 1-24). Chicago: University of Chicago Press.

NARRATIVE IN EARLY LEARNING: TRANSITIONING FROM PRE-SCHOOL TO KINDERGARTEN

KRYSTINA MADEJ

Children's experience and perception of narrative changes as they move into the formal learning environment of school. When children are very young, their experience of story is socially constructed and based in a multimodality that develops their imaginative, cognitive, affective, and physical capabilities through orality, imagery, interactivity, and performance. Stories create an encompassing environment that provides context for their actions and their involvement with the world around them. As children get older, and begin their formal education, the adult view that stories are structured literary entities is superimposed on their early narrative experience. This paper presents the study *The Dynamic of Young Children's Emerging Narrative Process.* The study observed young children in a preschool and in a kindergarten setting with two goals in mind: first, to identify the characteristics of children's early text narrative encounters in a contemporary setting (discussed in a separate paper), and second to identify if a change in approach to teaching narrative occurred between preschool and kindergarten (discussed here). The study revealed that a pronounced change occurred: in preschool story was used as an encompassing learning paradigm throughout the day's activities, in kindergarten story was used predominantly to teach literary structure within the Language Arts program. The study shows that as children move into formal schooling, stories are removed as a fundamental tool from their language of learning.

Introduction

Narrative has been used as a way to pass on experience and learning to others since time immemorial: it is inseparable from the context of human action. Psychologist Donald Polkinghorne says of narrative that it is "a primary form by which humans experience meaning." He shows in his book, *Narrative Knowing and the Human Sciences,* that narrative is ubiquitous to humans and a fundamental component of how they shape their worldview (Polkinghorne). Stories are the way we link our daily activities into a whole and provide for their significance within the entity that is our life. Literary critic Gerald Prince tells us "[narrative] does not simply record events; it constitutes and interprets them as meaningful parts of meaningful wholes...." (Prince). As such, when used in learning environments, narrative connects new knowledge to past experience, gives it context, and makes it more understandable and more memorable (Madej 2004)). It is a keystone in the development of our imaginative experience (Egan (1986), which, together with cognitive, affective, and physical experiences, provides for the schema that form our representations of the world, and allows us to adapt to and function in new situations (Bartlett). The way in which story has been used in learning over the years has changed to accommodate the social and political climate of the day. Educational theory at the time of the first school acts in England (second half of the 1800s) encouraged a move away from a contextual approach and towards an objectified and rational or scientific approach to ways of knowing. The "linguistic turn" in the fields of philosophy, the humanities, and the social sciences in the early-to-mid 1900s created a renewed interest in narrative as a basic learning strategy in fields as diverse as artificial intelligence and business. More than a learning strategy, narrative came to be seen as the contextual environment in which concepts evolved in a meaningful way, both for children and for adults (Madej 2007).

This essay begins with a brief historical account of narrative's use as a communication and learning tool and a discussion of narrative play in early development. It then identifies the purpose, methods, and results of the research study, and presents the children's and teacher's own words, and descriptions of their activities from the observation notes. In the concluding remarks examples are given of language arts strategies that continue to solidify an adult-oriented, formalized structure of narrative throughout elementary grades, and take children further away from one of their innate learning strategies.

Communicating and learning through contextual stories

In the days when our ancestors gathered around a fire to keep warm, the desire to bring stories to an audience through a media other than speech resulted in such dynamic scenes as those depicted in the wall paintings in the Chauvet Caves (France). Here, there are over 416 paintings of "bold lions, leaping horses, pensive owls and charging rhinoceroses" that are 32,000 years old, the oldest such paintings known, "a veritable Louvre of Paleolithic art" (Time Magazine). Continuously over the years, picture stories have been used as a vital part of communication between people(s). Over the centuries stories took on new forms of representation as individual cultures evolved–friezes, sculptures, daily objects such as the painted amphora of 5th century Greece (bce), all these were used to depict the ideas people wanted to share. These pictorial communications gave sway to the abstract symbols of the alphabet, which was first used to encode the facts and figures of daily commerce. Finally, at about the time of Homer, writing evolved to the point when it could bring story, with all its nuances of action and feeling, to a rapt audience.

The alphabet was a "code," in effect, a secret language that new initiates needed to master. Over the centuries the alphabet code became established and stories that had their origin with bards, the keepers of history and tellers of tales, were put into manuscript form and passed on to new "keepers" of these histories. Masters, charged with the education of young minds, knew this code as part of their stock-in-trade and passed on their skill to their pupils. As an example, going back only a thousand years, we find the *Colloquy*, written by the tenth century hagiographer, Aelfric to teach his students Latin. The *Colloquy* was written as a dialogue and encouraged students to assume a persona when responding to questions. Depending on what was asked, a student would respond as a monk, a ploughman, a merchant, or perhaps a fowler (Demers). The question was personalized: play-acting allowed the students to step into a role and connect with it affectively. Not only did children learn Latin, they did so within the context of the stories around them. In creating the story themselves, their understanding of both the subject they were learning and the nature of story itself changed. Aelfric understood that including an affective element in the basic nature of the learning experience would make learning more effective.

When printed texts became common and literacy a necessity for successful integration into society, ideas for encouraging learning also became more common. In the late 1600s, educators such as Thomas Tryon encouraged learning the alphabet code within the context of the home and with objects that were familiar to them, to children from two years on. Mothers were charged with the responsibility of ensuring that their children were literate; they based their literacy teaching in the objects of the home (Spufford). At the end of the 1600s, the philosopher John Locke, wrote disapprovingly of the scholasticism of the day and recommended learning be made more appropriate to children's playful interests. He suggested toys such as letter dice be used to engage them in learning the literacy "code," and felt that, once familiar with the code, they should be given books to read, books that were entertaining (Locke). He was hard pressed, however, to find books for children that were entertaining and finally settled on *Aesop's Fables* and *Reynard the Fox*, both published by the English publisher Caxton for adults a hundred years earlier (Meigs). Into the next century, Sir Isaac Watt, preacher, poet, and hymn writer envisioned children sitting cosily with their parents in a warm embracing environment while enjoying the rhythms and rhymes of his lyrical poetry (Demers).

These educators gave voice to ideas that reflected a growing nursery culture in which mothers supported the development of their children's literacy skills within the cultural, social, and political context of their home and local society using a range of strategies (Heath, Madej 2007). Books brought both the artifacts of literacy education (ABCs, letter combinations, verses) as well as stories to children. They consisted not only of the Lord's Prayer, though this was invariably the dominant text, but also of pictures, jokes, rhymes, and puns, and were visually and textually entertaining (Demers).

The traditional way of bringing learning to children in a culturally contextual manner through the stories of the people and things around them became difficult to continue in the large urbanized populations that were created by the industrialization of society and the move to cities by rural and small town citizens. One response to the problem of offering learning to a large disparate citizenship was standardization (Jackson, Vincent). Formulaic curricula that could be taught to larger numbers of students were created, and stories, with their contextual nature, were disassociated from the different subjects students were set to learn. The study of stories themselves, or literature, suffered the same fate. The formula for teaching about stories was reduced to teaching a normative structure that derived from Gustav Freytag's 1863 model of a five-act dramatic play. The model consisted of five elements (exposition, complication, climax, falling action, denouement) and had its basis in the Aristotelian story arc, also derived from the structure of the dramatic play. The approach to teaching how story was to be interpreted, and indeed, how it was to be written, was thus narrowed and mechanized. In addition, the 1800s saw a shift to a scientific method (direct observation, recording, and monitoring of the world) as a way of knowing that made storytelling suspect as a learning strategy. The new industrialized and scientific learning paradigm set boundaries for the teaching strategies used with the growing student population (a result of the new education laws) and that were also in tune with the social and political expectations of the day: to turn out "an obedient workforce who knew their place" (Minns, 183).

Early learning experiences

Children's literature and children's early learning strategies (toddler and preschool years) escaped these boundaries (for the most part). The late 1800s brought the nonsense tales of Edward Lear and the fantasies of Lewis Carroll: stories that went beyond "set" limitations (Demers). At that time as well, the moveable book, with its changeable story segments and figures that moved, engaged children in imaginative play (Brown, Shefrin). In the early part of the 1900s the development of the picture book provided a new genre that, in its combination of text and pictures, was an idyllic environment for imaginative approaches to sharing stories with children (Meigs).

In early learning settings, the ability to play, a key tool in our ability to learn (Winnicott), was fortunately maintained through the simple expedient that it was generally assumed children weren't sufficiently developed cognitively until they entered formal schooling to be confined and restricted in their learning activities. Children's earliest education, that is, before they entered formal school, escaped what the educator Kieran Egan describes as "the predominantly provincial trivia of the curriculum and the worksheet-oriented...activities of common teaching practice...." that have been the hallmark of traditional elementary school education and proven to be inadequate to the important task of developing the creative skills children need to successfully meet life's challenges (Egan 1997 p. 68). As a result, young children have been allowed to experience their way through their young life, at least until kindergarten, using all their senses, all their faculties, in creative and imaginative approaches to learning about themselves and about what is around them. In this world of exploration, engaging through stories that provide context for their actions, provides a significant means through which children develop cognitively, affectively, and imaginatively: it is the way they make meaning out of what they do (Bruner). During their pre-school years, the period when they become fluent in oral language, children develop their Mythic understanding (Egan 1997), in which story plays a reigning part. Intellectually it is a period when a sense of mystery, an interest in joking and humor, the ability to rhyme and play act, are engaged with through story. Story activities, which are encouraged in early education programs as a means for learning about many topics, are often lost once children enter traditional school and formulaic systems are put in place to teach a narrowly defined curriculum.

Young children's encounters with stories as part of their learning environment, and as a result, their perception of what stories are, begins to change in their first year of formal school: from one in which narrative is a broadly imaginative and inclusive experience to one in which narrative is a structured experience limited within the subject area of Language Arts. This change is one in which the cultural context and intrinsic connection to learning that makes it personal, and therefore sufficiently valuable to integrate and remember, no longer exists: children's access to an innate and vital way of making meaning is restricted.

The following pages present a study that follows preschool and kindergarten children through their day, describes the different activities that they undertake, and shows how their involvement with story changes. In presenting the observation, the children's words are used as often as possible to provide for the nuances of their understanding of and involvement with the activities, as well to give the children themselves a voice that is not interpreted by adults (or at least less so than normal).

Research Study

The study *The Dynamic of Young Children's Emerging Narrative Process* was conducted over three months from November 2005 to January 2006 (Madej 2006). It was the concluding study in ongoing research concerning children's use of narrative in digital environments being conducted as part of my Social Sciences and Humanities Research Council (SSHRC) Doctoral Fellowship that ran from April 2004 to April 2006. An earlier study had resulted in questions concerning the change in approach towards use of stories in learning that seemed to occur as children moved from early learning to formal school environments. This study was designed with two goals in mind. The first goal was to identify the characteristics of children's early print story encounters (discussed elsewhere); the second goal was to see if a change in approach to teaching narrative occurred between preschool and the more formal kindergarten that might cause a shift in children's perception of story.

The study used a qualitative approach based in Grounded Theory Method which is iterative and emergent. It was not intended to be definitive (and with such a small sample certainly couldn't be) rather the intent was to provide for greater understanding of what occurred in narrative education when children entered formal school, and to generate discussion, and perhaps change. A number of different strategies were used concurrently. Participant observations were conducted in two different settings: a preschool group of 3 to 4 year olds offered an example of the environment children enjoyed before entering formal school; a kindergarten group of 5 to 6 year olds provided the example of classes used to introduce and accustom children to traditional school environments. In the half-day preschool class, which consisted of 22 children, 13 girls and 9 boys, ages 3 to 4, the observation was conducted over four-weeks. In the full-day kindergarten class, which had 16 children, 9 girls and 7 boys, ages 5 to 6, the observation was conducted over two-weeks with a follow-up two-day observation of one project. (The difference in time in the classrooms was a function of what was permitted by the two educational authorities involved.) Two sessions of each observation were videotaped, and photographs were taken on three different days.

The two teachers of the preschool and the teacher of the kindergarten were provided a self-directed questionnaire regarding their approach towards the use of stories in their program. This was followed by an open-ended interview. There was generally a review of events of the day at the end of each day, and during that time activities were planned for the next day. Parents were given a self-directed questionnaire to answer to provide background information on the children's demographics and what story activities they engaged in at home.

The study found that in the pre-school the story was experienced as a comprehensive component of all aspects of children's daily learning activities. The children were involved in story through various modalities: orality, art, song, pretend-play, and playacting. They exhibited an openness to engaging with the story as an imaginative experience through all of, or any one of, these modalities. The kindergarten scenario treated story differently: though different activities were engaged in, these activities were subservient to story as a curriculum topic (Language Arts) with the learning goal of introducing the students to a formulaic understanding of story through the examination of sequence, character, and setting within the context of a plot.

Life in Preschool

In the preschool, story is presented and discussed as a way for the children to express their ideas. Children are encouraged to think about where stories come from, and who wrote them, and to think up stories and make books to share. They are encouraged to participate in making stories together from their own experience; many are fantastical. The teacher writes these stories down and then reads them back. She also helps the children make them into songs. Children are also encouraged to create (write, draw, make) stories at home and to bring these in to share. Print stories are used to support weekly program themes that are based on cultural or seasonal events. Art and craft activities are used to give children opportunities to express ideas in the story in non-textual ways: sometimes a special event in the story is used as an idea for an art project, sometimes a general theme, such as snowflakes, is used. Art, craft, song, dance, and playacting activities based on stories are initiated by both teachers and the children themselves. Both free time and quiet time after snack are available for children to read stories on their own, but most often during these times they share books with friends. Throughout a week, stories are an integral part of almost all the classroom activities and, within the routine of these activities, different aspects of a story experience unfold.

In the following examples, the first one shows the children being encouraged to think about themselves as story creators and stories as being made in different languages: spoken, written, sung. The second example provides a brief overview of how the story *Peter and the Wolf* is introduced through a number of different activities. Both examples use excerpts of the conversations as well as end-of-the-day summaries from the observation notes.

Preschool Observation 1

[Day 1] During activity time Heather and Alexis, the two preschool teachers, often encourage discussion about story by inviting comments and questions. On this day, after asking for suggestions about where stories come from, Heather leads the discussion to the topic of people making stories up out of their heads and children having the ability to make stories for themselves.

"Where do stories come from?" asks Heather.

"Paper...libraries...pencil...humans...TV...books," are some of the answers she receives.

"If stories come from humans, how do they come from them?"

"Brain...fun...imagination," the children pipe up with ideas about where stories might initiate.

Kyle offers a story about his grandfather. "My grandfather lives in Vancouver. He's an artist, he mainly draws."

Heather tells a story she makes up as she goes along. "Once upon a time there was a giant with a giant cornfield. Corn grew larger than the giant. He picked three cobs of corn that were huge and took them home. Do you know who was at this home? The crow and the ant. [More details are added]. That story is out of my head. You can make up stories too."

Heather has a number of items on the desk next to her, referring to them she asks her next questions, "Where does music come from? Which of these makes music?" She asks these questions as she shows the children a shaker, a stone, a bottle part-filled with sand. She then blows across the top of another bottle filled with water. She pours out some of the water which lowers the sound. "Sounds like a ferry horn," she says. Heather comments that Halle, who has just remarked that she has a shell that makes sounds, has the beginnings of a good story.

[Day 2] "Do you remember we talked about stories [yesterday]? Where do they come from?" asks Heather.

"Writer," one of the children replies.

"Where do writers get their ideas from?" asks Heather.

"TV, Africa," are two of the replies.

"What do you think you would be writing about if you were a writer?"

""You would write about some good animals." "You would write on a stone."

Heather tells a story about Africa and about pink flamingos. "I can turn this story into a song," and she sings her story about pink flamingos in a song voice. She points out that there are high notes and low notes in that song and talks about how a musical language was invented so that people could write songs. She shows the children musical notes: whole note, half note, quarter note and eighth note and talks about how they can be high, low, fast or slow, and how they sit on a staff. She says that the children will soon their own musical stories on a staff.

[Day 5] The children regularly bring in stories they have written at home (with their parents) and today Eric has brought one in. Heather says, "We have been talking about stories. We're going to read a "Haunted House" story. Eric made it up, his mom wrote it, and he made the book." After reading it once Heather helps the children make it into a musical story and they all sing it.

[Day 6]   Today [Heather] continues with her discussion about stories from yesterday, "stories come from our imagination and from our experience.... Sometimes before pencils and pens, people would sit in a circle and tell stories, that's a way to tell a story, to share information." "Eric made up a story and it was great, wasn't it everyone?" "And now Sophie has made up a story." Heather reads Sophie's story. "Did your mommy help you with the pictures? You are an illustrator and an author!"

[Later in the day] Today Heather tells the children that they will write a story.

"I've already written a story," says Kyle

"This will be a class story," replies Heather. She wants the children to each add to the story.

"I went..." "to the beach..." "all my mom's family and me..."
"What did you see at the beach?" prompts Heather.
"I saw a fish."
"Halle, what was the fish like?"
"It was a small blue fish."
"What was the fish doing?"

The story grows through questions Heather asks, "Where did they live? What did they do next?" She writes the story down as new additions are made and when it is complete she reads it out loud. The next day during Circle Time she takes out a bag of instruments and distributes them to the children so that each one has a drum, a bell, maracas, or another instrument that is available. "Shall we read our story to the music?" she asks, and directs each small group of children with the same instrument to begin. "I took a picture ..." reads Heather to the sound of bells and lots of noise.

[Day 7] "Tout le monde," Heather addresses the children, "We were writing a story, remember, it was about my family. My family went down to the beach. What a story you made, what a good story. Should we make an end to the story?"

"All right, 'The End,'" responds one of the children, "Read it again!"

"Shall I read it again?" says Heather, "You can make changes if you want to."

Heather reads the story to much laughter and changes parts of the story at the children's suggestions. The session ends as they move to another activity.

Preschool Observation 2

[Day 1]   Following a discussion about where music comes from, Heather introduces *Peter and the Wolf* by Sergei Prokofiev as a story which has sounds that represent animals/characters. The children listen to a CD which enthuses and animates them: they imitate the sounds of the orchestra instruments. They act out parts of the story, pretending they are grandpa and telling Peter not to go into the woods, or, they pretend they are Peter holding a rifle. Later that day, Alexa reads the print storybook and the children have the opportunity to listen to the story and look at pictures of the characters. The book is available for them to look at during free time. During outdoor time they pretend they are the animals, making loud animal noises and swooping about or stalking each other in a chase game,

[Day 2] Today is a musical day. Heather explains about musical notes and how they are used on a staff to make stories in music. For their art activity the children make large notes and place them on a poster -sized staff to make a musical story. Later, at the end of free time, when they are playing sound games, Alexa asks the children to sound out all the animals in *Peter and the Wolf*. Towards the end of the day Heather puts on an audio tape of the story which has music in the background; some of the children participate by shaking their heads, swaying their bodies, and acting out duck motions with their arms. They are following Heather's example. Heather comments that it is difficult to listen to a story without pictures and that they have done very well. The end of the day story is *The True Story of the Big Bad Wolf.*

[Day 3] The television is set up with chairs in front of it and today the children watch the 1946 Disney video of *Peter and the Wolf* with Prokofiev's music. They enthusiastically say it is just like going to the movies. The children comment to each other and there is lots of laughter. During Circle Time, Alexa initiates a discussion about the animals in the story that turns into an action song/game.

[Day 4] Day Four is occupied with a music teacher and a doctor's visit but the end of the day brings us another wolf story: *The Wolf's Chicken Stew.*

In the preschool class print story is changed from words on a page to an experience through a regular association of stories with music, with art/craft activities, and with other play activities. Whereas the words on a page may have a story sequence that the children can listen to, this sequence does not always seem of importance to them and is not highlighted by the teachers. Children express their preferences for parts of stories by asking for them again and again, ignoring other parts of the story as unimportant at the moment. When creating stories, the children use beginnings and endings (Once Upon a Time, The End) as brief rituals. The stories themselves are often a series of binary events without climax, but with resolution in a give and take situation (The Crago's 1983 study provides an extensive observation of these type of activities.). Often events which are at the forefront of a child's mind, such as a recent activity with a parent or friend, are included in their comments without consideration of relevance to the story at hand.While the preschool allows the children to experience story without explanations about how story is structured, the next example shows that the experience in kindergarten has children examining storyline and the structural elements of print stories.

Life in Kindergarten

In the kindergarten class, stories are used primarily as part of the Language Arts and Literacy programs. Once the story ideas are discussed, children are taught formal structural terms and shown that stories have different elements such as characters and settings. The children paint backgrounds and draw and color characters. They cut these out to use as large puppets in a performance they enact twice so that everyone has a chance to participate. Children are encouraged to consider the sequence of events in a story and then to draw a story map of these events. They compare their ideas about sequence with their peers' ideas, discussing, and arguing when events happened. Age-graded stories are used as part of a literacy program during which children have the opportunity to read stories on their own and to share with older children in reading-help sessions. Children read in the book corner when they have finished their work. Reading is an option during "Choosing Time."

The classroom routine offers the language arts program and the literacy program as separate opportunities for experiencing story and lesson plans are usually completed over a number of days. Two examples follow: the first encourages the children to understand sequence, character, and setting. The second has them working on a story map.

Kindergarten Observation 1:

[Day 4] Today the teacher, Lindsay, introduces the book *Brave Irene*. The discussion is first about bravery and what it means to be brave. The story is then used to introduce story elements and the first activity looks at sequence.

"In this story Irene is brave. I've copied out some of the pages for you and I'm going to divide you into groups and give you each one of these pictures. I want you to look at these pictures and put them in order of when you think things happens."

At one table the conversation goes like this:

"I think this one was first, then the one with the box."

"Then my picture," says Shayla.

"No Alex, that's not right."

"Yes it is, but it looks like they put the dress in the box."

After providing the groups with time for discussion Lindsay gathers the children and asks, "How was Irene being brave?"

Jackson replies, "Walking all by herself, and carrying that big box."

"Let's read the story and see what it is about," says Lindsay. While reading she stops a number of times to ask questions about what might be scary events. Then she says, "I'm going to stop here," though she is not quite finished, and starts a discussion, "What do you think Irene is going to do? How do you think she is going to get there?"

Shayla answers, "She might go back to her mother, and they would go look for the dress." There are other suggestions before Lindsay says, "I'm going to give you a piece of paper and want you to think about what is going to happen and then draw it. Guess, and we'll finish the story."

The children go to their tables with paper in hand discussing what they are going to draw.

"I think she's going to keep on walking and get to the palace. It's silver [the palace], no it's gold and blue," says Hannah. "That's the dress. It's back at the mom's house."

"I think she is going to find ice and slide to the palace. The wind is going to blow the dress," says Isabella as she draws ice with a dress in the air above it.

Sophia has drawn Irene (quite detailed) and given her red cheeks. "The snow has given them to her. She's not going to get wet because of her coat. And the [white] piece of paper is the snow," she tells me. She is using the white of the paper as the snow.

Jackson has drawn a snowplow. The snowplow will rescue her and "bring her to the dress."

[Day 5] Lindsay takes out *Brave Irene* and begins the literacy portion of the day.

"Yesterday you guessed some of the endings," says Lindsay. "Let's go over some of these endings and see if any of them are similar." Lindsay takes the drawings the children have done and asks each child to give us his/her ending.

"She catched the dress and makes it close to the castle."

"I thought she would be picked up by the castle."

"I knew she was going to get to the castle."

"She didn't."

"I thought the dress in the box she got it back."

"I thinked the girl going to the Palace but the stick thingy was locked."

"She was going to slide on ice."

"I thought that there would be a big storm and the dress would blow her away."

"A snowplow would pick her up and bring her home.

"I think she'll get to the castle and find the dress."

"So, did she end up getting the dress to the duchess? We'll have to find out." Lindsay reads the rest of the story. Then she goes on, "I'm going to get you to think about two things that you might not have heard of or you might have ... character and setting. So what are characters? A character is a person or could be an animal in a book or a movie. Who are the characters or the people in the story: [repeating children's comments] doctor, Irene, mother, duchess, servants, guests who were dancing."

Lindsay goes on to discuss setting. "Put up your hand if you think you know what the setting is. [She repeats the students' suggestions.] Snow...ah...the setting is where the story happens...the palace, the snow...the snow walk, her mother's room, her house. We're going to draw the settings. I'll give you each a partner and a paper to draw the characters and the setting and then we'll talk about them. So when you draw them make them with lots of detail. Make the character as big as the piece of paper. And here is an even bigger piece of paper for the castle and the house, Irene's house." Lindsay asks, "who wants to do the snow walk?" and who will be which character. The children take their pieces of paper to the tables. Individual students make the characters, and groups of three or four children make the settings. When the characters and setting are completed, the children act out the story.

During our discussion at the end of the day Lindsay says that she is really surprised at the detail the children remember. Things like the dress blowing into the tree. "I only expected one sentence, but they seemed to know the whole story." She tells me they will act out the story again the next day, and other children will get a chance to act out the parts.

Kindergarten Case Study: Story Map [Day 1]

After morning activities Lindsay says, "Everyone needs to turn around and face me. I'm going to read you a story. We're going to read *The Snowy Day*. When I'm reading it I want you to think about all the things the little boy does and all the places he's been. Because afterward we're going to talk about these things." Lindsay proceeds to read the story. When she reads she stops at specific activities the boy is doing and discusses these activities with the children. "How does he walk?" she asks.

"First he walks with his toes in, then he walks with his toes out."

"How come there's an arrow?"

"I don't know. Should we try to walk like he did…look at these marks…then he dragged his feet," says Lindsay.

When the story is complete Lindsay says, "We're going to finish the story now," and reads the last page. She then goes over the story, and writes the activities in a list on her flip chart. She provides an illustration of each activity. In addition, as she reviews the activities, she has the children enact them: "Where did Peter start his day? In bed. All right. Everyone lie down and pretend to be asleep. You are Peter. What happens now?"

When all of the activities have been reviewed Lindsay sets the children their next task, "All right, now we are going to make a story map. Does anyone know what a map does? It helps you find your way. We're going to make a map today … a map about what Peter has done, where he went." Lindsay takes a piece of white paper and pencil on which she draws elements of the story. "What should we make Peter? A triangle. Where was Peter at the start of the story? In bed, so we could put the triangle in the bed. What happened next? He went outside. It's a snowy day. How can you show a really snowy day … snowflakes! Then he made tracks through the snow and you could make tracks. He comes to a tree so you could draw the tree, then there is a snowball fight so we can draw some snowballs … keep the arrows going so we know which way he is going. Draw all of these in pencil, then you can color them." Lindsay calls groups of children to get paper and to go to sit at their place and begin their individual maps.

Most children draw Peter rather than the triangle as his representation. Some children draw Peter in every activity; others draw only the activity. Lindsay encourages the children not to forget their arrows so that they can see the connection between one drawing and the next. She helps by putting in many arrows that show how the events they have drawn are connected sequentially.

[Day 2] The next day Lindsay brings out the flip chart and gives everyone their maps to finish coloring. Lindsay then reads the story again and reviews the steps written on her flip chart. She says, "I'm going to put you with a partner and you're going to tell your partner about your story map. You might not [each] remember the story the same way so it's alright to share." The children are partnered and have the opportunity to tell each other the story.

Torri and Charlie are a team. "I'm going to go first, is that OK?" asks Torri. Torri races through the story, "First he got out of bed and went outside then he went to the tree, then he made a snowman then he made an angel, then he climbed a hill, then he went home. We're done." Charlie seems to feel pressure because Torri has been so quick. He hesitates, then rushes into a very clipped summary of the story based on his drawing, part of which goes as follows, "wacked the tree, made a snowman climbed a mountain, went to his room, we're done." Lindsay [seems to] take her cue from Torri and suggests that the class needs to finish. This means that most teams have not yet completed their task when they tell their story [to each other], in most cases neither person is finished. In another team, Alyssa is interrupted towards the end of her rendition and as a result her partner Jackson jumps into the end of her talk and hurries through his own map. The children do not have much time for interpretation and discussion.

These two examples show the kindergarten class in the process of learning about traditional story structure by being introduced to plot, sequence, character, and setting, and in the case study, story maps. Through a number of different activities, which include drawing and playacting, the children become familiar with the terms. Moments in the story are highlighted through action. Story is presented as chunks of information that need to be discussed and analyzed before new chunks are revealed. The idea of sequence is introduced and then reinforced by making story maps and discussing them. The activities surrounding the discussion around the narrative are still associated strongly with imaginative explorations through art and craft and with action and performance, and not only with text. The conversations show that at this age children have a personal perspective of what is important to them in the story, and of how to express it. The teacher provides activities that will lead this perspective towards the example she has drawn up for them, in many cases, adding to the chilren's drawings herself. Figure 1 shows the teacher's chart of the sequences of actions for the story map as well as representations of this sequence illustrated by the children. At this stage of their understanding of story each of the children has an affective attachment to the story, views the sequence of events differently because of this, and shows his/her emotional involvement in the drawing. The expectation is that the mapped sequences will reflect the example provided but there is significant individuality expressed in the children's ideas which they have been given some time to think about and develop. During their presentation, this individuality is reduced, because of peer pressure and a need to complete the project, to a formula that is quick and easy to deliver.

It is, without question, useful to provide children with ideas about the structure of narrative and to discuss ideas about setting, character, and sequence. And, as can be seen, at this age this can still be done in an atmosphere of creative multimodal activity. The undesirability of this direction comes when it is the only one provided. Encouraging a singular view of story as structure in the face of the importance of story as a maker of meaning demeans story's educational value; presenting story as having only one type of structure, in the face of the myriad story forms that exist, causes a disservice to its complex nature and restricts children's opportunities in using it to express themselves in their own way.

After Kindergarten

As children progress through school the formal structure introduced in kindergarten solidifies further. A concurrent research project into Language Arts programs across the U.S.A. and Canada showed there is consistency across the continent in how restrictively narrative is taught. As an example, the Champaign School District (Champaign Schools) has a reading and writing timeline that requires kindergarteners be able to "use prewriting strategies to generate and organize ideas (e.g., focus on one topic; organize writing to include a beginning, middle, and end). Reading goals for the end of Grade One include being able to "identify the literary elements of theme, setting, plot, and character within literary works." In Grade Two, students will "Give complete story retelling with characters, setting, problem, events, and conclusion." By Grade Four, students will "Describe how literary elements (theme, character, setting, plot, tone, conflict) are used in literature to create meaning." Although schools may be helping students develop analytical skills, they do so within the confines of one narrow view of story, using what has come to be seen as

Figure 1. The teacher's story sequence and children's story maps. In A the student has "bunched" the activities, B shows a neat sequence of events across the top of the page, in C the student has emphasized the arrows that provide direction in the sequence, in D the student has emphasized the character in each of the sequences.

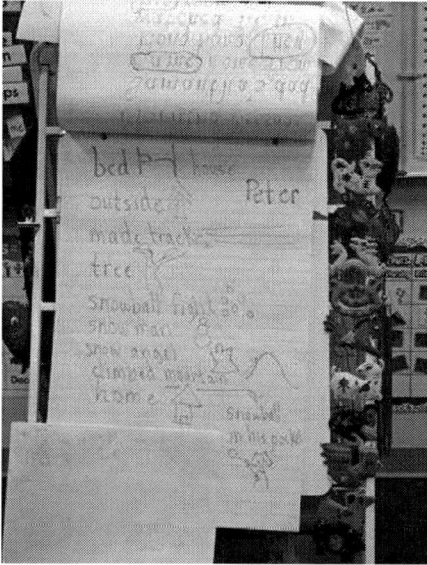

A.

B.

C.

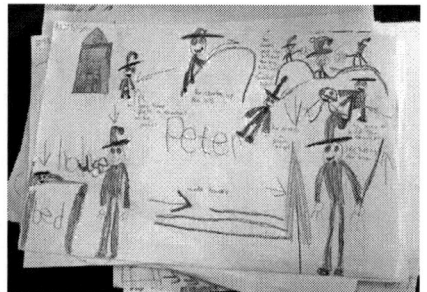

D.

"traditional" story structure (an easy formula) as a norm and presenting all other narrative structures as aberrant variations.

In addition, school boards provide suggestions for the type of books children should progress through on their way to becoming the adult-like silent readers they expect them to be eventually. As example, the Champaign School District provides characteristics of books in level A & B (kindergarten) some of which are: "single idea or simple story line, print clearly separated from pictures, most books have 1-4 lines of text per page." Characteristics of books in level M (end of Grade Two) include: "long, with lots of text per page, smaller print, and narrower word spacing." (All quotes from the Champaign Schools website.) To young children accustomed to different types of representation on a page, often augmented by social activity, such features can become insurmountable obstacles to overcome when asked to be interested in learning either the "code" of text literacy or the curriculum content presented.

Conclusion

The study found that in the pre-school venue the teachers exhibited an openness of approach to both the story structure and to the use of story as a part of the learning experience. The use of story was not restricted to a text with a specific structure. Print stories were used to support cultural or seasonal themes and were represented through a range of multimodal activities (or languages): song, craft, art, and playacting. Stories were also created aloud together in a group by the children and, though they came from the children's personal experience, they were fantastical. In the kindergarten venue, the teacher worked within a Language Arts curriculum that introduced children to a traditional linear story structure. Stories were discussed in terms of storyline and plot; associated activities included drawing storymaps, characters, and settings, and playacting the story. The children exhibited a varied perspective of story when initially introduced to story ideas. Through curricular activities, they were directed towards seeing story as one type of structure within a provided norm.

The study showed there is a change in the purpose of narrative activity from preschool to kindergarten: "teachers move from engaging with narrative as a part of the learning experience to introducing it as a structural form with elements that require explanation and study" (Madej 2007, p. 122). In this shift to an adult-oriented and structured literary view of narrative, story is removed from its important role as a means for engaging with learning and accessing knowledge: children are denied an important innate tool, that of personal reference as a signifier in situating their learning, from their repertoire of learning strategies. Possibly more importantly, they are taught that story and the context it provides is insignificant in their learning. They carry this narrowed perception with them into all their future learning, and indeed their lives.

This study was conducted as part of a Doctoral Fellowship awarded by the Social Studies and Humanities Research Council (Canada).

Bibliography

Bartlett, F. C. (1932). *Remembering: An Experimental and Social Study.* Cambridge: Cambridge University Press.

Brown, G. (2006). The Metamorphic Book: Children's Print Culture in the Eighteenth Century. *Eighteenth Century Studies,* 39.3, 351-62.

Bruner, J. (1990). *Acts of Meaning.* Cambridge, MA: Harvard University Press.

Champaign Schools. (2007). *English/Language Arts–CUSD #4* retrieved from http://www.champaignschools.org/, *Language Arts–Pacesetter English* retrieved from http:// www.picasso.cobbk12org/

Crago, M, & H. (1983). *Prelude to Literacy: A Preschool Child's Encounter with Picture and Story.* Carbondale: Southern Illinois University.

Demers, P. & Moyles, G. (1982). *From Instruction to Delight: An Anthology of Children's Literature to 1850.* Toronto: Oxford University Press.

Egan, K. (1986). *Teaching as Storytelling.* Chicago: University of Chicago Press.

—. (1997). *The Educated Mind.* Chicago: University of Chicago Press.

Heath, S. B. (1997). Child's Play or Finding the Ephemera of Home. In Hilton, M., Morag S., & Watson, V. (Eds.), *Opening the Nursery Door: Reading, Writing and Childhood 1600-1900* (pp. 17-30). London: Routledge.

Jackson, M. V. (1989). *Engines of Instruction, Mischief, and Magic.* Lincoln: University of Nebraska Press.

Locke, J. (1692). *Some Thoughts Concerning Education.* History Department, Fordham University. Retrieved November 2, 2006, from http://www.fordham.edu/halsall/mod/1692locke-education.html.

Madej, K. (2004). Report for SAGE: INE Collaborative Research Initiative project. *Narrative: Making Meaning in Interactive Digital Environments.* Burnaby, BC: Simon Fraser University.

—. (2006). *The Dynamic of Young Children's Emerging Narrative Process.* Unpublished Report, Simon Fraser University.

—. (2007). *Characteristics of Early Narrative Experience: Connecting Print and Digital Game.* Dissertation. Simon Fraser University.

Meigs, C., Nesbitt, N., Eaton, A. T., & Hill, R. (1969). *A Critical History of Children's Literature.* London: The Macmillan Company.

Minns, H. (1997). I KNEW A DUCK: Reading and Learning in Derby's Poor Schools. In Hilton, M., Morag S., & Watson, V. (Eds.), *Opening the Nursery Door: Reading, Writing and Childhood 1600-1900* (pp. 180-197). London: Routledge.

Prince, G. (2000). On Narratology (Past, Present, Future). *The Narrative Reader.* In Martin McQuillan (Ed.). p. 129. London: Routledge.

Polkinghorne, D. E. (1998). *Narrative Knowing and the Human Sciences.* Albany, NY: State University of New York Press.

Shefrin, J. (1999). "Make It a Pleasure and Not a Task" Educational Games for Children in Georgian England. *Princeton University Library Chronicle,* LX. 2, 251-75.

Spufford, M. (1997). Women Teaching Reading to Poor Children in the Sixteenth and Seventeenth Centuries. In Hilton, M., Morag S., & Watson, V. (Eds.), *Opening the Nursery Door: Reading, Writing and Childhood 1600-1900* (pp. 47-62). London: Routledge,

Time Magazine. 13 February 1995. Source: http://donsmaps.com/chauvetcave.html

Thursby, J. (2006). *Story, a Handbook.* Westport, CT: Greenwood Press.

Vincent, D. (1997). The Curriculum in Nineteenth-Century England. In Hilton, M., Morag S., & Watson, V. (Eds.), *Opening the Nursery Door: Reading, Writing and Childhood 1600-1900* (pp. 162-179). London: Routledge,

Winnicott, D. W. (1971). *Playing and Reality.* London: Tavistock Publications.

Wood, D. (1988). *How Children Think and Learn.* London: Blackwell Publishers.

Indigenous and Modern Epistemologies in the Learning of Mathematics

Kanwal Neel

This article explores the distinctive features and roots of Indigenous and modern epistemologies in the learning of mathematics. The frameworks for Indigenous and modern epistemologies are presented separately and the article concludes that there needs to be dual or multiple epistemologies. This does not mean, however, that these epistemologies cannot be bridged into a productive relationship with each other. The literature review uncovers some of the complexities of knowing mathematics, and the foundation of modern mathematics. This article embraces the complexities of responding to different worldviews that many Indigenous students straddle when they learn mathematics.

Introduction

How do children construct their knowledge of mathematics? Educational theorists and philosophers have attempted to answer this question for centuries, and the debate continues. The very word *mathematics* is derived from the Greek word *mathema,* which means "learning, study, science." There are many different definitions of the word mathematics including Keith Devlin's which states, "mathematics is the science of order, patterns, structure, and logical relationships" (Devlin, 2000, p. 74). Whatever the definition, there are different beliefs about how children construct their knowledge. Some believe that mathematics should be studied to better understand other objects within our world, and that knowledge can be gained through reasoning. Others view mathematics as the result of the study of those objects where knowledge is gained through sensory experiences. Still others believe that all knowledge is constructed through human perception and social experience. Educators have tackled this issue with a range of ideas and theories including: cognitive, socio-cultural, constructivist, behaviorist, multiple intelligences, and cooperative learning.

This article describes the foundation of modern mathematics and some of the complexities of understanding mathematics. It has been written in part to embrace the complexity that comes from responding to the different worldviews that many Indigenous students straddle when they learn mathematics. The word *Indigenous* as used in this article can be interchanged with the terms: Aboriginal, Native Indian, First Nations, Native, or Aborigine. The word *Modern*[1] as used here represents the Western or Eurocentric ways of knowing. Teaching mathematics is one thing but learning mathematics is another. Improving the learning of mathematics is connected with epistemology. This article presents some of the distinctive features, roots, and frameworks of Indigenous and Modern epistemologies. These have been established by answering the following questions: What are the distinguishing characteristics of each of the worldviews? What are the foundations of modern mathematics taught in schools today? The final section addresses whether it is possible to integrate these disparate worldviews within a single educational approach.

The modern epistemology of mathematics constructed with Cartesian-Newtonian ways of knowing used to be the only reality discussed in academic circles. Tarnas (1991) shows how the Cartesian-Newtonian worldview of linear, cause-effect logic exerts a strong influence throughout western thought not only in scientific thinking and methodology but also throughout philosophy. Recently, educators and elders of Indigenous knowledge have engaged in a critique of Modern epistemological predominance and the oppressive educational practices that follow it (Battiste & Barman, 1995; Cajete, 1999; Davison, 2002; Kavanagh, 2006). It is important to acknowledge that Modern pedagogy is not necessarily oppressive, just as Indigenous pedagogy is not necessarily empowering.

Indigenous civilizations have been compared to western civilizations using Modern epistemology. Educators are starting to challenge this status quo epistemology in order to make sense of the interconnection between social, physical, and spiritual ways of knowing.

Indigenous epistemology

Knowledge is the condition of knowing something with familiarity gained through experience or association. The traditional knowledge of northern aboriginal peoples has roots based firmly in the northern landscape and a land-based life experience of thousands of years. Traditional knowledge offers a view of the world, aspirations, and an avenue to "truth", different from those held by non-aboriginal people whose knowledge is based largely on European philosophies. (Department of Culture and Communications, Government of the Northwest Territories, 1991, p.11)

The work of Cajete (1994, 1999), Kawagley (1995), Ermine (1995), and Semali and Kincheloe (1999) provide perspectives on Indigenous worldviews and knowledge. Each author explores different aspects of the debate on Indigenous knowledge both in the west and elsewhere. It is difficult to encompass the whole meaning of Indigenous knowledge; each time we try to reconstruct Indigenous knowledge into another language we rewrite its meaning. Together with deconstruction, this strips a rich tapestry from Indigenous knowledge, as it is interwoven with thought, experience, language, and relationships that characterize Indigenous cultures.

Gregory Cajete

Cajete (1994) uses the metaphor of tracking and the symbol of concentric circles to provide a visual representation of the interconnectedness of knowledge.

> Knowledge grows and develops outwards in concentric rings. Concentric rings can also form the basis of learning; how to track ideas and intuitions; how to observe fields of knowledge; and how to see patterns and connections in thought and natural reality. (p. 123)

He also represents the integrated concentric rings of relationships among seven courses in the "Curriculum Mandala." The seven courses are founded on the shared metaphor and meanings of sacred directions among Native American tribal groups. Each of the circles represents rich sources from which to originate discussion of the nature and dynamic expression of creative thought based on metaphoric representations of Native American perceptions of the natural world.

Cajete (1999) states that the goal of basic education is to provide self-knowledge, "seeking life through understanding the creative process of living, sensitivity to and awareness of the natural world, knowledge of one's role and responsibility in the social order, and receptivity to the spiritual essence of the world" (p. 54). The contexts through which knowledge is gained are "through experiential learning (learning by doing and seeing), storytelling (learning by listening, imagination), ritual/ceremony (learning through initiation), dreaming (learning through the unconscious and imagery), the tutor (learning through apprenticeship), and artistic creation (learning through creative synthesis)" (p. 55).

Oscar Kawagley

Oscar Kawagley is a Yupiaq Inuit who, as an Indigenous person and Western-trained science educator and researcher, integrated respectful knowledge of the reciprocity of nature with his own education in science as it is taught in Western schools. Kawagley (1995) outlines how all learning and knowledge should start with what the student and community know and are using in their daily lives. To help students begin to understand these phenomena, Indigenous knowledge is connected with the five basic elements of the universe: earth, air, fire, water, and spirit. The sacred gifts of each must be understood, as well as the human activities that contribute to the sustainability or destruction of these life-giving gifts. To be holistic, the curricular activities must include Indigenous language and culture, language arts, mathematics, social studies, arts and crafts, and sciences. All must be interrelated as all of Earth is interrelated.

In using the five elements of life to teach, it is extremely important to assure that each element is a gift to the life-giving forces of the living Earth. The teacher must be careful to explain that those gifts are absolutely necessary for life on Earth to continue. Yupiaq people honor and respect these gifts in their rituals and ceremonies, incorporating all five elements in mutually reinforcing ways.

Yupiaq knowledge is based on a blending of the pragmatic, inductive, and spiritual realms. Mystical knowledge cannot be gained merely by observation, which is the main basis for rational knowledge. To obtain mystical knowledge, observation must be coupled with the participation of the whole being (mind, body, and soul) and with the universe. Culture influences our state of mind; stories and the imagination affect the attitudes and values of the mind (Kawagley, 1995).

Willie Ermine

Aboriginal or Indigenous epistemology requires an acceptance that knowledge exists in many forms, including the tangible and intangible. "Those who seek to understand the reality of existence and harmony with the environment by turning inward have a different incorporeal knowledge paradigm that might be termed "Aboriginal epistemology".... The inner space is that universe of being within each person that is synonymous with the soul, the spirit, the self, or the being" (Ermine, 1995, p.103). Indigenous Peoples do not seek understanding, nor convey cultural teachings within the group through objective processes. Rather, knowledge is provided so that the learner must integrate the intangible elements of self within the comprehension process. One's personal set of experiences, relationships, kinship, knowledge of community practices, spirituality and history are all part of Aboriginal epistemology. Indigenous Knowledge comprises a complex system of reciprocity that must be understood by the learner in order to maintain equilibrium within the world. Indigenous Knowledge differs from region to region and is grounded in the particular environment and culture from which it has emerged.

Ladislaus Semali and Joe Kincheloe

Semali and Kincheloe (1999) outline the dilemma faced in defining Indigenous knowledge, because context varies for millions of the world's Indigenous peoples. Central to the postmodern and postcolonial debates is "the origin of knowledge and the manner in which it is produced, archived, retrieved and distributed throughout the academy" (p. 4). Semali and Kincheloe (1999) urge caution and care with respect to who should be talking about Indigenous knowledge. The appreciation of Indigenous epistemology can provide Western peoples with "another view of knowledge production in diverse cultural sites," while at the same time situating Western knowledge in its own cultural setting, rather than a universal one. Studying Indigenous knowledge fosters "greater awareness of neo-colonialism and other Western social practices that harm Indigenous peoples," and serves as a reminder that "traditional knowledge has been lost and world views have been shattered."

Framework for modern epistemology

The framework for modern epistemology has been influenced by many educational theorists and philosophers. These forefathers[2] of modern epistemology include John Locke, Jean-Jacques Rousseau, John Dewey, Jean Piaget, and Lev Vygotsky. Their respective theories are defined, and their ideas create contradictions and tensions, which are very much part of the modern experience.

John Locke

John Locke (1632–1704) revived Aristotle's notion that all knowledge and learning originate in experience. His concept of learning was that the child's mind is a blank tablet (*tabula rasa*) that gets shaped and formed by his/her own experiences. He promoted natural learning methods that took into account an individual student's temperament, interests, capabilities, and environment. The mind makes connections through the senses and creates simple ideas from experience; these simple ideas combine to form complex ideas.

In *Some Thoughts Concerning Education* (1693), Locke posited that skills and knowledge are continuously learned by example and practice instead of by memorizing rules and principles. To have a sound mind in a sound body, a gentleman needs to develop the following: virtue, wisdom, breeding, and knowledge. Locke considered good morals and good manners more important than knowledge. "Learning must be had, but in the second place, as subservient only to greater qualities" (Locke, 1996, p.113). The knowledge taught should be usable and practical: for example, learning your own language, and foreign languages.

Jean-Jacques Rousseau

During the Age of the Enlightenment, Jean-Jacques Rousseau (1712-1778) wrote the novel *Emile* claiming that "God makes all things good; man meddles with them and they become evil." He insisted on educating children in a natural way. He asserted that since man possesses an inherent natural goodness, his nature should be allowed to develop from its original state. Rousseau advocated that people should learn naturally, with their natural gifts, and not be influenced by established cultural, moral, and religious teachings.

The main character Emile, learned about life through his experiences. Rousseau celebrated the concept of childhood and felt that children should be allowed to develop naturally. "The education of a man begins at birth, before speaking, before understanding, he is already learning" (Rousseau, 1979, p. 62). Rousseau argued that the impetus for learning is provided by the growth of the person (nature). He suggested that learning is developmental, and he devoted a book to each of the following stages in *Emile*: Infancy, The Age of Nature, Pre-adolescence, Puberty, and Adulthood. Rousseau's ideas emphasized that more attention should be paid to the education of the individual, as in child-centered education.

John Dewey

John Dewey (1859-1952) is considered one of the forefathers of constructivism. Constructivist theories of learning and teaching are based on the belief that students construct their own meaning and understanding from direct experience with content that is linked to their prior knowledge. Dewey's educational theory encompasses the psychological and the sociological. The psychological is the instincts, individual needs and desires, and natural capabilities a child is born with. The sociological is the society around the child: i.e., what society wants the child to achieve in life, activities such as reading, writing, or practical skills. Dewey felt that without a balance of the two sides, the process can not truly be called education (Dewey, 1944).

Dewey proposed that knowledge is attained in a community or social context with social and community-based subjects. One's life, personality, and experience all come from what a person does and how others relate to him or her.

Jean Piaget

Jean Piaget (1896-1980) was the first to state that learning is a developmental cognitive process[3], and that students create knowledge rather than receive knowledge from the teacher. He recognized that students construct knowledge based on their biological, physical, and mental stages of development. Piaget (1966) outlines four developmental stages of growth: sensorimotor (birth-2 years), preoperational (ages 2-7), concrete operations (ages 7-11) and formal operations (ages 11-adulthood).

The child, through physical interaction with his or her environment, builds a set of concepts about reality and how it works. As physical experience accumulates, the child starts to conceptualize and create logical structures to explain his or her physical experiences. This is followed by the ability to problem solve and engage in conceptual reasoning. During all developmental stages, the child experiences his or her environment using whatever mental maps he or she has constructed so far. From Piaget's work on the nature of children's intellectual development progressive educators sought to learn how to apply these insights to educational principles, based on genetic epistemology, and to look carefully at how knowledge develops in children (Egan, 2002).

Lev Vygotsky

The key to Vygotsky's (1896-1934) socio-cultural cognition theory is the concept that we learn from others in an environment that is culturally based because knowledge and learning are constructed in a social context. He emphasized a child's need to interact with others who have more experience and knowledge, usually older children or the teacher to solve problems. Vygotsky (1986) referred to the *Zone of Proximal Development* to describe the teachable range between what students currently know, and new knowledge that they are not yet able to learn on their own. He felt that children have their own understanding and beliefs based on their experiences and that it is the teacher's role to influence students to higher levels of thinking and knowing.

Integration of ideas

How do children learn to construct their knowledge? Depending on which educational theory one subscribes to or which educational stakeholder is raising the question, different tensions come to the forefront. Recent psychological, neuroscience, cognitive, imaginative, and educational research establishes the importance of learning with understanding, learning in context, and taking into account different learning styles. However, there are still many other issues that need to be dealt with. These issues continue to multiply with the explosion of knowledge, powerful new communication and information technologies, and the changing role of society. "Technology is essential in teaching and learning mathematics; it influences the mathematics that is taught and enhances students' learning" (NCTM, 2000, p. 24). Tools such as calculators and computers are not to be used as a replacement for basic understanding; rather, they can and should be used to foster understandings and intuitions.

In some ways, all the theorists agree that knowledge is gained through a form of reasoning and sensory experiences. Students need to be engaged both physically and mentally in their learning experiences. By using hands-on learning opportunities, they can learn in context. Physical actions and hands-on experiences may be necessary for learning, especially for younger children, but they are not sufficient. We need to provide activities that engage the mind as well.

Locke, Rousseau, and Piaget have generalized about learning being age dependent. As children grow up, they tend to move from one stage to the next. Dewey and Vygotsky also attributed individual differences to be a function of personal interests, abilities, and characteristics of the current learning environment. Vygotsky in particular extended the developmental theory of the individual's cognitive abilities to include the notion of social-cultural cognition: that is, the idea that all learning occurs in a cultural context and involves social interactions.

The experience that students bring to the classroom, the ways they interpret their learning experiences, and the knowledge, skills, and attitudes with which they leave the classroom will all vary. We need to acknowledge that students have multiple abilities, learn with different learning styles, and create meaning with multiple intelligences. In schools today, progressivist ideas have become central to educational thinking: attention is given to a child's nature, particularly to their modes of learning and stages of development (Egan, 2002). In order to engage students' imaginations, it is often necessary to present them with ideas and examples that are far from present day curriculum (Egan, 1997; 2005). Learning activities should build upon students' prior knowledge and present mathematics in an exciting and inclusive way. Egan's (1997) approach for engaging students in learning is to look first at the kinds of things that most readily seem to inspire the students' imagination and creativity. The use of story is one way of capturing a student's imagination and engaging them in participating in curricular activities. Both teachers and students must engage themselves in learning and teaching where imagination plays a vital part. Egan (2005) states "Imagination is too often seen as something peripheral to the core of education, something taken care of by allowing students time to 'express themselves' in 'the arts,' while the proper work of educating goes on in the sciences and math" (p. xiii). Context combined with content should direct teaching in the ongoing cultural quest for knowledge.

Foundations of School Mathematics

Many of the topics in school mathematics today are rooted in the epistemology of mathematicians outside Europe before the 14th century. The learning outcomes in the document *Common Curriculum Framework for K-9 Mathematics* (2006) are organized into four strands: Number, Patterns and Relations, Shape and Space, and Statistics and Probability. Mathematics related to the above strands was transmitted to Western Europe across many geographical and cultural boundaries such as India, China, and Egypt. The Egyptians and Babylonians were well versed in the basic operations of arithmetic, algebra, and geometry. The ancient Chinese, the Mayans, the Indians–all were competent mathematicians, with advanced numeration systems. Modern mathematics on the other hand is linked to European advances of the seventeenth century: the analytic geometry of Fermat (1629) and Descartes (1637); the differential and integral calculus of Newton (1666, 1684) and Leibniz (1673, 1675); combinatorial analysis (1654) and the mathematical theory of probability of Fermat and Pascal; the number theory of Fermat (1630-65); the dynamics of Galileo (1591, 1612) and Newton (1666, 1684); and the law of universal gravitation (1666,1684-7) of Newton (Marks, 1964, p.134).

Descartes and Fermat are credited with the development of analytical geometry. The roots that gave geometry a two-thousand year domination of mathematics began to erode during the course of the seventeenth century. The invention of algebra meant that various problem-solving algorithms were now available to solve complex problems. The development of notation meant that the supremacy of geometry was challenged. The union of the algebraic and geometric methods resulted in the invention of analytical geometry.

The differential and integral calculus of Newton and Leibniz provided a method for investigating continuity in all its manifestations. All continuous change problems, such as in dynamics or in the flow of heat and electricity could now be solved with the use of differential and integral equations. The ideas from algebra and analytic geometry were used to develop a meaningful understanding of the methods and intentions of differential and integral calculus. In calculus courses, even today, topics such as definition of the limit, simple function approximation, and approximation of definite integrals are taught. Such topics find their roots in the works of Newton and Leibniz. In recent years there has been more emphasis on applications that involve data, developing the idea of a mathematical model, and using sequences to study discrete dynamical systems.

Games of chance have been played for generations (the human desire to get something for nothing). Efforts to understand this activity led European philosophers and mathematicians to modern notions of chance and risk. Fermat and Pascal's collaboration started after Pascal asked Fermat's advice on a game of chance problem in 1654. Their solutions to probability problems led to the development of probability theory (Marks, 1964, p. 157). This mathematical theory of probability is not only taught in schools today but is basic in all statistical analysis from stock-market trends and insurance to Gallup polls and biometrics.

Today's mathematics curriculum from pre-Kindergarten to Grade 12 includes most of the topics outlined above. Several kinds of mathematical knowledge are needed to effectively teach these topics–knowledge about mathematical ideas, about how curriculum is unique at each grade level, about the challenges students will encounter learning these ideas, about how ideas can be represented to teach all students, and about how students' understanding can be assessed (NCTM, 2000).

Interconnectedness of epistemologies

It is not the intention of this article to argue that we should abandon one or the other worldview. Rather it is to suggest that it would be useful for us to connect the features of each epistemology in the journey of learning. The table below elaborates my interpretation of the interconnectedness between the epistemologies through the topics of Language, Visualization, Context, Learner Diversity, Integration, and Creativity. These six topics are my adaptation from the NCTM (2000) Principles, Gardner's (1983) Multiple Intelligences, Egan's (2006) Imaginative Framework, and Cajete's (1994, 1999) Indigenous Curriculum Mandala. These topics highlight some of the elements involved in the relationships among formal and informal learning in Indigenous and Modern ways.

Summary: Building epistemological bridges

The complexities that come into play when two fundamentally different worldviews converge present a great challenge. Most Indigenous peoples' worldviews seek harmony and integration with all life, including the spiritual, natural, and human domains (Knudtson and Suzuki 1992). These three realms permeate traditional worldviews and all aspects of epistemology. On the other hand, modern epistemology promotes a rationalist and dualistic knowledge production that analyzes and objectifies in a linear form.

Cajete (1999) in his book *Igniting the Sparkle: An Indigenous Science Education Model* describes a culturally responsive science curriculum. The curriculum integrates Indigenous (Native American) traditional values, teaching principles, and concepts of nature with those of Modern (Western) science. Every Indigenous culture has an orientation to learning that is metaphorically represented in its art forms, its way of community, its language, and its understanding of itself in relationship to its natural environment. Indigenous peoples have historically applied the thought process of creative science within cultural contexts, taking a holistic approach. In most schools, science is taught from a Western cultural perspective that is preoccupied with abstract formalizations and technical operationalization. Both worldviews relate to the social organization of science. The fundamental difference is that the Indigenous worldview takes place in a community context and serves the good of all; in the Modern worldview it takes place in specialized settings that is separate from everyday life. Thus, there is a mismatch between cultural perspectives

Figure 1. Interconnectedness between Epistemologies

Topic	Indigenous	Modern
Language	**Myths and Oral Lore** Learning occurs more frequently in informal, unstructured situations through observation and imitation rather than verbalization.	**Symbolism** Mathematics is a language: a way of communicating ideas. Students build links between their informal, intuitive notions and the abstract language and symbolism of mathematics.
Visualization	**Visual Images** Visual images, symbols, rituals and diagrams are used to acquire new information and understandings. Information is transmitted primarily through observation.	**Spatial Sense and Patterns** Visualization and understanding of measurable objects and their units, systems, and processes are created with the use of patterns and orientation.
Context	**Community Life** Counting, locating, measuring, designing, playing, and explaining are central to all indigenous cultures and to mathematics.	**Representation** Representation refers both to process and product. Representations should be used to model and interpret mathematical ideas.
Learner Diversity	**Learning Styles** Application of strategies that address the brain pattern of indigenous students should be used. Auditory learning, observation skills, and memory are part of the informal education of Indigenous students.	**Multiple Intelligences** Mathematics instruction should be done in multiple ways that help students develop confidence in their ability to reason and justify their thinking in multiple ways.
Integration	**Holistic Worldview** Indigenous Worldview is holistic or integrated. Everything is interrelated and all relationships are important.	**Connections** Models are used to represent and interpret physical, social and mathematical phenomena.
Creativity	**Cultural Traditions** Teaching creativity in mathematics by exposing students to creative problem solving techniques. Establish learning situations that are experientially based in cultural traditions and help students develop their inquiry skills.	**Problem Solving** Problem Solving is the key to mathematics instruction. Students learn the skills of effective problem solving in a variety of contexts and build new mathematical knowledge through it.

that results in many young Indigenous students becoming alienated from science and mathematics.

Many elders talk about the importance of children growing up learning two worldviews, Indigenous and Western. Recognizing their interconnectedness, they wish their young people would seek knowledge from both worldviews. There is a tension between maintaining culture and letting culture evolve. There is also tension about how school mathematics should connect with daily numeracy practices. Many Aboriginal communities feel that student performance in schools is usually measured with a different cultural lens. This artificial polarization should not distract us from what the elders are calling for: to situate the learning in student's own culture to help them learn, as well as to help them measure up to school mathematics standards in order to succeed in the modern world.

Many Aboriginal students find themselves participating in two cultures–the culture of the home/community and the culture of the school. Students see little connection between the two cultures; hence many rich learning tasks from the community are lost in the school. This is particularly true in mathematics, where Aboriginal students feel alienated from the de-contextualized mathematics curriculum. Therefore, teaching mathematics with the use of authentically engaging situations and examples can help students attach meaning to the concepts that they learn in school mathematics. For students to learn in dual epistemologies it would be helpful if the students could learn from the land with integration of cultural activities. For example, the concept of patterns could first be learned through button blankets or the collections of shells, and then with the use of pattern blocks or algebraic functions. The elders talk about "what is" on the basis of their lived experiences. On the other hand many of the teachers talk about "what should be" in part because many of them have been in the community for only a short period of time and have limited knowledge of the Aboriginal worldview.

Figure 2. Visual comparison of Indigenous and Modern epistemologies in the Learning of Mathematics with the metaphor of a *Haida Canoe*.

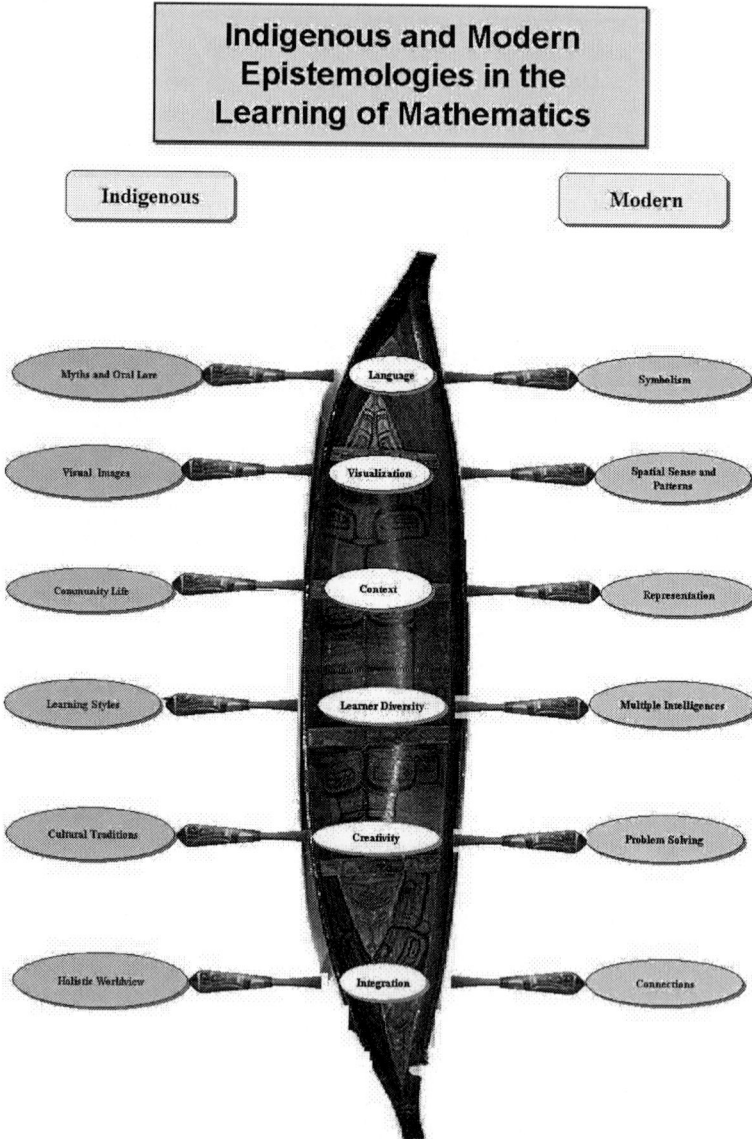

Indigenous and Modern Epistemologies in the Learning of Mathematics

Indigenous		Modern
Myths and Oral Lore	Language	Symbolism
Visual Images	Visualization	Spatial Sense and Patterns
Community Life	Context	Representation
Learning Styles	Learner Diversity	Multiple Intelligences
Cultural Traditions	Creativity	Problem Solving
Holistic Worldview	Integration	Connections

As I started this article I was thinking of finding a merged or common epistemology, but now I conclude that there need to be dual or multiple epistemologies. This does not mean, however, that these epistemologies cannot be brought into a productive relationship with each other. Figure 2 presents a framework that shows the connected features of each epistemology. The metaphor of a Haida canoe is a means of visualizing the connectedness of the two worldviews in the learning of mathematics. In many Indigenous communities the canoe represents the whole community, where many people work together to build it and then use it. If you paddle the canoe only on one side it turns to the opposite side, but if you paddle on both sides then the canoe moves forward in the direction you want it to go. Paddling on both sides enables one to stay on course.

End notes

[1] It is important to note that we do not assume the term Modern equates to advanced or sophisticated, and the term Indigenous equates to primitive. Each term represents a different worldview, and there is no single unified Indigenous worldview.

[2] In this section the works of five educational theorists is identified, but there are others like Immanuel Kant and David Hume who have also been influential about European mathematical and scientific thinking. The works of Descartes and Newton are discussed later in the article.

[3] Egan (2002) identifies the essays and works of Herbert Spencer (1820-1903) as playing a crucial role in the formation of progressivism, and influencing much of modern day schooling.

Bibliography

Battiste, M. & Barman, J. (Eds.). (1995). *First Nations education in Canada: The circle unfolds.* Vancouver, BC: UBC Press.

Cajete, G.A. (1994). *Look to the mountain: An ecology of indigenous education.* Skyland, N.C.: Kivaki Press.

—. (1999). *Igniting the sparkle: An Indigenous science education model.* Skyland, NC: Kivaki Press.

Davison, D. M. (2002). Teaching Mathematics to American Indian Students: A Cultural Approach. In J. E. Hankes & G. R. Fast (Eds.), *Perspectives on Indigenous People of North America* (pp. 19-24). Reston, VA: National Council of Teachers of Mathematics.

Devlin, K. (2000). *The Math Gene. How Mathematical Thinking Evolved and Why Numbers are Like Gossip.* New York: Basic Books.

Dewey, J. (1944). *Democracy and education.* New York: Macmillan.

—. (1938). *Experience and education.* New York: Macmillan.

Egan, K. (1997). *The Educated Mind: How Cognitive Tools Shape Our Understanding.* Chicago: University of Chicago Press.

—. (2002). *Getting It Wrong from the Beginning.* New Haven: Yale University Press.

—. (2005). *An Imaginative Approach to Teaching.* San Francisco, CA: Jossey-Bass.

—. (2006). *Teaching literacy: Engaging the imagination of new readers and writers.* Thousand Oaks CA: Corwin Press.

Ermine, W. (1995). Aboriginal Epistemology. In Battiste, M. & Barman, J. (Eds.), *First Nations education in Canada: The circle unfolds.* Vancouver, BC: UBC Press.

Gardner, H. (1983). *Frames of Mind.* New York: Basic Books Inc.

Kawagley, O. (1995). *A Yupiaq worldview.* Prospect Heights, IL: Waveland Press.

Knudtson, P. & Suzuki, D. (1992). *Wisdom of the elders.* Toronto: Stoddart Publishing, Ltd.

Locke, J. (1996). *Some thoughts concerning education.* Indianapolis: Hackett Publishing Company, Inc. (Original work published in 1693).

Marks, R. (Ed.), (1964). *The growth of mathematics.* New York: Bantam Books

National Council of Teachers of Mathematics. (2000). *Principles and Standards for School Mathematics.* Reston, Virginia. Available On-line: www.nctm.org/standards/

Rousseau, J. J. (1979). *Emile or On Education.* New York: Basic Books, Inc. (Introduction, Translation and Notes by Bloom, A. from original work published in 1762).

Semali, L. M. & Kincheloe, J. L. (Eds.), (1999). *What is Indigenous knowledge? Voices from the Academy.* New York & London: Falmer Press.

Tarnas, R. (1991). *The Passion of the Western Mind.* New York: Ballantine Books.

Vygotsky, L. (1986). *Thought and Language.* Cambridge, MA: MIT Press. (Original work published in 1962).

Vygotsky, L. S. (1978). *Mind in society: The development of the higher psychological processes.* London: Harvard University Press.

Western and Northern Canadian Protocol. (2006). *The Common Curriculum Framework for K-9 Mathematics.* Alberta: Alberta Education.

CONTEMPORARY HEROES AND STUDENTS' MOTIVATION FOR LEARNING

STEFAN POPENICI

In students' lives, education is related to inspiring role models and heroes who shape the students' motivation, values, and choices for the future. This article looks at the results of a nationwide survey on role models and motivation for learning for Romanian students. We will analyze what the findings of this survey tell us about the influence of students' imagination in the public education of today. We will try to find an answer to the question of whether or not students still value school learning, and how, if at all, imagination is connected with the motivation to study, learn, and develop skills for the future. We will present an analysis of major implications of our findings and provide a sketch of some of the possible avenues of development in curriculum design. Because of the various creations of the media, "street mythology" or value-empty heroes often capture the imaginations of our students, this study will briefly look at consequences and challenges for education as it is today.

Introduction

Often there is an enormous difference between how public education is portrayed by political rhetoric and statistical data and the realities in schools. We can see the willingness to create a good education system; it is particularly evident in the competition between institutions or countries for improved results in literacy and mathematics, sciences and humanities; but rarely is the way clear to achieving these results. The common challenge for our schools today, in different societies and geographical places, is to find an effective method to dialogue with disengaged students, to speak to their imagination and connect them to school's narratives. Our team of researchers wanted to see to what extent our new generations have an intrinsic motivation for learning and education, if the imagination of today's students is a powerful mechanism connected to education, and how they imagine their future. If experience shows that students do not see real-life connected with school then educational institutions are placed in a difficult situation struggling to inspire the imaginations of students.

We applied quantitative and qualitative methods of research for a nationwide representative survey of Romanian students. Our choice was determined by various factors: we had the chance to conduct research in a school with a large student population, on the first generation at the end of the upper-secondary education or vocational education studies (ISCED 4), which started school when Romania changed its political system to democracy. Another appealing characteristic was related to the fact that Romania is now an active part of international trends in education as a European Union member and one of the first signatories of Bologna accords and implementers of reforms for the European Higher Education Area. (We note that the general characteristics of the population we studied here present common variables and trends identified in comparative studies or professional activities we developed in other geographical and cultural areas, such as South East Asia, North America or other European countries.)

It is known that we commonly imagine *past* in idyllic colours and develop utopian illusions of perfect cities or societies that are long gone. It seems that politicians are particularly attracted to building their rhetoric on imaginary ancient times, constructed realities of a glorious past with perfect cities, and precedent, virtuous societies. This can be a powerful weapon for public figures, as is any symbolic instrument of communication based on the involvement of imagination. Nevertheless, it is important to look more closely at how important it is to imagine our future, especially when we talk about education. Starting from childhood, we naturally look for heroes and we shape our life in relation to role models or undesirable characters that embed within us a set of specific values. Bruno Bettelheim (1989) pointed out the fact that a child will never ask himself "Do I want to be good?" but *Whom do I want to be like?* A child will try to imitate and replicate the desired behaviour of a hero, in consonance with all values attached to this complex model. In other words, a child emotionally attaches him or herself to the behavioural model of a character he or she holds in high esteem, and the child adopts values represented by this model as their own axiological scale. Later, as teenagers look for different reference points, a different set of heroes becomes their symbolic "teacher," presenting and indicating the limits of revolt, clothing styles, mannerisms, values, and lifestyle. The relationship between individuals and role models is not a simple cause-and-effect relationship; various codes, cultural settings, archetypes, contextual conditions and psychological mechanisms weave the fabric of this formative dynamic process.

Bettelheim points out the profound significance of role models for education and how they shape the future structure of individuals' personalities. At the social level, the most visible heroes represent, in essence, the moral and behavioural codes used by the youth as reference marks for their present actions and for the future. In a similar vein, villains are the embodiment of undesirable behaviours and personalities. Therefore, youth will study or not, develop themselves spiritually and professionally or choose street gangs and disruptive behaviour, in synchronization with the "symbolic recipe" of the adopted role model(s). Villains are very important because they have the power to seize the imagination and–more importantly–to clarify values by confronting us with a choice of the moral coordinates we choose to follow: if the "villain" is an uncultured and uneducated individual, there are more chances to orient the child toward school and study in order to avoid a predictive and imagined future fall into a reprehensible life. A sports star lost to drugs and alcohol can be a powerful example for teenagers, allowing them to make choices which would help them avoid similar mistakes. However, if a "baddie" becomes a "hero" surrounded by a romantic aura, admired for money or flamboyant lifestyle, it will be hard for those fascinated by this class of idols to see school and learning as desirable goals. Nevertheless, it is clear that role models inspire and give individuals energy and motivation to achieve a similar level of success (Lockwood & Kunda, 1997). Their moral and axiological coordinates are extremely important from the educational point of view. Role models or models of success are directly related to cultural features, which are and will be perpetuated, determining behavioural and lifestyle models that are likely to be imitated. Therefore, this code of symbolic reproduction creates social roles and status configurations; it is a clear and powerful mechanism of imagining success in life as a formative process.

Imitation is embedded in our human nature and this is no surprise for schools and public education. In *Learners for Life, Student Approaches to Learning: Results from PISA 2000* (OECD, 2003), the authors underline that the OECD's international evaluations of students in mathematical, scientific or reading literacy reveal that motivation is one of the main factors for students' success in school. Therefore, it seems valid to consider that part of our goal is to address the challenge of finding what can engage students' imagination and on the basis of what we find to try to design practical ways to build and strengthen their motivation for learning. This challenge started with the idea of exploring whether or not our hypotheses about the importance of heroes and life models for social success are valid, real, and powerful for students' life. We decided to initiate a comprehensive study on students' heroes and values with the Institute for Educational Sciences in Romania.

Following these hypotheses, our team of researchers began to develop a questionnaire to survey a nationwide representative sample of students in the final year of upper-secondary education, with the aim of identifying students' attitudes to school, their values and role models, and how these relate to education. Interviews and questionnaires were conducted in 2004 and 2005 and the margin of sampling error for the poll's results was +/- 2 percent. A number of 2007 students represented the final sample, with 1834 from urban areas and 173 from rural schools. This study looked at what students envision as a formula for success in their future, and focused on their perceptions of school and learning and the connection of these constructs. The study involved quantitative research and qualitative methods of investigation (focus groups and interviews). The results speak about influences rather than causes of educational success and reveal some connections between how Romanian youth imagine success and about the predominant sources of students' role models. It was not our intention to assert that there is a certain causal relationship or a specific order of cause and effect between role models and students' behaviour. However, our data seem to suggest quite clearly that the "contemporary mythology" has a very powerful influence on students' performance in school and their future careers.

The first set of data from our study reveals a surprising fact, which opposes the common myth that asserts that only very young children emulate heroes: most students (88.9%) between 17 and 19 years of age have role models and clearly identify their heroes as a source of motivation and inspiration for their lives. Only a minority of 6.4% claims not to have a role model. As we can see in Table 1 the percentages show that a vast majority of students clearly identified, named, and detailed their role models.

The data reveal that students search for role models and this exerts a certain influence on their own choices, on their performance in school, and on their attitude towards learning and educational trajectories. In this contemporary mythology, students operate using binary oppositions because *"the human brain is innately 'hardwired' to build understanding on the binary discriminations"* (Egan, 1997, p. 39). Dividing their reference points into good and bad, ideal and evil, or their role models into "goodies" and "baddies," students clarify and bring order to their choices, motivations, and moral coordinates for the present and the future.

Table 1. Distribution of students who say that heroes inspire their life and goals

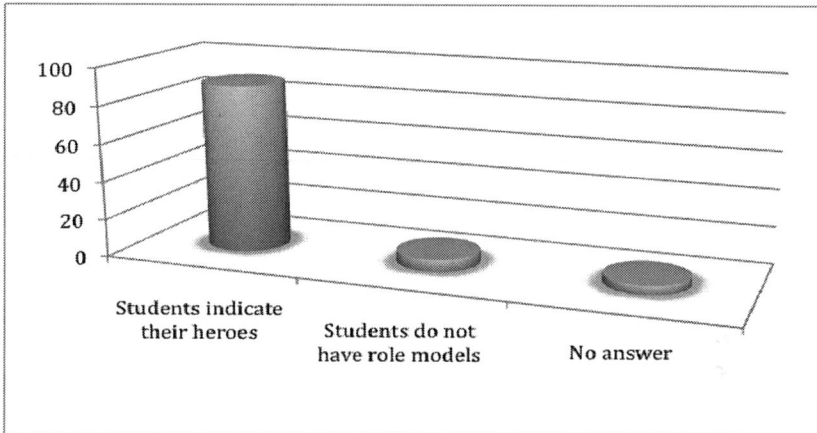

Collecting data brings us the possibility of arriving at a more accurate picture of motivation for learning in a representative cohort and a glimpse of the imagery structure of a generation. Answers to questions such as "Whom do I want to be like?" and "Whom do I not want to be like (and why not)?" coupled with responses to interviews and multiple questions within the survey reveal a disturbing reality: the existence of two parallel but very different worlds–that of the school and its teachers and, equally complex and "valid," that of the students. Students build their motivation and shape their identity in consonance with their imagined model of existence. The majority (90.8%) indicates they want to have negative heroes as models for their life. One of the most interesting findings of the survey was the extent to which negative heroes are actively used as reference points, helping individuals to identify and define failure or unacceptable conditions (social status or set of behaviours). Table 2 shows a representation of this distribution.

Table 2. 90.8% of students specify having negative role models

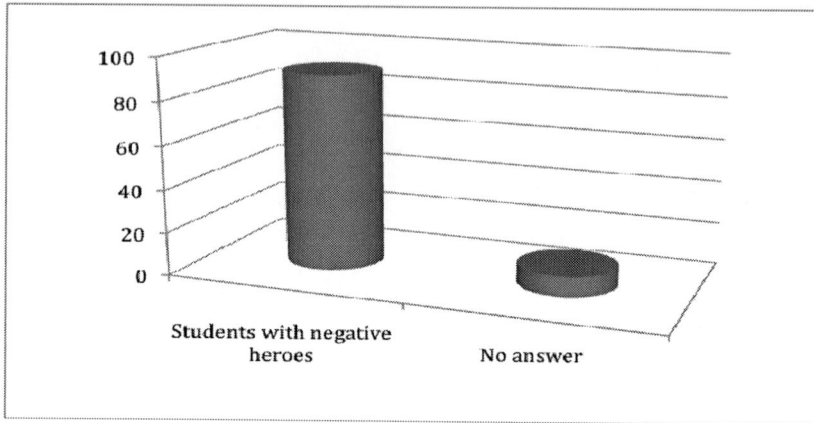

This study did not focus on specific characters mentioned by respondents as role models or their opposites, but on specific categories of heroes and how, if they are adopted, they inspire students' lives and motivation for learning. Notorious celebrities such as Britney Spears, a character from "American Idol," and a popular actor were all included in the "TV stars" category regardless of gender, nationality, or factors other than notoriety achieved through exposure on television. The students' mothers, uncles, brothers, and other relatives were grouped under the "Family members" umbrella. Adopting and using these general categories provides for the comparative distribution of students' preferences in choosing heroes and their opposites.

Table 3 shows that the most "visible" heroes in what we have referred to here as "contemporary mythology" are TV characters. The peculiar aspect of the top rated category of role models is that they are significantly more visible and popular than any other group, even than Family, the second-place group.

Table 3. Distribution of students' role models

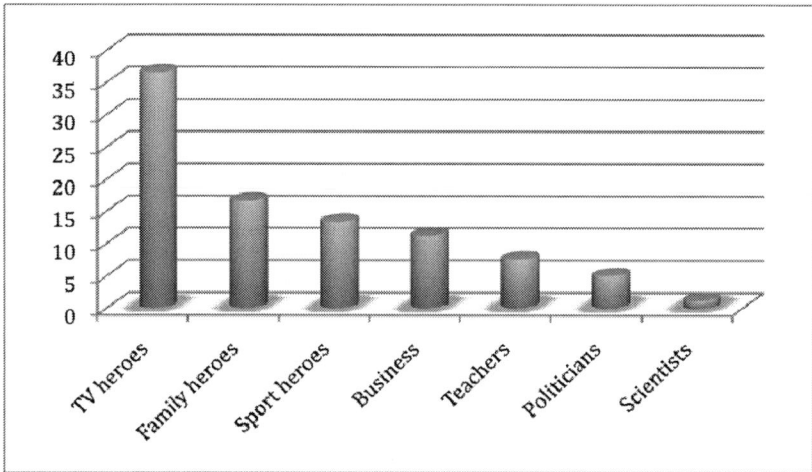

The comparative distribution of data presented in Table 4 reveals that mass media, an efficient, but morally irresponsible educator, shape the most visible category. On the other hand, it indicates that teachers are not able to stir students' imagination or interest even by half in comparison with the first three categories. Using heroes and their opposites in this comparative analysis proved to be a very useful approach, especially as during the interviews students indicated clearly how their hero represents "an ideal situation" they "dream to achieve" and their opposites are "paths to be avoided." It is revealing to see how their choices reflect what is important in their life and who is shaping their symbolic meanings, values, culture or counter-cultures.

The data showed, even from the beginning of the analysis, that media is the most powerful educator in this sense and that students' imaginations were actively engaged by television productions. In both positive and negative positions, teachers are less visible than TV, sport or family heroes and even politicians, which were mostly placed at the undesirable positions. From this perspective, they are close to "scientists," a category almost invisible for students as "interesting and inspiring characters/models."

Table 4. Role models and their opposites

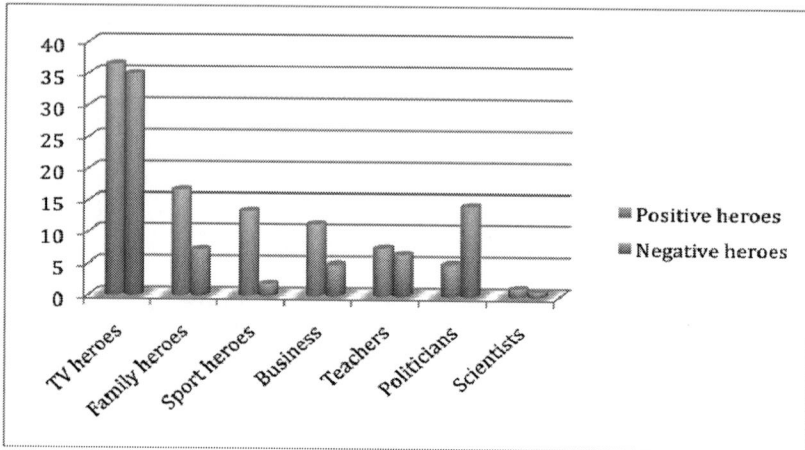

This distribution is highly relevant for many reasons. First, it is possible to see that TV stars capture students' imagination both as positive role models and as opposites. The explanation for this is that a significant part of students named a character from a category as a role model and another one from the same group as a clear undesirable model of life and values. For example, in the case when Justin Timberlake was identified as the hero, the question about the unacceptable role-model was answered by "I do not want to be like *Eminem*." "Family members" placed as the second major group though a large percentage separates the two groups: "TV stars" provided 36.5% of role models for youths (opposites to role models: 34.9%), "Family members" accumulated less than half, with 16.6%. Close to second place, we find "Sport heroes" with 13.3% and "Business" with 11.2 percent. Teachers remain mostly "invisible" for an entire generation: they are neither loved nor hated; in students' symbolic space, academics simply do not have sufficient relevance or interesting features to drive youths' imagination for a future career or any kind of adventure. Unfortunately, with 1.2 percent, "Scientists" were below the margin of the poll's sampling error. A specific set of questions was focused in our study on the reasons why a specific role model was chosen.

It was interesting to see the reasons that lead every student to choose a specific character as a model worthy of inspiration. The general values for the main reasons to follow the hero identified by students are presented in Table 5.

Table 5. Reasons to choose your hero

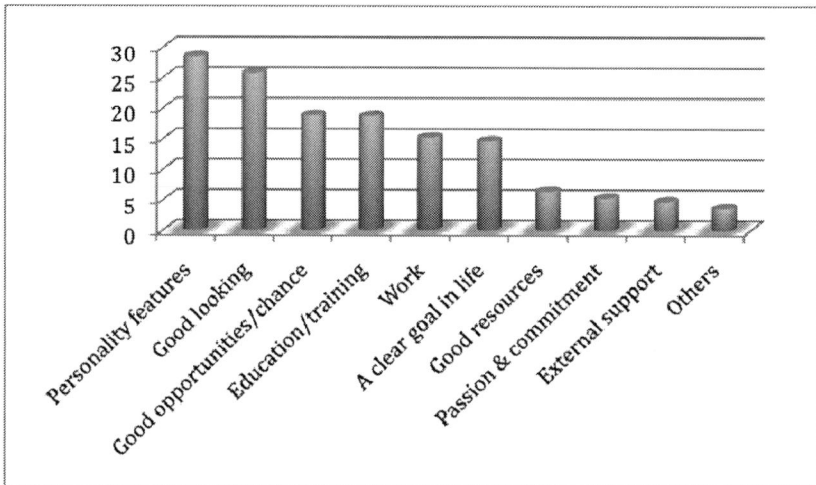

As we have shown in Table 3 TV stars are the most visible and important group of students' role models. Therefore, we looked at why students chose them as "models to follow in life." The answers' distribution rank reveals that the most important was that these stars are notorious, have "professional success," are "good looking" and are "intelligent/smart." The least important reasons were their education, religiosity, altruism, or credibility/sincerity. Students' perception seemed to be that education had little or no importance in leading to success in life, at least in comparison with other factors such as notoriety or good looks.

Even before being part of a comparative and comprehensive analysis, these data show that, on a nationwide scale, dominant role models are not found in schools or spaces that are symbolic of schools or school life. Very few students find role models within school life or in other areas symbolically connected with education, learning, or academic culture. Most popular heroes that inspire students and are able to shape ideas, moral choices, and motivations were found in commercial entertainment. These findings show the schools' do not have the capacity to stimulate students' imagination and only a partial capacity to offer and promote alternative role models (or models of success)–ones that are able to speak about learning as an exciting journey and a key of personal and social development.

Table 6. Reasons to choose your role model: TV heroes

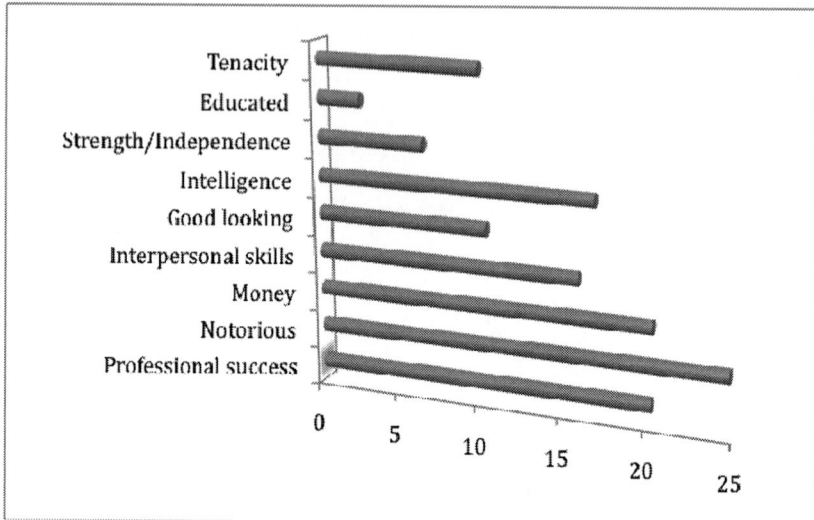

Undoubtedly, this perspective is based on evidence that shows youth has an extrinsic and instrumental motivation for learning and are disengaged and in moral confusion: external attributes are set above intrinsic value, and attractiveness and a commercialized idea of "fun" are set up as opposite to intellectual endeavors and creativity. An entire generation signals here that schools exist apart, in a parallel life to the students, and their response is to ignore these institution as much as students' interests and visions are themselves ignored. This generation openly chooses to follow "notoriety" and–following the commercial pre-packaged products of an industry–has almost completely lost interest in school as a partner and mentor: public education is oblivious of this fact and there is little to indicate that anyone cares about the imaginative lives, dreams, and hopes of their students. Public education's influence on students to choose a role model or a specific set of values is rated as very low. Teachers and schools are the lowest in students' perceptions as influential factors for choosing their points of reference in life.

Table 7 presents the main factors influencing the choice of a role model; these were organized into two main categories: community groups and the mass media. In the first group, we can see that family and friends are the most influential in shaping or orienting students' choices. In the second group, television is indicated by students as the most influential factor that influences their choices.

Table 7. Factors of influence when choosing a hero

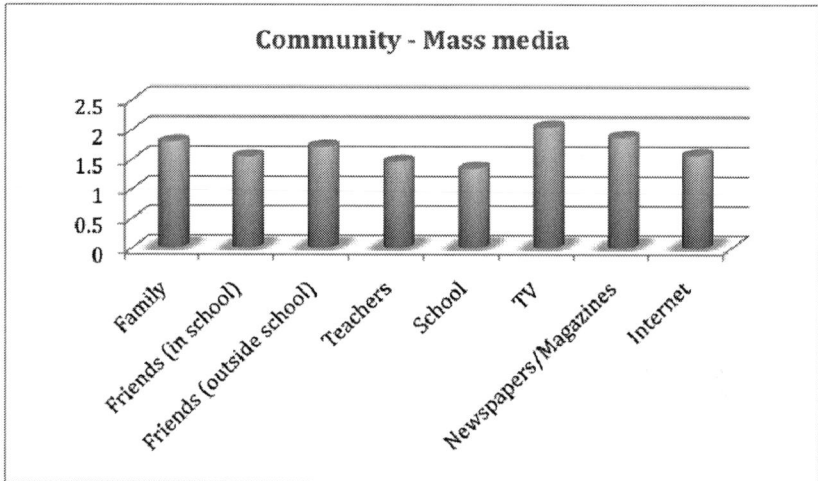

Community - Mass media

As our study reveals, television is undoubtedly the main source for youths' role models. The mass media confirm their informal teaching role, inculcating values, preferences, behaviours, and "role models" as recipes for success. It is obvious, at least in Romania, that the sense of moral responsibility for this important role is missing completely from television; that a media which exerts tremendous symbolic force over our youth is used without any ethical (or at least decent) reference. Nevertheless, it is very important to see that here is a clear sign for a major transmutation: the educational role is taken from the school and often from the family by the media. Family stands only in third position (after television and magazines) in students' ranking of factors of influence in choosing role models in life. Previous Gallup International studies in Romania show that youth prefer to spend their free time in front of the TV (Gallup, 2004). Almost 90% of Romanian children watch television at least 4 to 5 days a week and 79% watch TV every day. The average child living in Romania watches television for 151 minutes during weekdays and 214 minutes during weekends. The average time is almost equal to the average time spent in school by a child. International studies reveal that this trend is common to most industrialized countries and the only difference is the increased time spent in front of personal computers, playing games, or watching video content online. This is, in fact, a significant change with major implications for educators, but entertainment is still the dominant content accessed by youth and the effects are the same. Daily exposure to television/entertainment is directly associated with no interest in reading: only 3 percent of the children mentioned reading (books, magazines, and other printed texts) as their favourite way of spending time enjoyably. Television, the gaming industry, and the internet shape the values and capture the imagination of young people who are not yet able to independently distinguish right from wrong. In spite of this, public education is still trying to advance its agenda of moral literacy by using a decrepit industrial model of rational goals, contents, and facts that are delivered in the same unattractive forms. The first set of our data tells us that new heroes provided by the media are rapidly adopted by students as role models.

Consistently the data in our study have revealed that students' motivation for learning in school is predominantly external, and public education is neither capable of nor really interested in, creating intrinsic motivation for learning. Moreover, students' imaginations are not attracted by the public education discourse or by school life. When their imaginations are not engaged in school, youth simply follows the human desire for reference points in life and looks at any available attractive space where they can access characters that will engage and inspire their imaginations. TV stars or computer-game characters, "American Idols," or street heroes are better than a school curriculum empty of valued symbols and imagination. In our target group 36.3% felt that educators are generally indifferent towards role models adopted by the students. Teachers never asked this significant proportion of students about their interests, dreams, or their real-life projections for the future. Imagination continues to be a fashionable buzzword for most of the teachers we interviewed, but it proved to be a fuzzy and unsuitable concept when we asked how they engage students' imagination in learning or teaching.

School is perceived as being uninterested in students' real needs, interests, and aspirations. In this representative cohort, 33.2 % of students considered education as responsible for their role models' success in life, while 24.8% opined that school was not connected with success in life. The largest percentage (40.5%) of the students questioned could not say whether or not there was any connection between education and their models' success in life. Again, education and learning–at least in an institutionalized context–is not perceived as a condition for personal development and a large percent of students revealed confusion or lack of interest in this issue (or both).

Table 8. School's influence on personal and social success

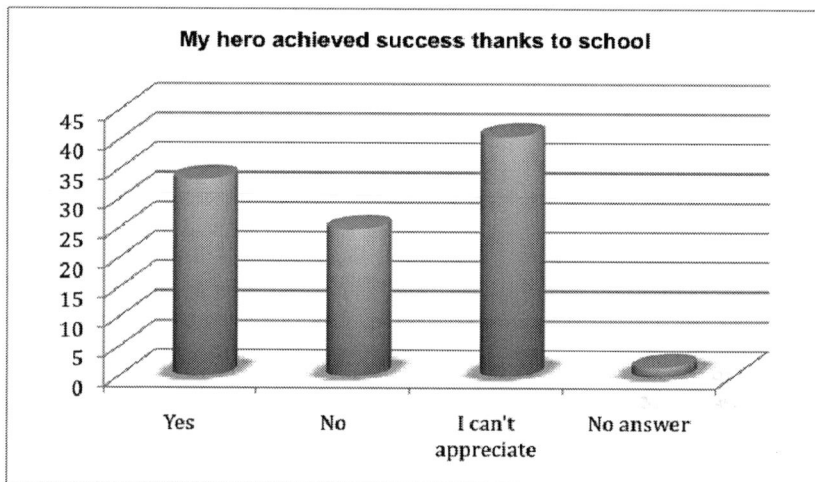

My hero achieved success thanks to school

Unfavourable feelings among students about school are significant. Data reflects that a significant number of students see a gap between their interests and needs and the school curriculum and practice. Critical views towards school rise to 26.4% among students in the specified cohort. Among those who are critical, 36.9% indicate that school is not student-centred and is uninterested in or unresponsive to students' interests and needs. Moreover, 21.6% consider that school is "not fair" and does not provide opportunities for a better future and 5.5% consider school as boring and useless. Through extensive interviews and questionnaires, we documented the fact that a significant percentage of survey participants felt that they did not belong at school and attended for external and instrumental reasons. During our interviews some of the students clearly expressed that they felt they were part of a mechanical process with compulsory procedures and requirements. In a very flexible reality, where new ideas, challenges, and possibilities have been opened by the knowledge society, schools appear to maintain a didactic paradigm. Even for students who are oriented towards academic performance there is separation between their real interests and what is being taught and what is happening in school. Imagining their future is an active and important part of students' life and influences different sides of school life as well as individual careers.

Stakeholders should understand and value how education systems prepare students for life. In fact, today's parents, students, and stakeholders in different parts of the world are beginning to realize that schools are losing connection with students' imaginations. Drained of passion and emotion, curriculum is far from students' lives and real interests. A recent study released by the World Bank reveals that:

> Abstract, fact-centered, and decontextualized narrative knowledge prevails in the secondary curriculum and continues to be used for selective purposes in a setting of scarce educational and job opportunities, causing high dropout and high failure rates among secondary school students. (World Bank, 2005, p. 78)

Comparing our data findings in Romania with statistical results from comparative international studies around the world made it possible to document the fact that lack of engagement and the challenge of re-thinking curriculum to bring back passion, emotion, and imagination is a common problem for schools all over the world. Although these international studies say very little about students' heroes and how those heroes influence the students' motivation for learning, we were able to find consistent data that show specific relevance if we look at it in light of our findings. For example, the Organization for Economic Co-operation and Development (OECD) revealed through a 41-country survey conducted in 2003 that a significant percentage of students agree with the statement that school has done little to prepare them for adult life. They also agree or strongly agree that school has been a waste of time:

> A significant minority of students, 8 per cent on average across OECD countries, consider school a waste of time and an average of 32 per cent consider that school has done little to prepare them for life. In Germany, Hungary, Luxembourg, Mexico, Turkey and, among the partner countries, in Hong Kong-China, Liechtenstein, Macao-China and Uruguay, those agreeing or strongly agreeing that school has done little to prepare them for life exceeds 40 per cent. (OECD, 2004, p. 125)

In other words, a surprisingly large number of students today follow a different model than that represented by their school's axiological and developmental codes and ignore public education's role as a potential positive factor in life. Students who think that school is a waste of time cannot develop a sense of belonging in school, and they do not believe that academic success will have an effective bearing on their future. These feelings and attitudes may result in their turning away from school and abandoning the idea of continuing their education (Finn, 1989; Jenkins, 1995). Characters that represent the symbolic personification of their desired moral, behavioural, and developmental features often capture students' imagination; these characters are often opposed to the idea of schooling or even the idea of civilization. Youths, even in remote areas of the world, are subject to strong media influence that is morally irresponsible and is not concerned about lifelong learning, life skills, or moral values. It is the responsibility of the school to rethink its paradigm and mission to become appealing for students' imaginations, to be able to inspire dreams that are connected with pro-social and learning values, to restore faith in schools' ability to be interesting and relevant. Facing major ecological, humanitarian, and cultural challenges we cannot afford the enduring moral indifference that makes schools comfortable with the perspective of building its discourse and realities on a paradigm created more than a century ago for fledgling industries in their primitive forms. At the same time, we as educators have the awesome responsibility of bringing solutions for students who are unable to find resources to live in a parallel existence and simply refuse to go to school for the legitimate reasons that school is boring and has no relevance for their lives. It is a crying shame when a school loses even one bright young mind simply because, by its very structure, it focuses on its own processes and mechanized didactics, rather than on the interests and needs of its students.

Worldwide, educators must accept the challenge of building metacognitive capital, oriented to culture, civilization, and humanistic ideals of education, a capital able to lure even an already captured imagination. Education stands now, at the beginning of a new century, major tasks in front of it: one is to face, and reverse, the unfortunate trend of increasing numbers of children being excluded from education not only in some developing countries like the Philippines, Romania, India, but also in developed nations such as the United States, New Zealand, Australia, and the United Kingdom. In countries such as Jamaica, the proportion of out-of-school children has been rising for the last decade. Moreover, in countries that usually place well in international tests–like New Zealand–it is accepted as a fact that one in five students will leave school before the end of compulsory education. Moreover, it has proven that, often, local governments' or World Bank's ideas of educational reforms and so-called "structural development" are not functional in reality. This is a story about institutions with little desire to imagine the worst and to think "outside the box" or even face the reality that the entire paradigm of planning and implementing education should be changed through the educational reform. This is, in fact, just another chapter of "captured imagination," but at a different level. In short, education as it is today presents many reasons to look for a change of its obsolete paradigm.

In other words, we can say that education is now facing the challenge to…educate. Public education is called on to rebuild its narrative with a focus on knowledge and values capable of providing equal chances to all in a globalized world, and of motivating students to learn on their own under the accepted jargon of "lifelong learning." If youths are left with no heroes, no role models, or points of reference in life by the school's unengaging and unstimulating curriculum and by its unmotivated (or untrained) teachers, then they look, in a natural impulse, for a new source for all of these. Enter the mass media as an aggressive, but flexible and creative institution, with the self-proclaimed goal of capturing the imaginations of its consumers. The problem is that television usually does not motivate students for lifelong learning or personal development, and its programs motivate the viewers to buy not to learn. The industrial approach of education in schools is replaced by a highly consumerist culture promoted by television and media products where motivation for learning is too often trivialized and ridiculed. Internet, even if we take into consideration all the amazing opportunities opening there, cannot be seriously regarded as the driving force of education or as an educator oriented to building learning throughout life. Education should be fed with good quality products, inspiring stories of hope and emotion, passion and moral values, and creative ideas will arise naturally for learners who truly enjoy what they are doing. This way we will also enable youths to imagine different alternatives and to choose independently as educated and responsible human beings. The chance to choose when you ask yourself "Whom do I want to be like?" and the seeds of passion and motivation for learning are the most important parts of a genuine education. It really doesn't matter if youths' imaginations are nourished sometimes with low-quality products.

If we sacrifice the imagination of our youths on the altar of rationality through a profoundly inadequate curriculum, we leave them exposed to worthless dreams (such as provided by television stars) or destructive imagery. School is still the institution called upon to help all students develop themselves and the first step towards this goal is to begin imagining a better future. In our work with disadvantaged students, in Romania or the Philippines, we found that step one was to rebuild hope in youth, a real and strong belief that their future can be built together and in this future education plays a major role in finding success. This was more important than content and objectives, because content was lost if their imagination was working for something else. Only after that was it possible to talk about curriculum and we tried to keep this hope alive through a continuous reference to their imaginations and creativity; we found in practice that any student who is engaged in what they learn will show, in a remarkably short time, improved school results. Thanks to this experience, we strongly believe that it is the educator's responsibility to speak to students' imagination as part of our commitment to provide equal chances and opportunities for all.

If we do not speak to students' imaginations, how can education prepare students for the increasing need to be creative and flexible for a future that will require the use of knowledge in a very flexible and imaginative way? In order to be an effective educator it is necessary to know what students truly love and look at practical ways to engage their imagination in educational stories and journeys, such as mathematics, science, music, and literature. It is the right time to put aside for a moment all learning theories and consider whether it is not important to bring back into school the joy of learning and the natural need to follow an ideal. It is a good time to seek practical ways to awaken and engage the imagination of our students through curriculum. Bringing back imagination, looking at students' ideals as they are, and cultivating creativity remain as the greatest challenges for schools, and require a blend of skills, information, and creativity in an independent educated mind. All of these comprise what Einstein called "the creative imagination" as a means for science and seems to be the real goal of an education mandated to develop responsible citizens and skilled members of a society that will be dramatically different from what we have now in the most accelerated time of change in history.

Bibliography

Bettelheim, B. (1989). *The Uses of Enchantment.* New York: Knopf.

Egan, K. (1997). *The Educated Mind: How Cognitive Tools Shape Our Understanding.* Chicago: The University of Chicago Press.

Finn, J. (1989). 'Withdrawing from school'. *Review of Educational Research,* 59(2), 117-142.

Jenkins, P. H. (1995). School Delinquency and School Commitment. *Sociology of Education,* 68, 221–239.

Lockwood, P., & Kunda, Z. (1997). Superstars and me: Predicting the impact of role models on the self. *Journal of Personality and Social Psychology,* 73(1), 91-103.

OECD (2004, b). *Learning for Tomorrow's World: First results from PISA 2003.* Paris: OECD.

OECD, (2004, a). Problem Solving for Tomorrow's World. First Measures of Cross-Curricular Competencies from PISA 2003. Paris: OECD.

Gallup International (2004). Expunerea copiilor la programe radio si TV (Children's exposure to television and radio programs). Romania: The Gallup Organization.

The World Bank (2005). Expanding Opportunities and Building Competencies for Young People A New Agenda for Secondary Education. Washington DC: The World Bank.

Gender and Achievement Through the Socio-Cultural Lens: Implications for Research and Curricular Design

Sean McLaughlin and Tim Waddington

A research gap exists in Vygostkian theory regarding gender and development, in particular about issues concerning boys, curricula, and brain research. These issues have recently been problematized by such popularizers as Leonard Sax and Michael Gurian. With an eye towards addressing issues that impact boys and curriculum, the authors provide a framework of study for examining the role of gender in child development that includes the ethno-cultural and socio-economic factors Vygotsky considered critical. They relate these research interests to Imaginative Education as a model.

Introduction

This year marks the thirtieth anniversary of the English-language translation and publication of *Mind in Society: The Psychology of Higher Mental Functions*. Since then, more of Lev Vygotsky's work has been published in North America, and many now have the opportunity to study his theory of child development which is centered in social and cultural relations. His theory has effected change in understanding how children develop, and new views on the roles played by parents, educators, and society at large.

While Vygotsky's contribution to the field of developmental psychology is significant, his short life left the possibility for a full extrapolation of his ideas unfinished. First in Russia, and now in the West, psychologists and researchers studying Vygotsky's theories, bring new consideration to how ethno-cultural and socio-economic factors affect development. An area that has been largely ignored in English-based Vygotskian scholarship is the role of gender in development (Tudge, 1999). In recent studies, when gender is mentioned, it is only peripherally, and comments are "tentative and speculative" (Ibid., p. 1376). If one is willing to contend that gender is a developmentally significant factor in all cultures, then a gap exists in Vygotskian theory that requires attention.

Recent years have witnessed an intense and growing interest in gender-based studies. Gurian (2005) often speaks of a "crisis" of engagement and scholastic outcomes in what has been called the gender achievement gap. His thesis suggests that boys are lagging behind. He feels our collective challenge as educators is to address this slippage. How we conceptualize the causes of the problem will impact our ability to make effective and pedagogically defensible interventions. This paper's broad focus is the concern that cultural-cognitive explanations have been, so far, underrepresented in these discussions, to the favor of more physiological ones. Dominant strains of research usually present what may yet prove to be a socio-cultural issue that stems from physiological factors; in turn, the solutions they prescribe rely on biologically-minded Piagetian notions of child development rather than on more balanced approaches. This paper provides an alternative framework of study for examining the role of gender in child development.

Current research

Two dominant voices in the issue of gender development in North America are Michael Gurian (2003, 2005) and Leonard Sax (2005). An educator and family therapist, Gurian began investigating gender differences after experiencing personal turmoil during school. Sax, a psychologist and physician, became alarmed by the rising number of boys being referred to him with questions of ADHD and requests for those boys to be medicated. Both authors have published some disturbing statistics indicating that developmental needs, particularly for boys, are not being met. In his description of "The Current Crisis," Gurian (2005) includes statistics showing gender inequity in development and school. For example, as high as 70 percent of failing grades in school are given to boys, 80 percent of behavioral disorders are diagnosed to boys, and nearly five million American boys are prescribed Ritalin, accounting for over 80 percent of the total prescriptions (Gurian, p. 22). Gurian and Sax both conclude that boys' needs are not being met, and they ultimately attribute such failure to a lack of understanding of the innate biological differences between the genders.

With the use of PET scans, researchers have started looking at the differences in brain function between the genders. Brain research shows that boys' corpus callosums are upwards of 25 percent smaller than girls', that girls' frontal lobes are generally more active, that the hippocampus works differently in boys than girls, and that boys have more dopamine and testosterone while girls have more estrogen and oxytocin (Gurian, 2005, p. 48-49). Findings also demonstrate that brain tissue is different between the sexes, that the brain's functions are compartmentalized differently, and that the visual system is organized differently (Sax, 2005, p. 14, 20). These research results drive the recent direction of gender based study and the implications for child development and academic performance. The discovery of hormonal differences, as well as brain size and activity differences, have led to conclusions that boys and girls process emotion differently and that boys take in less sensory data, while being more likely to take risks and show physical aggression (Gurian, 2003, p 10).

Certainly, we do not wish to discount the significance of such findings or discredit the linkages to be made between physiological factors and child development. However, reliance solely upon biological factors occludes other significant contributors to gender differences, such as cultural and social factors, from receiving their appropriate emphasis. Gender as a social-cultural construct is well documented (see, for example Butler, 1990 and Fuss, 1989). Noting that sex is a biological term and gender is, to a considerable extent, an encultured phenomenon, we intend to articulate a new avenue of study by relating Vygotskian concepts of development to gender study so as to broaden our collective understanding of gender in relation to child development.

Regardless of whether one accepts there is a crisis in child development and academic performance based on gender or not, the issue addressed here is the void in Vygotskian-based study. To date, socioeconomic status and ethnocultural factors have been studied with relation to Vygotskian notions of mediation, activity theory, and child development. However gender, while being mentioned as an area deserving of investigation (Hogan and Tudge, 1999, p. 48), has not been studied.

Reasons for this underrepresentation in the research are speculative, but in western society, one can perceive a reliance upon empirical measurement to support claims that boys are suffering in school and society. Explanations that rely on innate biological difference tend to reinforce the credibility progressive educational thought has traditionally afforded science. New brain research is treated as comprehensive fact and rationale for behaviour, without a detailed exploration of the implication of this research for classroom practice. For example, PET scans may be able to map certain brain functions, showing gender differences, but they fail to do so in the case of higher mental functions acquired through learning (Head, 1999, cited in Connolly, 2004, p. 35). There are biological linkages, but one cannot confirm how strong these connections are between structural brain function and gender development.

Only a few decades ago, popular theory held that girls were suffering in math and sciences, and attention was needed to bolster their performance. At the time, socialization was seen to be the cause of girls' poor performance. Girls were not encouraged to take these courses, as established roles for women did not require such study. The result was a push to make math and the sciences more interesting for girls. Since then, as evidenced by Sanders and Peterson (1999), school age girls' participation and performance in these subject areas have improved and, in relation to several indicators, equaled, if not surpassed, that of boys. Yet paradoxically, there has been tremendous resistance to answering the question of boys' developmental issues with socio-cultural reasoning. Vygotskian-minded research is needed to close the gap in the literature, and lend socio-cultural solutions to what is viewed as the crisis facing boys in our society.

Mediation

Mediation is central to all Vygotskian theory: "building a link between social and historical processes, on the one hand, and the individuals' mental processes, on the other" (Wertsch, 2007, p. 178). Gender is mediated both implicitly and explicitly, from birth.   Citing Harding (1996), Steiner suggests that, "Gender is now understood to be a relationship between women and men…not a property that women and men have apart from the other gender" (Steiner, 1999, p. 202). This definition entails a responsibility to collaborate in mediating the meaning of this relationship between women and men.

In general, children in Western society are mediated according to gender. Research has shown that socioeconomic and ethno-cultural factors influence the amount and type of mediation (Kozulin 2003). Gender must influence the amount and type of mediation as well. Gender is mediated in ongoing ways, when, for example, a boy, dressed in blue, is told that he doesn't cry and must play fair; or a girl, dressed in pink, is told she is to take care of the other children and that good girls are always kind. Gender-associated statements such as this are influential when a child is making meaning. Mark Tappan elaborates on Gilligan and Wiggins (1988) statement that "cultural norms and values that define masculine and feminine behavior affect the experience of equality and attachment…by making the moral voices of justice and care gender related" (Tappan, 1992, p. 109). To Tappan this means "that the words, language, and forms of discourse that our culture uses to describe men and women, and to define 'masculine' and 'feminine' behavior, mediate most experiences that boys and girls have" (Ibid.). Once internalized, these gender-laden statements allow boys and girls to interpret experiences differently. We could surmise that perceptions of inequality and procedural justice are more compelling for boys because a mediated precept of "play fair" has been internalized. On the other hand, experiences of attachment and detachment may prove more potent for girls because their understandings are more likely to have been mediated through the language of care and compassion.

Western culture mediates gender and research has shown that this mediation affects development and academic performance. Stetsenko et al. cite several studies showing that girls have a lower perception of their own abilities and performance expectations than do boys (Frey and Ruble, 1987; Parsons and Ruble, 1977; Stipek, 1992), and that girls are "(1) less likely to attribute success to their ability, (2) more likely to attribute failure to a lack of ability, and (3) less likely to believe that success can be achieved through effort" (Stetsenko et al, 2000, p. 517). The article does note that girls' negative self perception is more pronounced when girls have recently been exposed to failure, but this is also an example of how gender is mediated. One might fairly ask, by way of contrast, whether boys in the same situation may prove more resilient, having been exposed to mediating comments which extol the virtues of never quitting.

Gender mediation may also encourage biased gender stereotypes. An example is presented in a study by Thompson, Arsenault, and Williams (2006), in which high-help-seeking girls were rated by teachers as being lower in motivation and ability, while the reverse existed for the boys. Harry Daniels' work provides a possible answer to why teachers might see the same situation differently based on gender. Daniels postulates "boys experience a contradiction between cultural messages and practices associated with hegemonic masculinity and those teaching practices conducive to optimal learning within primary schooling" (Daniels, 2001, p. 151). The encultured view of masculinity encourages the notion that collaborative learning or eliciting help appears weak and goes against the perceived educational competition with peers. "Hegemonic masculinity" is a mediated idea, one that could be a main cause for boys' poor success in school. Reviewing such studies and hypotheses should encourage further study of gender mediation and stereotypes with the goal of aiding child development.

Our intention is not to sound an alarm and thereby eliminate early childhood gender mediation (as if this were even possible), but if mediation is a central theme for Vygotskian development, it needs to be examined from a gender perspective. If gender mediation were to be studied in intersection with critical periods, speech and language, leading activities, and perezhivanie, the results could lead towards more comprehensively reasoned resolutions to the "crisis" facing boys in school.

Vygotskian links to gender-based development

Vygotsky's theory of development can be interpreted for gender differences as it has been for socio-economic status and culture. In the following sections we will connect aspects of Vygotsky's theory–critical periods, speech and language, play, and perezhivanie–to gender and will then draw curricular implications.

Critical periods

Critical periods are central to Vygotsky's theory of child development. Critical periods are described as times of immense transformation in a child's mental processes and social relations that are so profound they lead to crises for the child (Mahn, 2003, p. 122). Unlike Piagetian stage theories of development, the five critical periods outlined by Vygotsky do not occur at set ages, although there are approximate ages for critical periods that correspond with major developments in the child's life. Crisis periods precede longer times of relative stability.

The crisis of the newborn separates the embryonal period of development from infancy. The one-year crisis separates infancy from early childhood. The crisis at age three is a transition from early childhood to preschool age. The crisis at age seven is a link that joins preschool and school ages. Finally, the crisis at age thirteen coincides with the turning point in development at the transition from school age to puberty (Vygotsky, 1998, p. 193).

Vygotsky viewed the onset of the different critical periods to be determined by historical and cultural development. How children make meaning changes during these critical periods and accounts for their developmental importance. Vygotsky viewed meaning as an internal structure that provides the connection between thinking and speech. He states: "Meaning is not equal to the word, nor equal to the thought. This disparity is revealed by the fact that their lines of development do not coincide" (Vygotsky, 1997, cited in Mahn, 2003, p. 126).

How, then, does gender play a role in these critical periods? Considering the developmental differences in language, speech, and social interactions, the linkages between thought and language suggest the onset of gender-based differences in the shaping of meaning. Girls are considered to be developmentally more prepared for entering school at the age of five or six, particularly in western culture. We can ask what the precise nature of meaning-making in the intersections of gender and critical periods, as well as what the temporal onset and durations of respective critical periods, are that would either justify or refute the claim that girls appear ready for school before boys.

Social interaction, central to critical periods, also deserves investigation from the perspective of gender. Vygotsky asserted that an interdependence of individual-internal and social-external processes existed in learning and development, that is, individual development occurs through social relations. During critical periods, changes to the child's social situations of development "result from and cause qualitative transformations in their perception, experience, appropriation, internalization, understanding and memory of interaction in and with their environment" (Ibid., p. 128). Without social interaction, a child's development would be stunted. There are differences between how boys and girls interact with one another, in mixed as well as in same-gendered groups (Hogan and Tudge 1999). Discrepancies made manifest through play and patterns of peer collaboration are explained below

Speech and language

Current research states that, on average, females use more words than males, and that, during the learning process, girls use more words when working both individually and in groups (Gurian, 2003, p.17). Laura Berk, in studying the language use of school children found that young children's use of private speech in grade one predicted greater success in second grade math (John-Steiner, 2007, p. 139). One study showed that, when given a task where assistance from a researcher was permitted, the girls spoke far more than the boys and engaged the researcher in "help-eliciting speech, including direct requests for their participation" (Thompson and Moore, 2000, p. 249).

Beyond such differences in apparently nascent abilities, language acquisition plays is an influential factor in the long-range education prospects and developmental trajectories of children. Vera John-Steiner and Paul Tatter write:

From birth, the social forms of child-caretaker interactions, the tools used by humans in society to manipulate the environment, the culturally institutionalized patterns of social relations, and language operating together as a socio-semiotic system are used by the child in cooperation with adults to organize behavior, perception, memory, and complex mental processes. For children, the development of language is a development of social existence into individuated persons and into culture. (John-Steiner and Tatter, cited in John-Steiner, 2007, p. 148)

Language intersects with gender, and allowing for variation within genders, the importance of language in relation to mediation as well as its relation to play and peer relations appears a significant area of inquiry.

Play as a leading activity

According to Vygotsky, play is "invented" as children realize that desires cannot or will not be immediately accommodated by others (1978). Play is a tool allowing the child to enter an imaginative realm in which they "think about the world in a way freed from the constraints that the world's normal forms, behavior, and everyday purposes impose on us" (Egan, 2005, p. 31). Generally, the motivation to engage socio-dramatic play occurs between the ages of three and six, at which time children enter school. At three, children become very interested in what is around them and are fascinated by the world of adults, a world they cannot enter (Karpov, 2003, p. 146). The motivation of socio-dramatic play is to enter the adult world, where valuable social behaviors are internalized.

Contrary to popular belief, play is structured, and laden with rules and roles to be followed as children make sense of the adult relationships they see. For example, if a child is playing the role of a mother, she must act according to the rules of maternal behavior. (Vygotsky, 1978, p.94)

Play, as a leading activity, prepares children for entering school. Maintaining the roles inherent in socio-dramatic play, for example, "creates demands on the child to act against immediate impulse" (Vygotsky, 1978, p. 99). As a result, a "child's greatest self control occurs in play" (Ibid.). Further, play creates a zone of proximal development in the child, for in play "a child always behaves beyond his average age, above his daily behavior; in play it is as though he were a head taller than himself" (Vygotsky, 1978, p. 102). According to Russian neo-Vygotskians, several years of socio-dramatic play develops skills required for engaging in learning at school, such as the ability to self regulate behavior and the motivation to learn (Karpov, 2003, p. 147). As Vygotsky suggests,

> At school age play does not die away but permeates the attitude toward reality. It has its own inner continuation in school instruction and work (compulsory activity based on rules). It is the essence of play that a new relation is created between the field of meaning and the visual field–that is, between situations in thought and real situations. (Vygotsky, 1978, p. 104)

An area of interest not examined by Vygotsky but investigated by others involves the relationship between gender and play. Janet Lever (1978), on observing play, found that boys' play involved games that left room for negotiation and conflict resolution. Girls, on the other hand, took turns playing and avoided conflict. When conflict did arise the girls would withdraw, whereas the boys would deal with the conflict. For boys, conflict made the games more enjoyable. In an earlier study, Lever found the rules and organization for play to differ greatly. According to Lever (1974), through their games boys are exposed to a richer variety of social contexts, whereas girls' play was dyadic parallel play. Continuing in this vein, Dipietro (1981) studied rough play and discovered that boys' play was characterized by physical aggression, whereas girls' interactions were characterized by more verbal interactions, suggestions, and play centering on novel interactions with toys (Dipietro, 1981, cited in Ausch, 1994).

Such studies appear to suggest that if gender differences exist in early play, there will be gender differences as children enter school. Jeanne Block (1984) contends that the gender differences in play lead to differences in intellectual and emotional development. This echoes Vygotsky: "At school age play does not die away but permeates the attitude toward reality" (Vygotsky, 1978, p. 104).

Perezhivanie

Perezhivanie is the word Vygotsky used to describe how children make meaning of their social experience. This Russian term does not have an adequate English translation. Holbrook Mahn defines it as "the way children perceive, emotionally experience, appropriate, internalize, and understand interactions in their environment" (Mahn, 2003, 129). Through perezhivanie, "the same objective situation may be interpreted, perceived, experienced, or lived through by different children in different ways" (Ibid.). The power of perezhivanie, from a developmental perspective, is that it is a socially mediated experience. Together with their mediator, the child co-constructs a unique meaning for themselves.

Perezhivanie, a commonly overlooked idea in the West, has gender implications. If one sees gender-based differences in perception, emotion, and memory, there should arise marked differences in individual perezhivanie with a relation to gender. An example of a relevant research project in perezhivanie would be to investigate the mediation of compassion across gender, for example, to what extent are girls socially mediated towards compassion and to what extent does this affect their perceptual abilities to identify with the plight of others in response to literature such as *The Diary of Anne Frank.*

Curricular implications

Vygotsky's theories of child development have had a great impact on developing pedagogies over the last century, and his influence continues to grow as his works are translated and disseminated through the West. Bernstein's definition of pedagogy provides a suitable framework for looking at this impact and establishing a link for gender based education:

> Pedagogy is a sustained process whereby somebody acquires new forms or develops existing forms of conduct, knowledge, practice and criteria, from somebody or something deemed to be an appropriate provider and evaluator, appropriate either from the point of view of the acquirer or by some other body or both. (Bernstein, Cited in Daniels, 2007, p. 308).

This definition identifies educational practice not as a means for simply transferring knowledge but as a relationship between the acquirer and provider, important factors in a Vygotskian educative process.

This definition of pedagogy provides a reason for gender-based practice based on what is "appropriate" in terms of conduct, knowledge, practice and criteria for both boys and girls. According to Mahn, educators using a Vygotskian framework should be "creating comfortable, stimulating, and engaging environments where teaching-learning is built on students' prior experiences, natural curiosity, and developmental processes" (Mahn, 2003, p. 123). The National Research Council defines what is included in this prior knowledge: "Prior knowledge also includes the kind of knowledge that learners acquire because of their social roles, such as those connected with race, class, gender, and their cultural and ethnic affiliations" (Ibid). Any developmental differences between boys and girls that can be attributed to gender should be considered when planning curriculum.

Central to Vygotsky's pedagogical beliefs is the impact socio-cultural and environmental influences have on development as such influences are interiorized to the developing person:

Every function in the child's cultural development appears twice: first, on the social level, and later, on the individual level; first between people (interpsychological), and then inside the child (intrapsychological). This applies equally to voluntary attention, to logical memory and to the formation of concepts. All the higher functions originate as actual relations between human individuals. (Vygotsky, 1978, p. 57)

The development of higher psychological functions can be evaluated from a perspective of gender. The vehicle by which this could happen, would be the formation of concepts, what Vygotsky commonly referred to as the primary function of education. Vygotsky delineated concepts into two distinct categories: scientific and spontaneous. Lee describes spontaneous concepts as "the knowledge we develop through participation in everyday practices" (Lee, 2003, p. 394). Scientific concepts, alternatively, are introduced in school by a teacher and "form a coherent, logical hierarchical system...[and] are characterized by a high degree of generality, and their relationship to objects is mediated through other concepts" (Daniels, 2007, p. 310-311). Vygotsky argued that instruction cannot proceed directly to scientific concepts without first being mediated via everyday concepts, even though this remains the current practice in many classrooms. Spontaneous concepts should provide the link to scientific concepts in true concept development:

If concept development is to be effective in the formation of scientific concepts, instruction must be designed to foster conscious awareness of conceptual form and structure and thereby allow for individual access and control over acquired scientific concepts. It must also foster the interaction and development of everyday concepts with scientific concepts. (Ibid., 312)

In gender-based classrooms (that is to imply, single-gendered classrooms), the spontaneous concepts used to mediate these scientific concepts could be selected according to the everyday experiences characteristic either to boys and girls. A core assertion of gender-based instruction is that the level of engagement is likely to be heightened when students are inspired through shared experience. Once again, these assertions need bearing out in inquiry. Will separate gendered settings allow for greater levels of engagement? Will the appropriation of scientific concepts be facilitated by a more common frame of everyday reference? What are the connections that can be enhanced through the lens of gender-based education?

Vygotsky's views on thinking suggest how important gender-based learning experience could be: "[Thought] is not born of other thoughts.

Thought has its origins in the motivating sphere of consciousness, a sphere that includes our inclinations and needs, our interests and impulses, and our affect and emotions. The affective and volitional tendency stands behind thought" (Vygotsky, 1987, p. 282). If curriculum could be adapted according to gender, both boys and girls could be more successful in school (John-Steiner and Souberman, 1978, p. 131). In an English curriculum, this might mean choosing novel studies with which the students will be most engaged: for example, *Into the Wild*, for a boys' class. Such topics elicit themes relevant to boys' frames of reference, and provided a deeper engagement in the educational process.

The use of the Cultural-Historical Activity Theory (CHAT), used with success by Carol Lee in the Cultural Modeling Project, could also reference gender-based education. CHAT developed from psychological theories of Vygotsky, Luria, and Leontiev (Lee, 2003, p. 393). Lee outlines several tenets of CHAT, including, "mutually constituting influences of social interaction in participation in jointly constructed activity across multiple settings and the functions of mediating artifacts. CHAT places culture at the centre of human sense-making activities" (Ibid.). Rather than just a theory for cognitive development, CHAT provides for "the whole person–body mind and spirit" (Wells and Claxton, 2002, p. 4). From a gender-based perspective, CHAT could become a means to investigate differences between what are relevant learning artifacts for boys and girls. The use of such tools gives the opportunity to mediate healthy, non-hegemonic ideas of masculinity and femininity. CHAT appears to provide a promising resource for developing effective gender-based instruction.

Finally, one area that has received some academic attention from a Vygotskian perspective is peer collaboration (Tudge, 1992). Most Vygotskian research focuses on the role of dyadic interaction as a means of developing thinking and concept formation. Gender should be considered as a factor when conducting these studies. In two studies Ellis and Gauvain conducted (1992), differences were discovered in the way boys and girls exchange information while working in gender-based pairs. This lends to the gender comparisons that are evident between dyadic play and dyadic work in the classroom setting. In Tudge's study (1992) boys and girls were pre-tested individually to discover the "rule" used by children for predicting the outcome of a balance beam test. Children then worked either alone, with a partner that followed the same rule, or with a more competent or less competent partner. Children were given two post-tests. The study concluded that children were just as likely to progress with a more competent partner, as they were to regress with a less competent partner. Gender did have an effect on the outcome of the results. Tudge reported that while there were no differences in rule usage between genders, there were significant differences between the multivariate analysis of variance MANOVA time x gender interaction. The time the girl dyads used in determining an answer was longer, due to the length of time spent discussing the options. If girls generally tend to avoid conflict, it is plausible that the length of time used results from the importance of maintaining good relations over the importance of determining the answer. This could affirm Block's (1984) assertion that gender differences in play lead to differences in intellectual development.

There was also a gender difference in the performance following peer collaboration. The results from the second post-test revealed that while boys did not "significantly improve" on their pre-test scores, the girls who worked with other girls actually regressed. This provides a link to the differences in dyadic play because during their collaborations "girls seemed more interested in preserving good relations with their partners than in arguing with one another" (Hogan and Tudge, 1999, p. 48).

When studying six year olds on a spatial relations task, Bearison et al. (1986) found that "male dyads produced more 'verbal with explanation' type disagreements, while female dyads had more enactive type disagreements. The former, but not the latter, type of disagreement was significantly associated with positive cognitive change" (Ausch, 1994). Considering such a study from a gender perspective, the results from the post-tests could be less important than the process the children utilized to reach their results, insofar as they suggest a general mode of instructional strategy likely to both engage and provoke development in male learners. This is an area in need of further study.

Implications for imaginative education

Mindful of the mediation of gender and roles, a boys' IE classroom could be quite different from a girls' classroom not only in content, but also in the presentation. In such a setting, the concerns associated with the notion of "hegemonic masculinity" could be considered through the teaching methods and class content. The particular heroic qualities studied in a romantic framework, for example, could be tailored for greater engagement. Here, we might envision the use of heroic qualities such as tolerance, generosity, and concern for others, in addition to the more traditionally minded male notions of persistence and fair play. The "heroic narrative" ultimately chosen to deliver the content would be intended to reflect the developmental needs of boys. Identifying the most useful cognitive tools becomes important. For example, within the framework of Romantic Understanding, Egan's "extremes of reality" appears to align with boys' penchant for risk taking and adventure, and therefore may prove more likely to create an environment where boys experience a deep sense of engagement.

The differences in speech and language, play, and mediation provide a basis for inquiry for such a classroom or curriculum model. A boys' class could combine high levels of structure with specifically defined goal-oriented activity. In a boys' class, once an acceptable structure is in place–with its rules, roles, and expectations–learning activity could proceed with very little subsequent direction, an environment analogous to the process of boys' play where discussion, disagreement, and conflict are part of the process. An engaging, imaginative learning environment focused on goal-directed activity would require participants to actively engage in discussion and conflict as they strive to formalize their understanding. This idea reflects Egan's description of play as one of the cognitive tools for learning (Egan 2005). As a learning tool, the use of play could be more effective for boys in a split-gendered classroom as opposed to a gender-mixed setting as boys may be more comfortable assuming various roles and engaging in the productive conflict and disagreement characteristic of their styles of play with each other. A girls' class may also benefit from a gendered setting for a similar reason: the cognitive tool of play could be utilized to engage girls through their general characteristic of process, collective goals and empathetic consideration.

Certainly one could continue to discuss both the theoretical and practical implications of gender-based instruction for Imaginative Education, which is premised to some degree on Vygotskian theory. The brief examples included here are intended only to demonstrate possible directions in the range of research that can be undertaken to consider the intersection of Vygotskian concepts and gender-based scholarship.

Conclusions

If Vygotsky could comment on the perceived gender gap in western schools, his response to the concerns might be quite different from present physiological explanations. Though it may still be too soon to comment on the relationship between what the new brain research is reporting and how it affects gender, it is not likely Vygotsky would agree that the problem is based in physiology, that is, in biological sex differences. Vygotsky would most definitely look at the problem from a socio-cultural perspective. The mediation of gender itself is, we believe, the central issue and Vygotskian researchers needs to examine the role of mediation in the unique development of boys and girls, in particular as they reach adolescence, when Vygotsky noted "self consciousness is social consciousness transferred within" (Vygotsky, 1998. Cited in Karpov, 2003, p. 150). A second area for study is how gender specifically impacts development regarding critical periods, speech and language, play, and perezhivanie because these aspects affect children's academic performance. A final area deserving study is using CHAT to foster positive educational connections for both boys and girls. The use of common spontaneous concepts in specifically gender-based classrooms could provide a strong link for engagement, and ultimately success, at school. If boys are at risk of "falling behind in school and life," there must be an effort to consider how our scientistic theories and our socio-cultural constructions of gender and their varying connections to pedagogic practices, negatively impact boys development. Enlightened by cultural-cognitive perspectives, we may come to change current practices for the better.

Bibliography

Ausch, L. (1994). Gender Comparisons of young children's social interaction in cooperative play activity. *Sex Roles: A journal of research*. August.

Butler, J. (1990). *Gender Trouble: Feminism and the subversion of identity*. New York: Routledge.

Connolly, P. (2004). *Boys and Schooling in the Early Years*. New York: Routledge Falmer.

Daniels, H. (2001). *Vygotsky and Pedagogy*. New York: Routledge Falmer.

—. (2007). Pedagogy. In Daniels, H., Cole, M., & Wertsch, J., (Eds.), *The Cambridge Companion to Vygotsky* (pp. 307-331). New York: Cambridge University Press.

Egan, K. (2005). *An Imaginative Approach to Teaching*. San Francisco: Jossey-Bass.

Fuss, D. (1989). *Essentially Speaking: Feminism, nature and difference*. New York: Routledge.

Gurian, M. (2003). *The Boys and Girls Learn Differently: An action guide for teachers*. San Francisco: Jossey-Bass.

Gurian, M. (2005). *The Minds of Boys*. San Francisco: Jossey-Bass.

Hogan, D. & Tudge, J. (1999). Implications of Vygotsky's Theory for Peer Learning. In O'Donnell, A., & King, A., (Eds.) *Cognitive Perspectives on Peer Learning*. Mahwah, NJ: Lawrence Erlbaum Associates.

John-Steiner, V. (1999). Sociocultural and feminist theory: Mutuality and relevance. In Chaiklin, S., Hedegaard, M., & Jensen, U., (Eds.), *Activity Theory and Social Practice.* Oxford: Alden Press.

—. (2007). Vygotsky on thinking and speaking. In Daniels, H., Cole, M, and Wertsch, J., (Eds.), *The Cambridge Companion to Vygotsky* (pp. 136-154). New York: Cambridge University Press.

Karpov, Y. (2003). Development through the lifespan: A Neo-Vygotskian approach. In Kozulin, A., Gindis, B., Ageyev, V., & Miller, S. (Eds.), Vygotsky's *Educational Theory in Cultural Context* (pp. 138-155). New York: Cambridge University Press.

Kozulin, A. (2003). Psychological tools and mediated learning. In Kozulin, A., Gindis, B., Ageyev, V., & Miller, S. (Eds.), *Vygotsky's Educational Theory in Cultural Context* (pp. 15-38). New York: Cambridge University Press.

Lee, C. (2003). Cultural Modeling: CHAT as a lens for understanding instructional discourse based on African American English discourse patterns. In Kozulin, A., Gindis, B., Ageyev, V., & Miller, S. (Eds.), *Vygotsky's Educational Theory in Cultural Context* (pp. 393-410). New York: Cambridge University Press.

Mahn, H. (2003). Periods in Child Development: Vygotsky's Perspective. In Kozulin, A., Gindis, B., Ageyev, V., & Miller, S. (Eds.), *Vygotsky's Educational Theory in Cultural Context* (pp. 119-137). New York: Cambridge University Press.

Sax, L. (2005). *Why Gender Matters.* New York: Doubleday.

Sanders, J. & Peterson, K. (1999). *Mind Matters,* Fall Issue, 1-5.

Stetsenko, A. et al. (2000). Gender Effects in Children's Beliefs about School Performance: A Cross-Cultural Study. *Child Development,* 71(2), 517-527.

Tappan, M. (1992). Texts and Contexts: Language, Culture and the Development of Moral Functioning. In Winegar, L., & Valsiner, J., (Eds.), *Children's Development Within Social Context Volume 1: Metatheory and Theory.* Hillsdale: Lawrence Erlbaum Associates.

Thompson, R & Moore, K. (2000). Collaborative Speech in Dyadic Problem Solving: Evidence for Preschool Gender Differences in Early Pragmatic Development. *Journal of Language and Social Psychology,* 19, 248-257.

Thompson, R., Arsenault, S., and Williams, D. (2006). The Effects of Preschool Girls' And Boys' Help Seeking on Adult Evaluations of Dyadic Problem Solving. *Journal of Language and Social Psychology,* 25, 146-167.

Tudge, J. (1992). *Processes and Consequences of Peer Collaboration: A Vygotskian Analysis.* Child Development, 63 (6), 1364-1379.

Vygotsky, L. (1978). *Mind in Society: The Development of Higher Psychological Processes.* (M. Cole, V. John-Steiner, S. Scribner, & E. Souberman, Eds.). Cambridge, MA: Harvard University Press.

—. (1987). *Thinking and Speech: Collected Works of L. S. Vygotsky, Vol. 1.* New York: Plenum Press.

—. (1998). *The Collected Works of L. S. Vygotsky. Volume 5: Child Psychology.* (R. W. Rieber, Ed.). (M. J. Hall, Trans.). New York: Plenum Press.

Wells, G. & Claxton, G. (2002). Sociocultural Perspectives on the Future of Education. In G. Wells & G. Claxton (Eds.). *Learning for Life in the 21st Century.* Blackwell Publishing.

Wertsch, J. (2007) Vygotsky on Thinking and Speaking. In Daniels, H., Cole, M., & Wertsch, J., (Eds.). *The Cambridge Companion to Vygotsky.* New York: Cambridge University Press.

TEACHING AS GAME PLAYING

QINGYU PAN

Games can be used to inspire children to dedicate themselves to certain exploratory operations, and games can provide the most effective ways to release all kinds of human potential. The purpose of the teaching procedures derived from games described in this article is not to discuss how to make effective use of games in the classroom, but rather to explore how to re-organize the content and teaching processes into the form of games, and so better engage students in learning.

Stories, games, and teaching

Like listening to stories, playing games is an activity much loved by children. Usually, children can, with rapt attention and a generous dose of fantasy, be engaged in listening to stories. Similarly, games can be used to inspire children to dedicate their attention to an exploratory operation, sometimes in co-operation, and at other times in competition with their classmates.

In one form or another, games have, for generations, played a central role in early childhood education. Young children's minds and bodies are developed with the help of fairy tales and a variety of games. Unfortunately, however, when children enter elementary school, the opportunities to teach by means of stories and games are greatly reduced, most likely due to the pressure on teachers to impart content knowledge. Because written language is generally believed to be the most important learning tool, a lot of time is spent on learning how to read and write in the primary grades in elementary school. Although stories and games continue to be used in teaching, they are no longer the necessary elements of teaching. Still, many educators teach without stories and games, because they have mastered the basic "formal" approaches to teaching and they do not believe it necessary to use games and stories in their classrooms. As children's writing, reading, and communication skills develop, such teachers no longer see stories and games as necessary tools of teaching. In middle school, and especially in high school, we find hardly any stories and games in the classroom. However, there are still some teachers who, in order to maximize students' enthusiasm, persist in using stories and games as approaches to teaching in their classrooms; what's more, they constantly improve on the way they use stories and games in the classroom. They have found that, although both children's understanding of and expression in written language have become quite mature, there is still value in continuing their teaching with stories and games.

As long as we can design teaching processes reasonably, stories and games are still capable of producing a powerful driving force for learning. No doubt, the book *Teaching as Story Telling*, written by Kieran Egan, provides teachers with an opportunity to recognize the value of stories in teaching. In recent years, Egan has upgraded the story model to a higher level by reforming the structure and changing the direction of teaching. He is not concerned with the telling of moving stories; rather, he focuses on ways to make the best use of the binary opposite concepts, the main organizers of a good story, as a means of organizing the content of a certain topic. He advocates the examination of how to tell a series of non-fictional stories based on the process of resolving the conflicts produced by the opposite concepts, by asking with regard to any curriculum material "What's the story on this?" The teacher can think of curriculum content just as the journalist thinks about events that need to be organized into an engaging form for the TV news item, which is organized into a non-fictional "story."

This model greatly enhances the effectiveness of stories because it integrates fragmented materials into a compact teaching unit with a tight logic. In this model, finding the appropriate binary opposite concepts is the initial and most important step; following this, the teacher selects the material deemed most appropriate to encourage the process of proposing, developing, and settling the conflicts generated by the binary opposite concepts in the story. From Egan's model we can take a new approach to planning teaching. Essentially, teaching involves people, knowledge, environments, and processes. What people have discovered and invented over the centuries will be associated with other elements of the world, and can be used to inspire teaching through stories.

It is clear that games feature prominently in children's life; but what is gained by using games in the classroom? Here, following Egan's example, I will attempt to design a model of teaching based on the forms of games. This model is not about how to effectively make use of games to teach well, but how to explore ways to re-organize the teaching content and processes in terms of the forms of games. A good game relies on a certain set of rules. On the one hand, these rules do impose a limit on the actions of the participants; on the other hand, the same set of rules also makes the actions meaningful. Games cannot continue in the absence of rules.

What I am concerned with is how to organize and regulate students' learning activities in accordance with a system of rules which organize knowledge and skills. Just as teaching as story telling is based on the conflicts of concepts that are binary opposites, the model of teaching as game playing will also be organized in light of the conflicts between understanding both implicit and explicit rules to resolve a question. This means that we may face greater challenges, because a rule is a category more abstract than a concept. I cannot guarantee that my research will succeed; but I would like to give it a try, and perhaps, should it fail, which I hope it will not, even so we will learn a valuable lesson.

Understanding and performing: the integrity of the learning process

What Egan is concerned about is the promotion of students' logical thinking ability with the help of imaginative and emotionally attractive teaching approaches. If designed properly, teaching as story telling can also inspire students to participate in practical operations. However, I think that focusing on students' understanding is the central feature of teaching as story telling. Similarly, teaching as game playing is concerned more with performance, design, and creativity in the learning process; that is to say, it focuses on ways that will lead students to not only understand but also perform the creative "silent knowledge" which is usually based on a system of rules.

Here, I would like to say something about the complete process of learning, which will help us to recognize the value of teaching as game playing. I would argue that understanding and performing are two indivisible aspects of the learning process; in all disciplines learning involves both understanding and performance. In fact, understanding means making sense of the astonishing "process of performance" of human intellectual activity in specific areas. On the other hand, performing is essentially the most effective method to examine the volume, depth, sensitivity, and creativity of understanding.

Learning in the Arts and in the Humanities, such as writing, lectures, performances, painting, music and dancing, focuses on performance-based learning. Does this mean, then, that the focus of learning mathematics and natural sciences is on understanding rather than performing? No. Mathematics and natural sciences should focus both on understanding and performing. If we take the principle of knowledge as our basic theory, then the theoretical formulas derived from this basic theory will be looked upon as the lively "performance" of the principle of knowledge which demonstrates its applications in specific conditions. If we take all kinds of scientific theories as the basis of technology, then the entire panoply of scientific and technological inventions and creativity will be looked upon as the best practical "performance" of these scientific theories. As the wonderful "performance" of scientific theory, the rapid developments of technology have dazzled us. Imagine what the world would look like without scientific technology!

In general, the goal of understanding in education is objective systemic knowledge; however, Egan is concerned with an underlying logic of the knowledge to be learned, and begins with the binary opposite concepts in teaching as story telling, which I interpret as "re-statements" and "re-performances" of knowledge. I consider performance-based learning to be the creative use of knowledge and rules in order to solve certain problems under specific conditions. We can understand the knowledge of understanding-based learning as symbolic knowledge; correspondingly, we can understand the knowledge of performance-based learning as tacit knowledge. This is because we have difficulty in accurately expressing in language how we can creatively solve complex problems by means of applying knowledge and rules, just as it is hard to satisfactorily explain how we can control our fingers to write a word on a piece of paper. Tacit knowledge is silent and automatic; it occupies a central position in some kinds of performance-based learning, such as creation, design, expression, performance, production, problem-solving, and so on. It used to be the most effective way to test the depth, breadth, accuracy, and sensitivity of understanding.

Tacit knowledge is usually easily ignored in school education thanks to the popular, yet mistaken, view about knowledge. In general, we look to knowledge in books stored in the library and in artifacts displayed in museums as the standard forms of knowledge. It is often forgotten that, in addition to libraries, museums, and centres of science and technology, there are other, more extensive forms of storing knowledge, which are embedded in all scientific, technological, cultural, and artistic products. Students in schools mainly acquire text-based symbolic knowledge, which is considered highly effective, simple, and compact. Here, the literal language assumes an important role, and is looked at as the entry to and channel for all understanding, or even seen as the end of all understanding (written exams have existed for thousands of years). Therefore, the ability to manipulate language in writing is given the same weight as cultural competence. The result of all this is that the educational values of the knowledge stored in all kinds of products of scientific technology, culture, and arts are not given the consideration, recognition, and legitimacy they deserve.

Egan reminds us that we should not take the familiar world around us for granted. He says that even the most insignificant products of our modern life, in fact, embody the highest achievements of our civilization. For example, the simple plastic bag into which our groceries are put at the supermarket is a product of the development of the modern chemical industry, based on centuries of careful and ingenious investigations by scientific researchers. Nevertheless, we often turn a blind eye to the everyday products of human knowledge, and take it for granted that there was no miracle. But, if you lived in medieval times, when you saw a substance so thin, light, translucent, and strong, you would probably think this could only be God's treasure. Why do we deny students the opportunity to marvel at the world with eyes and minds that do not take everything for granted? Why don't we show them the beauty and wonder only slightly hidden in all things? In my opinion, the reason is very simple: it is because of the general belief that the principle of manufacturing knowledge has been written down in textbooks, and consequently, it is not necessary for students to investigate these innumerable products. In effect, we erect an invisible wall between understanding the symbols of knowledge and experiencing the magic of knowledge in our school education. The status of symbols as representatives of scientific knowledge has been inflated to such an extent that nothing can be added; accordingly, the technologies which created all kinds of products are belittled and are considered dispensable by school education. The reason behind this is that people think technology is the direct product of applications of scientific theories, and as long as we can grasp scientific theories, we will have no difficulty in learning technology. We can learn technology at the institute or in the factory, so it is not necessary to learn it in school. As a result, technology as a form of knowledge has been reduced to less than written language as a form of knowledge. This is very harmful to education, because it not only leads to a great deal of scientific knowledge being poorly understood in the classroom, but it also teaches students to discriminate against technology. And since technological innovations are closely linked with creative thinking, the widespread discrimination against technology as a form of knowledge means that students are missing the best opportunity to develop their creative imaginations.

Our above analysis of technological products can also be made regarding the products of literature and art. Only the copies of most works of art are shown in schools, and students rarely see the original art works. The reason is that we do not think that students will understand art only by accessing the original works. In many cases, art, for children, is another symbol of knowledge. In education, remembering the critical evaluation of a particular work of art is far more important than understanding the work of art itself. This is somewhat reminiscent of the story of Lord Ye's love of dragons. In that story, Lord Ye professes a love of dragons and has dragons depicted on all of his possessions. But when a real dragon comes calling, he runs away. Similarly, a lot of tacit knowledge embedded in technological products, as well as in literary and artistic works, have always been "silent" in education. My purpose in suggesting teaching as game playing is to awaken this silent knowledge by means of discovering sub-rules. Only after this has been accomplished can we motivate our students to develop such tacit knowledge and skills in the process of performance-based learning.

Dedicated and preoccupied: the core value of teaching as game playing

Teaching as story telling, as designed by Egan, draws attention to the important role conflicts between opposite concepts play in encouraging children to understand knowledge in depth. What, then, is the most valuable idea for teaching that we can extract from games? Indulging in learning physically and mentally is the most powerful enlightenment to teaching that I can derive from games. Listening to stories creates good listeners, just as playing games creates good players. In other words, when a person is involved in games he will be wholeheartedly engaged in the operation, and sometimes will even continue to work on the problem all through the night, long after the game has officially ended. Under normal circumstances we rarely encounter the kind of "crazy" passion in education that we can easily find in playing games, but if we successfully make use of the form of games in teaching, we will.

Why do games have such magical attractive power? In my opinion, the reason is simple: games provide the most effective access to releasing various human freedoms and potential abilities, which will be stimulated only when they are effectively challenged. On the one hand, this challenge requires that people should comply with clear, universally recognized and commonly binding rules; on the other hand, it encourages people to operate and explore freely and actively within the parameters set by the rules. Not only does this challenge require a deeper understanding of the rules, but it also encourages people to be well-versed in these rules through concrete actions in order to grasp the fine skills needed to control the rules. Therefore, knowledge and practice, minds and hands, mental and physical activities are all integrated into a whole process in teaching as game playing.

It is now clear that the rules are the core elements of game. Next, we turn to discussing the role of rules in playing a game.

The rules of a game are not only negative constraints, but also positive and empowering, which means that the rules will give the meaning and value to free action and also unite free operation into coherent events. Most games, such as chess, hide-and-seek, various cards games, and so on, are based on clear rules. Therefore, we experience a sense of awe because the rules make our behavior meaningful. If we discover that someone has won the game by violating the rules, the winner will be considered immoral and no longer eligible to play. In other words, success does not necessarily bring us happiness, only when such success has been achieved by following a set of well-recognized rules, and received some public recognition, can the real joy and a sense of achievement occur. For example, when we play with a child, he may be unhappy if he realizes that we have deliberately lost to him, because he believes that it was not a true victory, since the regulations were violated. Therefore, the rules are the source of meaning of all actions.

In game playing, we also find that when the rules of the game are simpler, clearer and more consistent, the operations will be more dynamic and more exploratory. In other words, the simplicity and clarity of rules is the secret of the game's success. If the rules are vague and can be freely modified, the joy of playing the game will be basically lost.

Rules are not only expressly provided, but also indirectly implied in the adjustment process during their operation. Only through their specific operation do rules demonstrate their reality and constraints. Essentially, the rules are set up in order to regulate people's behavior, rather than to improve people's understanding. Without playing, the value of the rules cannot be fully appreciated. Playing and operating is the ontology of rules. In the process of playing and operating, a simple rule will be an ever-changing form and become a non-exhaustive action regulator. We can call this the "invisible rule"–the changed form of the rule in concrete operation. Invisible rules have a decisive effect on a game. Invisible rules display their roles primarily through the use of high technology to solve those unexpected detailed and delicate issues. It is not the written rules that determine the outcome of a game; it is the invisible rules, the settlement of detailed questions, and the concrete application of technology that do so.

Only with the use of rules can the game go on. The important prerequisite for playing games is that before a player enters the game he should know not only what the specific task is, but also what kind of performance will be considered a success, which means that everyone must make it clear what the purpose of the game is and what its evaluation criteria are. Only that way can the game become naturally competitive and challenging. Even if a person plays a game by himself he will challenge himself in terms of a certain specific task. This clear and unequivocal design of a task is what gives a game its infinite charm.

If we make a summary of the above analysis, we can derive four aspects of instruction. First, dedicate yourself to a specific operation; second, creatively apply the rules in a practical situation; third, deal with those unexpected details and delicate issues by virtue of high technology; and finally, have a clear and specific task design and evaluation criteria.

The guiding principles of teaching as game playing

If we want to design a model of teaching inspired by games, we should begin with the four aspects above. Perhaps we could see the four points of enlightenment as four guiding principles of teaching as game playing.

The first principle is for the student to dedicate himself to a specific operation. This is absolutely crucial. Today, if we look back at teaching in the classroom, we must admit that there is a disconnect between students' physical and mental development: the two are not coordinated. In most cases, we have separated children's mental activities from their physical activities; we even believe that hands-on lessons are only included in physical education, home economics, wood shop, and technical classes. Here, the physical activities we refer to are not only visible body movements, but also internal skills, such as the skills embodied in the process of problem-solving, writing, lectures, design, production, painting, and other creative activities, which are not immediately obvious at first. In other words, these skills essentially co-ordinate processes of physical and psychological operations. Even in math class, for students to unconsciously play, multiply and divide, and remove some figures and graphics is also a good way to trigger inspiration. Scientific observation and hands-on activities in the lab play an important role in the science curriculum. In other words, this model focuses on indulging in learning both physically and mentally. The five cognitive forms, the somatic, mythic, romantic, philosophical, and ironic understandings proposed by Egan, are equally applicable here. The learning process in which students indulge in both physically and mentally is, in fact, a process of mutual cooperation between each of the above five cognitive forms.

The second principle is to creatively apply the rules in a practical, complex situation. This draws attention to the necessity of guiding students to understand the rules in depth by working on a task until it is completed, using the rules. We have to motivate students to change the literal rules into flexible operational strategies, rather than just remembering them. In education we place more emphasis on the restrictive aspects of rules than on their ability to empower. We should lead the students to grasp the essence of the rules of knowledge: it is not only a kind of positive constraint, but also a kind of sensible freedom, which has infinite constructive and generative power.

In general, we give much more weight to the written abstract rules than to the invisible rules in education, which too often results in students' failure in performance-based learning. As we said earlier, invisible rules should be thought of as a self-regulating process of written rules in specific situations. Let me illustrate this with an analogy: the written rule is like a lens, while the invisible rules are the micro-principles used to debug the lens according to specific scenarios. Through this sophisticated debugging action, the image of the object in the camera lens will become increasingly clearer. The image cannot be made clear with a static lens; only by constantly adjusting can the camera take clear photographs. For example, when we read poetry, novels, biographies, or essays, despite not knowing in the beginning what genre of text we are about to read, after having read the first two or three lines, we will automatically select a specific mode of reading style. Then we will be able to judge the format and style of the text. Why can we do this? Because in everyone's mind there is a very intimate personalized system of rules about writing, in addition to the standards of writing, as invisible rules. They enable us not only to identify the genre initially but also to allocate meaning to the specific context.

For individuals, invisible rules are the most real, direct, and effective learning tool. Invisible rules have great power to generate and create meanings from activities. To say a sentence is to create a fact of language, as well as to create an existence of a spiritual activity. However, because they are invisible, the present education system does not recognize their value. It is generally considered that as long as the students can clearly understand those universal, written, and well-established rules, they will be able to use those rules to explain things or to demonstrate their ideas. Thus, just as when teaching mathematics and science we place special emphasis on the theorems, when we teach language, history, geography, and other disciplines, we also place particular emphasis on the "general rules," such as grammar, the law of historical development, social structures, the rules governing the process of climate change or the distribution of vegetation–general rules which occupy a central position in teaching. But the question is, does learning these "general rules" in light of the literal understanding and application lead students to develop the appropriate capabilities? This is similar to a student of Chinese middle school who may be able to clearly analyze the grammar of an English sentence, but cannot fluently say a single sentence in standard English, and even the sentence that he writes in English reads more like a Chinese-style English sentence. Despite the fact that we find the invisible rules of reading play a great role in automatically selecting a specific mode of reading, we do not acknowledge it in writing. If we are to understand the text in depth and have a detailed appreciation of its artistic standard, or if we are to carry out a literary creation, then, the invisible rules necessary will far exceed the earlier level of rules. Without specialized training, I think these invisible rules are only a relatively rough guide regulating our behaviour.

The third principle is to apply rules to deal with those unexpected details and the delicate issues by means of a superb technology, which is a further extension of the second principle. These complex and delicate issues are unpredictable, which provides the incentive to continue game playing. Without corresponding technical support, we cannot solve these unexpected, complex, and delicate issues easily. As such, the application of rules is inseparable from technical support; in other words, the rules are more or less technology-related, and the techniques are more or less associated with the delicate issues. What we must pay attention to is the fact that these complex and delicate issues are essential in the course of completing tasks, and to some extent, they even determine the outcome of activities. Like in the game of Chinese chess, one careless move can lead the whole game into a passive situation, causing irreparable damage, and it is very difficult to make up for that single instance of carelessness. Therefore, in game playing, how one deals with complex and delicate issues is a basic reflection of one's proficiency in using the invisible rules. When we try to master language skills, or mathematics problem-solving, or creative design and so on, we can clearly feel that the corresponding technical skills play an important role in the process, or even, in many cases, the level of technical proficiency determines the player will ultimately win or lose (succeed or fail). There is a misunderstanding about the knowledge of technology and skills; that is to say, we only look at technology and skills as a more ingenious way to solve the specific problem, but fail to recognize that they represent a fundamental cognitive style–flexible and multi-faceted thinking. In performance-based learning, the technique is not only a tool, it also presents the value of pursuing excellence. We as educators should focus on skills that are valuable to our students' intellectual development. For example, students will experience a specific stage when they are learning to sketch–drawing a ball, for instance. Why should we draw a ball? It seems that people do not care about this issue, but feel that drawing a ball is somewhat more complex than drawing a cube.

Sketching mainly depends on the binary opposite colours, black and white, which are extreme colors. One of the reasons why we choose a ball as the object to be drawn is that the ball can completely reflect the changing volume between brightness and shadow on its surface–there is a well-lit, bright area, there is the junction line between brightness, and then there is the shade, the dark, reflective side. All elements of sketching are in place here, and are demonstrated in a continuous, gradually changing, and intuitive way. Until students can understand that we give the ball a three-dimensional sense through changing the shading of the drawing, and until they recognize that changing the hue in tone with the changing light is what determines the three-dimensional sense, rather than drawing rows of beautiful lines on paper, we cannot consider this training a success. Unfortunately, most students only learn how to draw rows of beautiful lines in the classroom. In fact, the value of the lines is in the service to the hue; independent lines have no value in spite of their potential beauty. The skills we want to develop are not how to draw lines, but rather to teach the students how to show the changes of hues accurately by the means of drawing lines. Of course, drawing lines is a part of artistic expression, because different textures of lines really conjure up different experiences and feelings. Therefore, the skill of drawing lines is important, but such a skill should be built on the basis of the "rules" about changes in light and shadow.

The fourth principle is that the task of design and the criteria of evaluation must be clear and specific. Only when the learning tasks and the criteria of evaluation are clearly defined and specified can we challenge students to dedicate themselves to performance-based learning. Ambiguous tasks and vague, ill-defined standards of student performance are the primary reason for the declining interest in learning. The same goes for playing a game: if players do not know their specific tasks and the scoring criteria, their desire to play games will decline. This is why the games players most often like to play and never tired of are those most familiar to them.

We put forward this principle because we feel that the traditional teaching plan of performance-based learning is often lacking a clear task to solve, and its evaluation standards are too often vague, the guidelines pointless and too broad. The writing requirements often put forward by language teachers are as follows: the theme should be clear; the structure should be reasonable; the language should be fluent and smooth. But such empty standards will hardly inspire students. If we ask our students to write a letter to the suffering children in the earthquake-stricken areas of western China's Sichuan province, what exactly does a "clear theme" mean? Until we put this topic into a specific and clear situation, it will be unlikely to challenge students' writing skills. For example, we could make some suggestions regarding the theme by providing students with some key words: shock, sadness, worry, loss, hope, encouragement, support, love, faith, unity, helping oneself and helping others, persistence, and optimism. The best way to inspire students to write meaningful letters of condolence is to provide them with words such as these, in particular, to make the transition from one part of the letter to another naturally and harmoniously, rather than mechanically stitch the content of the various parts together. In other words, in writing, changing the mood from one of sadness to one of optimism must not be mechanical and stiff; rather, it should be organic and natural. Such unclear and abstract guidelines would deflate the students' desire to write.

Let's look at another example. In a history classroom we would usually ask students to analyze the significance of the first industrial revolution, for instance. If we do not give the specific standards and requirements of analysis, students probably feel that they are unable to grasp such issues. However, if we change the form of questions and ask instead: what are the common characteristics of the areas where the first industrial revolution took place? What areas did it subsequently extend to? What major social and cultural impacts did it have on all sectors of society? Were these changes lasting or temporary? Such questions can stimulate students' curiosity and interest, and thus their motivation to learn, because students will find directions of research from these structured problems which can give them the guidelines.

Egan is somewhat reluctant to include objectives in teaching as story telling. While I agree with his claim in regards to story telling, I feel that his reasons for the exclusion of learning objectives do not apply to teaching as game playing because performance-based learning would not promote the learning qualities without the guidelines of the sophisticated mission objectives, as well as clear evaluation criteria. Rules themselves cannot keep the game going in the absence of clear and specific aims.

Therefore, in this mode, the objectives of mission and criteria of evaluation are a necessary impetus to promote teaching.

The model of teaching as game immersing

The task of designing a universal mode of teaching as game playing is not easy. But if we give up on very strict requirements, we can offer some general procedures of teaching based on games. After all, no matter how nice the theory and inspiration, if they are separated from the process of teaching practice they will be meaningless. Which is why I am proposing a relatively simple mode of teaching. I have to quickly add that this model is just one of the many possible models. I believe that experienced teachers will be able to design more effective and more motivating modes of teaching after reading this article.

The following is the procedure of a teaching process based on games.

1. Identifying the basic rules:
1.1. What kind of basic rules seem most likely to organize the subject into an organic whole?
1.2. How can the relationship between the basic rules and the sub-rules be coordinated?

2. Organizing the content into a structured activity:
2.1. Access: What kinds of issues, scenarios, and activities demonstrate most vividly the basic rules of the secret; and then inspire students to discover the basic rule?
2.2. What kind of classical works, materials, or activities can show a variant of this basic rule or its extreme forms most clearly and forcefully?
2.3. How is the basic rule coordinated with the sub-rules in works or in actions?
2.4. What changes did the basic rules undergo historically? What did these changes mean?
2.5. Who can summarize the basic rules in their own language most accurately and most powerfully? (Students can do this cooperatively, in groups.)

3. What kind of tasks can be designed to most effectively stimulate students' creativity and imagination?
3.1 What kind of mission design can best embody the basic rules?
3.2. What kind of task design can best inspire all of the students' physical and mental power?

3.3. What kind of task design can best stimulate students to apply the basic rule creatively?
3.4. What kind of task design can best showcase the most important of the exquisite rules?
3.5. What kind of techniques can best contribute to solving the task?

4. How to conclude the topic:
4.1. Display and share the results.
4.2. Make the evaluation interactive and competitive.
4.3. Improve the students' works and publish them online.
4.4. Create a future-oriented design.

We can take the topic of "Still Life Sketch" as an example to conduct some necessary explanations of the mode, which we select from the art textbooks of a junior high school.

1. Identifying the basic rules:
1.1. What kind of basic rules seem likely to organize the subject best into an organic whole?
1.2. How can the relationship between the basic rules and other sub-rules be coordinated?

The main purpose of performance-based learning is to understand the basic rules and then apply them to solve problems. The basic rules are not single and fixed, but can be chosen from a number of rules. In general, we have to choose as the basic rule the one with the greatest influence on the action. With the topic "Still Life Sketch" not only the rules of the art will be expressed, but also the rules of changing light and of perspective. Taking into account that we portray the three-dimensional nature of objects mainly through changes in shading, this would constitute a basic rule, while perspective and the skills of artistic expression would be considered supplementary rules. In this way, our focus is on how to express the changes in light and shadow on the surface of an object by means of changing the density of the lines. On this basis we can analyze what roles the principles and techniques of expression and perspective play. For example, we can allow students to compare the differences in light and shadow from different locations, thus helping them to understand the relationship between perspective and the rule of light and shadow. Also, in order to help students understand the relationships between the skills of artistic expression and the rule of light and shadow, we can allow students to observe how the density of the lines drawn change according to the change of light on the surface of the object.

2. Organizing the content into a structured activity:

The main task of this part is to understand the changed forms of the basic rule and the development process of the basic rule by means of demonstrating specific works, products, or activities, and then to sum up the general form of the basic rule.

2.1. Access: What kind of issues, scenarios and activities most vividly demonstrate the basic rules and then inspire students to discover them?

Generally, it is easy to arouse the students' curiosity by reflecting on and questioning the familiar viewpoints of a given topic. In the topic of "Still Life Sketch," we can begin with the question, How do you draw a three-dimensional sphere? We can guide students to think of such questions as: We know the ball is round, but it is not a flat circle, it is a three-dimensional one. Since our sketch paper is a flat, two-dimensional space, how can we draw a three-dimensional ball on a two-dimensional paper? What can help us to make a difference between a ball and a circle on a piece of paper? In other words, if we just draw the outline of a ball on the paper, how can we distinguish a ball from a circle? At this point, we can encourage students to think about what role the light plays here. Yes, just by examining how light and shadow appear on the ball–because the light changes on the surface of the ball according to its location–we can infer that the ball is three-dimensional. Through this process of inquiry, students will discover an important basic rule: the sketch cannot be separated from the light. In other words, the drawn image is an interactive product of the light and the object. What we draw in the form of a sketch is not a purely "objective" object, but an object which is placed in a particular light. This is a very important discovery.

2.2. What kind of classical works, materials, or activities can show a variant of this basic rule or its extreme forms most clearly and forcefully?

The role of light helps students to discover the mystery of the art of sketching. In order to deepen the students' understanding of the role of light, we should also display variations of the basic rule of light and shadow in as many situations as possible. We can accomplish this through an in-kind show, and then demonstrate it through concrete works. In particular, we should guide students to analyze the visual influences on the object which are exerted by different sources of light, light coming from various directions and angles, light of differing intensity, varying levels brightness of light, and finally, the reflectivity of the object itself. When we demonstrate specific works in the classroom, we can allow students to analyze such factors as the angle of the light source, intensity of light, environmental reflection, and so on.

2.3. How is the basic rule coordinated with the sub-rules in works or in actions?

After mastering the rules around the source of light, we can guide students to analyze the relationships between changes in light, taking the perspective of the object, and the skills of drawing each other.

2.4. What changes did the basic rules undergo historically? What is the significance of these changes?

Rules are a product of history; therefore, understanding the development process of rules will contribute greatly to grasping the rules in depth. We can display original painting and Oriental painting works to students in order to help them think about how to show three-dimensional effects in drawing before the discovery of the rules of light and shadow. As we know, light had little to do with Oriental painting, and in particular with Chinese painting, so there were many conflicts of light in these paintings. We may ask students how these older Chinese painters could draw a three-dimensional ball since they did not express the sense of three-dimension in accordance with the rule of light and shadow. Can students figure out the way to make a ball appear three-dimensional? By analyzing the ancient Chinese works, students should find that it is through the variation in the thickness of the lines and in the depth of the colour that an object is made to appear three-dimensional. Then, we can discuss Leonardo da Vinci's outstanding contribution to the art of sketching. We can explore how the principles of perspective and the rules of light and shadow powerfully promoted the development of the arts during the Renaissance.

2.5. Who can summarize the basic rules in their own language most accurately and most powerfully? (Students can do it by cooperative learning in groups.)

We can ask students to summarize the basic rules of sketching in groups; after each group has submitted their own conclusions, it will be useful for them to comment and debate each other's findings and finally to reach a consensus. Of course, different positions on some of the rules can still be retained.

3. What kind of tasks can be designed to stimulate students' creativity and imagination best?

3.1. What kind of mission design can best embody the basic rules?

3.2. What kind of task design can best inspire all of the students' physical and mental power?

3.3. What kind of task design can best stimulate students to apply the basic rule creatively?
3.4. What kind of task design can best showcase the most important aspects of the exquisite rules?
3.5. What kind of techniques can best contribute to solving the task?

If I were an art teacher, I should not hurry the students to draw their sketch; instead, I would ask them to do an exercise with "imaginary light" before I would ask them to do anything else. One way to do this is to ask students to close their eyes and imagine the following: We are going to place some geometric plaster models on the desktop. The light is assumed to be coming from the top right. At first we will place a cube on the desktop. Now we will ask students to imagine what occurs on the surface of the cube, and then let them draw a simple schematic to record their findings as quickly as possible. Next, we place a plaster sphere to the left of and behind the cube, so that the cube casts his shadow upon the sphere. Next, we will ask students to imagine how the light changes on the surface of cube and sphere, and then ask them to sketch the relationships between the two objects. Now, the teacher may ask: is the shadow line that the cube's edge casts on the surface of the sphere straight or curved? Also, we can ask students to think about whether the relationship between brightness and shade on the cube has changed. Finally, students can exchange their schematics with each other, and then discuss whose work reflects the relationships most accurately and truthfully. Following this, we can demonstrate the whole process in-kind, so students can carefully observe and compare their works with the actual situation. Teachers can ask students to find out the differences, even to analyze the reasons.

Then, ask students to close their eyes and imagine again. However, this time we will exchange the locations of the cube and sphere, with the same light source, and then ask students to repeat the process. In addition, we can consider how to challenge students' imaginations and abilities by continuously adjusting the directions, brightness, colors, as well as the numbers of the light source.

On the basis of accurately understanding the rules of light and shadow, we can explore the important role the sketch skills play in expressing the three-dimensional sense and the texture of an object. We should encourage students to try to apply a variety of styles of lines to portray the same object, and then teach them some specific painting techniques. However, it must be stressed that sketching skills do not work in isolation, and should be associated with the principles of perspective and the rules of light and shadow. For example, the edge line of object near the direction of disappearance from perspective is rather ambiguous and vice versa.

Similarly, the edge line of an object is rather clear under a powerful light, while it is rather gentle under a weak light. An object seems hard and rough under a glare, while it seems soft and delicate under a dim light. We can express the corresponding feelings of light through performing and displaying the sketching skills, and so on.

Finally, we can layout the task for students to sketch "the plaster models." The light settings and placements of plaster models will be sophisticated enough to challenge students' creativity.

4. How to conclude the topic
4.1. Display and share the results.
4.2. Make the evaluation interactive and competitive.
4.3. Improving works and publish them virtual online.
4.4. Create future-oriented design.

The last part of the model is most familiar to teachers. It aims to deepen recognition and understanding of the rules mainly through their positive interaction, and at the same time to enjoy and share a wide range of artistic techniques of expression. This part of the model can effectively stimulate in students a sense of achievement and a sense of honour, and then provide a broad frame of reference for learning. In a sense, it plays the role of an art museum. We can even carry out some simulation "auction" activities to further enhance the learning atmosphere. It is worth noting that the final step–future-oriented designing–is a unique form of conclusion that belongs to this model. In order to conclude this topic, we can allow students to think about issues such as the following:

We have now figured out the relationships between the rule of light and shadow, the principle of perspective and drawing skills. If we take coloured objects such as some kinds of bottles, cans, fruits, and flowers instead of the white plaster model, how can we express the sense and texture of their three-dimensionality? What impact would replacing the white light with coloured lights have on sketching? These issues will lead students to explore in further depth the relationships between the light and sketching.

Conclusion

The structure of games can tell us much about what attracts and engages children's minds. It is clear that some central features of games are also of value in structuring lessons and units of study in schools, if we hope to bring out their inherent attractiveness and engage students with them. This is no mystery and may be said to be quite obvious at one level. We are not setting out simply to entertain students in the ways that some games do, even though some games have much more serious purposes as well, but we are drawing on some insights into the way games work to draw out the inherent engaging qualities of the content of the curriculum. Too frequently educationalists have focused too much on the logical form of the content itself and have failed to recognize how other principles that are truer to students modes of psychological engagement are ignored. I have tried to show how attending to some of the structural components of games can transform how we might be able to teach more effectively.

Imagination and Teacher Formation: The Experience at the Museum of Childhood

Gladir da Silva Cabral, Celdon Fritzen, and Maria Isabel Leite

Concerned with the qualification of educative practices, considering museums as important partners in the pedagogic task of school teachers, and understanding that education cannot occur separated from culture, the Museum of Childhood has proposed a series of actions centred on imagination. The Museum, created by a Postgraduate Program in Education at a Brazilian university, intends to be a place of education and research with focus on artistic, scientific, and cultural production for, about, and by children. In the activities proposed to schools, the relevance of imagination in the formative process can be observed in two different gambits: in the workshops offered to children (with games, painting, sculpture, story-telling, films, etc.) and in teacher formation (with emphasis on the importance of imagination and aesthetic experience in children's relation with the museal objects). In addition, this museum intends to be an inclusive place and wants to find alternative strategies of art fruition especially directed to individuals with visual deficiencies. Stimulating different senses and the imagination, these strategies (relief, texture and three-dimensional images, hands-on displays, sound experiences) will be used to help individuals to make sense of the objects and images exhibited. Also, for the sake of inclusion, the height at which objects and images are placed is controlled for physically disadvantaged viewers and small children. The Museum of Childhood thus becomes an ally to teachers, schools, and municipalities in achieving their educational goals.

Introduction

The Museum of Childhood, created by the Graduate Program on Education at the Universidade do Extremo Sul Catarinense (UNESC), located in Criciúma, in the state of Santa Catarina in the south of Brazil, intends to be a space of education and research that focuses on the scientific, artistic, and cultural production for, about, and by children. Since its creation in 2005, the Museum of Childhood has worked towards establishing closer contact with its public through different ways: workshops, series of debates, exhibitions, etc. Concerned with introducing to educational practice the understanding that museums can become important partners of teachers in schools so that education does not work in isolation from culture, the Museum of Childhood has been proposing to this public a series of specific actions centred on imagination. But why imagination?

> According to the sociologist Niklas Luhmann, today imagination occupies a place that once belonged to religion: the position from which we perceive that "we do not understand what we do not understand," that is, a place of uncertainty, of the arbitrary, after all "a potential place for liberty." (Girardello 2003, p. 1)

This means having the freedom to create, to produce meanings. Museums and formal spaces of education, such as schools, should be seen as privileged places of creation and production of meaning, therefore of imagination.

After the Irish philosopher Richard Kearney,[1] Girardello (2003) speaks of the metaphors that describe the role of imagination in different times. Imagination, understood as a reflection of reality, would be like a *mirror*, "in which the mental image and its artistic representations are considered mere copies of the original divine creation" (p. 2). If imagination is considered a possibility of production of the real, it would be compared to a *light bulb*, in the sense that "the power of forming images does not result only from what the physical senses perceive, but also from invention and imagination. Furthermore, imagination can be taken as a *labyrinth of mirrors*, "in the sense of an illusion that must be broken" (p. 3). Girardello believes that what Kearney is saying is that nowadays even the idea of a *labyrinth of mirrors* is insufficient to accommodate the intricate social relations involved and wrapped up in the webs of imagination. He is in favour of the search for a "narrative identity, by which human beings tell and retell their own story"; thus, the narrative of some individuals who speak about themselves to others is able to lead them beyond the labyrinth.

Therefore, the relation between narrative and imagination that Girardello proposes implies the understanding that narrative should be "considered an intermediate instance between imagination and culture" (p. 4), that is, as we narrate we are "also attributing meaning to the facts of culture, in a continuous strategy of reading and cultural production. The oral narrative seems to be a valuable material for the reflection about the imaginative life of subjects of reception" (p. 5). Thus, the author says, the word "is a road to the imaginary meeting between individuals." Interaction among people usually requires the sharing of narratives; and between the images of those who tell and those who listen to stories "some common-sense meaning vibrates, although certainly limited" (p. 5).

We also understand museums as privileged spaces of narratives, replete with memories and subjectivity–therefore special places of imagination. As a place of narratives, imagination, and memory, the greatest treasure of a museum is its collection and forms of access, and the issue of accessibility has become very important in the museal field. Therefore, giving visibility to the physical collection of the Museum of Childhood has become its first challenge to ensure that its different social roles are successfully fulfilled. Lacking adequate space, the Museum's visibility has been limited because its expositions are temporary, partial, and fragmented. In order to transform a limitation (that is, the lack of space) into an advantage, the team of the Museum developed, in partnership with the visiting professor Dr. Julio Romero Rodriguez, of the Universidad Complutense de Madrid, a concept called "museum without walls." Dr. Rodriguez sees difficulties (such as the lack of space, in our case) as opportunities for development as well:

> If we see them [the difficulties] as restrictive for the creative process, we should recognize them as guiders as well, since it is from inside limitations and through them that we find alternatives to continue, widen and even find new directions to our work. In fact, only by admitting and respecting the determinants of the material with which we work as essential, can our spirit create wings and search for the unknown. (Ostrower *in* Oliveira 2008, p. 87)

Thus, turning the lack of space in the Museum of Childhood into an advantage and exploiting its great communication potential, we used insulating tapes to draw lines and colours as spatial markers for a new museal proposal. This concept is based on aesthetic references found in different artistic languages–such as the scenery from the films *Dogville* and *Manderlay*, directed by Lars von Trier, from Denmark, the works of artists like Ana Mendieta (1948-1985) from Cuba, Alberto Greco (1931-

1965), from Argentina, Susy Gómez (1965), from Spain; and the photographs of Florentine Diaz, also from Spain (1954). We also employed as reference resources commonly used for marking spaces in parking lots or lines in bank offices, as well as elements from childhood culture, such as toys and labyrinths in playgrounds. This profusion of lines and colors limits and simultaneously opens the empty spaces, transforming them into an entirely accessible Museum for the whole day.

Based on this proposal, the Museum of Childhood started to see itself, in its physical dimension, as a space without definite borders: flexible, porous; merged into the university campus; a place permeated by interchanges, receptive, open; a locus of discoveries and awakening of the senses of all who pass by bringing their cultural, social, and historical marks that gives meaning to what is seen, felt, and heard in the Museum. This is a daring proposal, which "works in the limits of the body, in the limits of physicality. Just a little more and it does not exist" (Farias in Oliveira 2008, p. 55).[2] In the process of making strange the dialectics of quotidian life, we came across another strong aesthetic reference for the concept of the proposed museum: some modern and contemporary sculptures and installations. According to Oliveira (2008, p. 58), "the concept of sculpture has been so much tested and expanded that it has fallen apart." Besides, "among its fragments different modalities emerged as well as the concept of installation." This is the concept of installation that the Museum of Childhood borrows in order to think its new proposal into physicality: "it is not a piece that we see from the outside, like a traditional sculpture. The installation is a sculpture in which we enter, and it involves the various senses: the sense of smell, vision, and touch. It is a sensation of synesthesia," according to Oliveira (Oliveira 2008, p. 8).

Almeida sometimes treats sculptures as "characters that talk with the visitor and sometimes as objects that create ambience to a scenery" (Oliveira 2008, p. 112). The author argues against the idea of sculptures as objects destined only to contemplation and suggests that we "open space for the ludic contact with sculptures, an invitation to the poetic interpretation and to the use of the body" (p. 112). The concept of ludic sculpture draws the artistic object (a sculpture) near to the ludic object (a toy)–both loaded with symbolism, awakeners of subjective images, and facilitators of aesthetic, delicate, and imaginative experiences. According to the concept formulated by Oliveira (2008, p. 127),[3] sculptures can be considered "sensory, time and spatial, corporeal, imaginative adventure."

If we consider art and its plurality of significance, contemporary art specifically, is based on a proposal that disturbs the spectator, wakes him from the torpor of routine, from the fortuitous circumstance of just passing by, and invites him to take a position. This same posture can be associated with education, to the process of learning and producing knowledge–a movement that always starts from the point of discomfort in the direction of the new. We can say, then, that art places the spectator–and education places the apprentice–in a "state of suspension." Thus, paraphrasing Oliveira in her reflections about the sculpture, we propose an almost immaterial museum, one that can be confounded with the space itself, something that can be understood "not necessarily as an object, but as an attitude, an action, [...] as an action of formalization of the human being, who works, operates in the world, in the matter" (Serra in Oliveira 2008, p. 52)[4]–a special area of production of meaning and imagination of spaces. The concept of museum without frontiers has become the foundation for the 2008 exhibitions: *Childhood and School Cultures* and *Childhood in the Iberian-America*. Both expositions were structured in an open way: they were scattered in different passageways throughout the UNESC campus, inviting and receiving users and visitants from various blocks.

In the first exhibition, *Childhood and School Cultures*, a multiplicity of forms of being, representing childhood and school cultures were exhibited: photographs (old and new); objects; fragments of theoretical texts; poetry; children's stories; literature for adults; images of works of art; cartoons; illustrations; texts and drawings made by children; interviews etc. The objects were displayed as part of the museum collection and were used as support for children's artistic expressions; in addition they were used as scenery and ambience for the objects, texts, and images, becoming at the same time ends and means of the exposition. "They are not volumes that, in the traditional way of sculptures made of matter and opaqueness, open clearings in the emptiness of space. It is as if the matter from which they are made [how the samples are organized] wanted to be mingled with the air."[5]

The theme proposed by the exposition was, on its own, extremely inviting to students and teachers, who found materials there for critical discussion about their own reality. They were also the most important contributors of material for the exhibition: many schools offered children's works, desks, tables, seats, that is, "familiar objects [...] were now presented in a new configuration, breaking with the regular composition, situation and habitual dimension. They are new three-dimensional 'aesthetic' objects [...]" (Oliveira 2008, p. 64). This way the school community was dislocated from the perspective of an external visitor to the position of co-author of the exposition. In this way, the Museum of Childhood offers to the public many opportunities for direct participation and encourages them to record and report their memories of school, to define a position in pedagogical controversies, or even to solve logical, mathematical challenges.

The other exposition developed by the Museum of Childhood was about children in the Iberian-American culture, a very opportune theme because 2008 is celebrated in Brazil as the Iberian year of museums. "The theme chosen for the Iberian Year of Museums is a challenge for the debate and understanding of the important role museums play in defense and promotion of identities, memory and the cultural patrimony," affirms the Minister of Culture in Brazil, Gilberto Gil Moreira[6]. The objective of the exposition was to think critically about the production for, about, and by children in the Iberian-American countries. The exposition made available to the visitor, poems, paintings, toys, books for children and adults, postcards, and a variety of diverse objects as well as images of children making art. Bringing to the surface different views about childhood is a way of affirming that there is not a unique and standardized childhood, but rather a multiplicity of forms a child can take in different times and spaces.

These two exhibitions provoked a dialogue between many "selves" and many "others"; between routine and art; popular and scholarly art; two- and three-dimensionality; between seeing, listening to, and touching... using imagination as a main thread of meaning production. Although we understand that the mere observation of the public implies a position of active contemplator who interacts with what is seen vis-à-vis their previous repertoire, and, thus, establishes a dialogue with the significance of the texts, objects, and exposed images, these two exhibitions also intended–in accordance with their physical museological configuration–to give to the visitors more freedom to participate as authors of the production of meaning. Another strategy used to amplify the communication with the public and open more ways of access was making available, through the Web, texts and bibliography about subjects proposed in the expositions. For this task, we welcomed many suggestions of bibliography as well as authorial texts sent by different collaborators which are available in our website.

A museum, in order to fulfill its role, should obviously have a public. But how can we attract the public to the Museum of Childhood, if that public is not yet accustomed to visiting museums on a regular basis, considering that the number of visitors in Brazil's museums these days is fairly low? The challenge of forming a museum-going public and offering them a visual education are, then, inseparable parts of the educational mission of this Museum. Preparing the exhibition and expecting a positive reaction from the public is not enough. The educational mission of the

Museum includes the intention of transforming momentary uneasiness into assimilated reality, in reiteration, in frequency, in production of meanings through the development of imaginative processes and improvement of the gaze. In this sense, the educational institutions (schools and universities), with their teachers and groups of students, are the great focus of attention, since they are the most important locus of education. The Museum of Childhood builds its politics of public education with this prerogative.

The Museum is structured to receive and encourage the visits of adults, particularly pre-service teachers, as well as groups of children. In both groups, the relevance of imagination in the formative process can be observed in the workshops offered to children (with games, painting activities, sculpture, story-telling, films, etc). In one of its educational activities, the Museum of Childhood is visited by school children who are helped by monitors attentive to their reactions and commentaries on the collection exhibited, always with great care lest they influence their reading, since our intention is only to provoke the dialogue between the children and the objects exposed. As part of this dialogical attitude, the Museum offers workshops aimed at, through the aesthetic elaboration, offering children the opportunity of exercising their prerogatives as producers of culture.

During the children's visits, the Museum offers activities like clay modeling, story-telling, games, sculptures, painting with natural ink, building toys from recycled material, etc. Besides the contact with aesthetic experiences, the main objective of these workshops was to make available opportunities for the exercise of imagination as a form of elaboration and appropriation of knowledge. These activities were based in the concept that imagination is one of the two instruments by which the children deal with the world, and it is imagination that re-elaborates children's experiences with the world (Sarmento 2005).

The activities proposed to teachers were planned to overcome a concept of continuing education that characterizes it as the simple transmission of information. Faced with the low qualification of graduate teachers, the Brazilian government offers training programs on educational theories and practices, but usually these programs are created without prior discussion with teachers about their experience (Kramer, 2001; Zilberman, 1988). By contrast, our intention was to build with the teachers an opportunity for reflection based on the themes proposed in the exhibitions, and on the debates and activities promoted by the Museum of Childhood. This is possible because we understand the museum to be an educational space in which the contact with aesthetic and cultural objects makes a dialogue with the experience, memory, and imagination of the spectators possible. This opportunity allows us to think of "continuing education less as a training or qualification process and more as a dynamic historical movement, as a cultural formation, which is essential if we wish that teachers become autonomous individuals in history" (Kramer, 2001, p. 65).

This is why in the continuing education program prepared for the exposition called *Literature and Enchantment* (which we offered in 2007) we stressed the importance of imagination and aesthetic experience in the relationship that children established with the objects. During the scheduled visits, we asked the teachers to encourage the children's dialogue with the collection. We also wanted to open a discussion about the conception of childhood, its representation in and reception of literature, the ways by which the virtual museums establish their relation with the infant public, and the uses of literature in the school. Particularly in the continuing education program entitled *Learning in Museums*, we were interested in reflecting with the teachers about how, when reading is not strictly subordinate to pedagogical demands, reading literature can become an important moment of aesthetic fruition, and how the intense exercise of imagination set in motion by the children in contact with narratives and poems produces knowledge of the world. The exhibition of a book cover, a title, and illustrations, as a warm up exercise, as a form of provocation to children's curiosity before the effective reading of the text, helps them to imagine and create new narratives connected with the experience they have in the world. Besides recognizing the importance of literary reading for children, we saw how important it was for teachers as they started to better understand themselves through literature because of the childhood memories activated during those reading moments.

> The role of memory, of narratives and of life story is fundamental as education politics, and shall not be denied during the educational process and in the teachers' stories, schools and projects. Learning with experience, revising the journey through reading and writing, rereading what was once written by each–not only what we learned to write and read–can have an important formative dimension. (Kramer 2001, pp. 186-7)

Connected to the educational function that the Museum of Childhood tried to develop in its teachers' education activities, we must mention the visits of undergraduate groups of students, including those from other universities, and groups of graduate students in the Post-Graduation Program on Education, as well as students of extension programs like *Art in the School*. Our monitors were oriented, on such occasions, to follow a schedule of visitation and, through dialogues, to challenge the visitors to imagine, remember, and reflect upon the elements that constitute each thematic exposition that the Museum offers. The objective is always to develop a formative relationship with the objects in the Museum by widening the cultural experience that books, pictures, drawings, toys, videos, among other objects linked to childhood, can provide when considered not for the sake of their utility, but from the perspective of their aesthetic and cultural meaning.

While promoting discussion about childhood, museums, and the aesthetic experience, we want to highlight another event that has been promoted since 2006 in Florianópolis, capital of the state of Santa Catarina, in partnership with the Art Education Sector of the Museu de Arte de Santa Catarina (NAE/MASC) and the Department of Education at the Universidade Federal de Santa Catarina (CED/UFSC): the *Cycle of Debates on Museum, Education and Culture*, which is in its third year. During monthly meetings researchers from all parts of Brazil committed to the themes presented above are invited to give free lectures to the general public.

In addition, the Museum of Childhood, understands the importance of cinema as an aesthetic experience that helps to represent the historical and social diversity of childhood, and it promotes films exhibited on campus that are open to the public in general. The program is always organized around a theme suggested by contemporary debates. For example, for the Iberian Year of Museums in 2008, we developed a list of films produced in Iberian-American countries in which childhood was treated as a theme. We chose films that met the criteria of having a certain aesthetic quality and which were not available for the public commercially, a very important fact in a city of 180 thousand inhabitants such as Criciúma.

As well, the Museum intends to be inclusive for all, following United Nations guidelines, which, since 1980, have underlined the importance that individuals with special needs also have "the same opportunities that other citizens have of enjoying the economic and social dynamics and participating in cultural activities in equal conditions" (Castellan & Carlsson 2008, p. 1). Therefore, the Museum of Childhood looks for alternative strategies especially addressed to this public.

> It was during the 16th century that governments started to think about the education of students with special needs, and at that time the solution was the segregation and the confinement of so called different people in asylums and mental hospitals. [...] During the 19th century the first classes in regular schools were opened to students considered "difficult." (Mendes in Kirst & Hisses 2008, pp. 2-3)

In 1996 the Brazilian government proclaimed Law n. 9.394–Law of Directives and Bases of the National Education (LDB), which requires the inclusion of children with special needs in classrooms in regular education. As a result, bringing all the students to visit museums is part of the most recent pedagogical indicatives that suggest the recognition of museums as non-formal spaces of education that can facilitate a different form of knowledge production. This, together with the Museums National Politics[7] that, since 2004, is being implemented in Brazil in order to transform the Brazilian museums into more accessible places to everyone, created the necessity of thinking, researching, creating specific strategies that make the process of appropriation and reception of this new contingent of visitors easier .

Some Brazilian museums have accepted this challenge, like the Museum of the Contemporary Art of the Universidade de São Paulo (MAC-USP), and the Pinacoteca do Estado de São Paulo, both in São Paulo, the richest and most populous state in Brazil, which houses the greatest number of museums in the country. Following their example, other initiatives have gradually been developed. According to Bornelli and Silva (2008), we still have "the necessity of production of pedagogical objects in order to amplify the possibilities of inclusion in regular schools" (p. 4). The museums can and should be seen as allies in this process. In Santa Catarina, the Museum of Art of Santa Catarina (MASC), located in Florianópolis, is implementing projects of inclusion, particularly to people with visual deficiency, in partnership with the Universidade do Estado de Santa Catarina (UDESC). In a similar vein, the Museum of Childhood seeks to create some alternative strategies that can help teachers in their educational mission. To better attend to wheelchair users, the Museum proposes that paintings in the exhibitions should be placed in a lower position than what is usual in museums. An example of this is the reproductions of works of art on childhood exhibited at the University Library during the exposition entitled *Childhood in the Iberian-America*. Another strategy used in this exposition was to search for alternative spaces, ones less commonly used to house museum projects such as the nucleus regarding the iconographic map that presents images of artwork portraying childhood in the different countries of the Iberian-America. It was placed inside a large map drawn on the ground of the hall of Block XXI-C in the campus.

The other major group of people to whom expositions have traditionally been less accommodating other than people in wheelchairs, is the visually impaired. With the exception of interactive expositions, museums and exhibitions appeal primarily to the sense of vision. "Sacks indicated clearly that the blind individual only perceives as reality a whole objects that fit in his hands, this is, objects that he can feel at one time, with one touch" (Duarte in Bornelli & Silva 2008, p. 3). Thus the Museum of Childhood initiated, timidly, the creation of museal alternatives in which, through the different senses, in dialogue with imagination, the individuals can give significance to objects and exhibited images. Another strategy is the use of labels in Braille. The museum organizes expositive nuclei with touchable and interactive pieces–as seen in the two expositions cited–as well as "tactile boxes"–as in the exposition called *Childhood and School Cultures,* which contained copies of some of the displayed objects. In the same exposition, two photographs of two three-dimensional objects–tactile matrices–were specially created.

> The blind visitor requires the greatest number of adaptations in an exposition, but, on the other hand, he also evinces the possibilities and innovations new forms of apprehension and fruition of the object. Thus, the up-to-date art museum, besides providing for inclusion, must be conscious of the contribution brought by visitors with special needs, to the extent that it challenges the comfort of the museum professional and makes him think about his role in society. (Tojal in Kirst & Silva 2008, p. 7)

Inasmuch as the Museum is seen as an installation–an open work–new pathways are revealed and the historically established perception of art as an untouchable, eternal, sacred work is broken. These notions were established and reinforced during the Renaissance and based on the concepts of masterpiece, work of art, and artistic genius and structured at the moment when the artist became aware of his creative power.[8] Art, once understood as the expression of and for an elite and separated from other aspects of life, is now re-signified and appropriated by everyone. The same has historically occurred with education, originally offered for a few privileged people and now democratized and accessible to everyone. In this sense, the actions of the Museum of Childhood here reported, show diverse proposals for the education of children and adults, in addition to the creation of in-relief, textured and three-dimensional images, hands-on objects, sound experiences, and others which aim to facilitate and qualify the processes of appropriation of knowledge by the different audiences. These activities consolidate the Museum of Childhood as an ally of teachers, schools, and municipalities for achieving their educational goals: to offer qualifying, imaginative, and creative education. Paraphrasing Girardello (2003): we can express our wish that the Museum of Childhood and the schools work together to offer re-imagined activities and bloom as spaces open for critical transformation.

Endnotes

[1] Richard Kearney (1988). *The Wake of Imagination: toward a postmodern culture.* University of Minnesota Press.

[2] This commentary was made in relation to the sculptures by Waltércio Caldas.

[3] Based on the book *Escultura Aventura*, by Kátia Canton.

[4] He is talking about the concept of sculpture.

[5] Farias *apud* Oliveira 2008, p. 31.

[6] In: http://www.cultura.gov.br/site/?p=10290.

[7] "In Brazil, the Federal Government, through the Ministry of Culture (MinC) and through the Department of Museums and Cultural Centers (DEMU/IPHAN), established a bridge, a dialogue with entities and professionals involved with the museal sector in order to discuss and institute a proposal of Museum National Politics: the creation of the Brazilian System of Museums, an articulation and development net that incorporates state and municipal museums; the organization of formation workshops throughout the national territory, in the several areas encompassed by the museum; and the installation of a museum observatory. This process started in 2003, with a document that indicates the conceptual basis for a Museum National Politics, Museologic Formation and Capacitation Program, and the Museologic Institution Record." (Reddig 2007, p. 66).

[8] Michelangelo was the first artist to be conscious of that.

Bibliography

Bornelli, M. C., & Silva, M. C. da R. F. da. (2008). Uma experiência de ensino de arte: a trajetória de uma estudante cega. In *Anais do IV Seminário Educação, Imaginação e as Linguagens Artístico-Culturais.* Criciúma (SC): UNESC. Available at: www.gedest.unesc.net. Accessed in 14 June 2008.

Castellen, C. M., & Carlsson, M. L. (2008). Um toque de percepção: o Museu de Arte de Santa Catarina para além da visualidade. In Leite, M. I., & Ostetto, L. E. *Educação, pesquisa e arte: a formação cultural na contramão do instituído.* Santa Catarina, 2008. [mimeo]

Girardello, G. (2003). A imaginação no contexto da recepção. In *Anais do XII Encontro da Associação Nacional dos Programas de Pós-graduação em Comunicação–Compós.* Recife, 2003. [mimeo]

Kirst, A. C., & Silva, M. C. da R. F. da. (2008). Museu de arte: possibilidades de inclusão da pessoa cega. In *Anais do IV Seminário Educação, Imaginação e as Linguagens Artístico-Culturais.* Criciúma (SC): UNESC. Available at: www.gedest.unesc.net. Accessed in 15 July 2008.

Kramer, S. (2001). *Alfabetização, leitura e escrita: formação de professores em curso.* São Paulo: Ática.

Oliveira, A. M. R. de. (2008). *Escultura e imaginação infantil: um mar de historias sem fim.* Doctoral Theses. Florianópolis (SC): UFSC/PPGE.

Sarmento, M. J. (2005). Crianças: educação, cultura e cidadania activa. *Perspectiva.* Florianópolis: Editora da UFSC), 23 (1), 17-40.

Reddig, A. B. (2007). *A infância representada nos espaços museais de Santa Catarina: reflexões sobre educação, identidade cultural, museus, arte e infância.* Master's Dissertation. Criciúma (SC): UNESC/PPGE.

Zilberman, R. (1988). *A leitura e o ensino da literatura.* São Paulo: Contexto.

CONTRIBUTORS

Gadi Alexander earned his BA and MA at the Hebrew University in Jerusalem. He completed his PhD at UCLA with John Goodlad in 1976 as a Fulbright exchange student. He has been a member of the department of education at Ben Gurion University in Beer Sheva, Israel, since that time, and currently serves as head of the graduate program in curriculum and instruction. He has co-headed several intervention projects in schools and published articles and chapters in books about educational technology and creative thinking.

Gladir da Silva Cabral is a Professor and researcher at Universidade do Extremo Sul Catarinense (UNESC) and member of the Museum of Childhood (Criciúma, Brazil). He is also the president of the Editorial Board at UNESC. His research interests focus on cultural identity, language, literature, and education.

Kieran Egan is a Professor in the Faculty of Education at Simon Fraser University. He is currently Director of the IERG. His interests include trying to sketch a somewhat new educational scheme based in part on Vygotskian ideas, and also working out ways to help students and teachers find the regular subjects of the curriculum more imaginatively engaging. He graduated from London University with a B.A. in History, and from Cornell University with a Ph.D. in Education.

Mark Fettes is an Assistant Professor in the Faculty of Education at Simon Fraser University and Executive Director of the Esperantic Studies Foundation. His research focuses on how educational systems engage with different ways of knowing and being, and with the integration of such systems in wider cultural patterns. He holds a Ph.D. in Theory and Policy Studies in Education from OISE, University of Toronto, a M.Sc. in Biochemistry from the University of British Columbia, and a M.A. in Natural Sciences, from the University of Cambridge.

Celdon Fritzen is Professor and researcher at Universidade Federal de Santa Catarina (UFSC), collaborate professor at UNESC, and coordinator of the Museum of Childhood. His research interests focus on literature, literacy, literary theory, and education.

Lisa Gjedde is an Associate Professor in ICT, Media and Learning, at the Department for Curriculum Research, at the Danish University of Education. Her research interests focus on exploring and developing the creative and inclusive learning potentials in ICT and Media based learning environments. She is also involved in research and development of digital storytelling and innovative learning strategies.

Michael Herriman is Professor of English Language in the Faculty of Foreign Languages at Nagoya University of Commerce and Business. Previously he was director of the English language centre and coordinator of graduate programs in Applied Linguistics at the University of Western Australia. He has held visiting professorships at universities in England, Canada, Russia, Germany, and Holland, and conducted research in Thailand and China. His main research has been in language acquisition, language testing, language policies, and academic writing by university students. He completed his PhD at Cornell University.

Maria Isabel Leite is a collaborate professor at UNESC, and member of the Museum of Childhood. Her research interests focus on childhood, children's culture, museum, and education. She has published many books in Portuguese on these subjects.

Krystina Madej is an Adjunct Professor at the School of Interactive Arts and Technology, Simon Fraser University. She was recently a Postdoctoral Fellow with IERG. Her research is concerned with how narrative is mediated by different technologies and creates meaning for us, in particular in the areas of digital narrative and video games. She holds a BFA from Concordia University, a MAPW from Kennesaw State University, and a PhD in Digital Narrative from Simon Fraser University.

Concettina Manna completed her degrees in Pedagogy and in Italian Literature at the University of Naples. She became a Primary School teacher in 1999. She is currently a PhD student in Methodology of Educational Research at University of Salerno. Her research focuses on narrative knowing and, in particular, on the role of autobiographical practice and of "life history" in learning and in teaching. She is particularly interested to know the philosophical and hermeneutic structure of this practice.

Rod McKellar is a high-school classroom teacher (29 years) and recent PhD graduate from Simon Fraser University. He worked with the Imaginative Education Research Group's LUCID project and is currently developing an overview of district literacy practices among the three participating communities to contrast them with the project's conception of "romantic understanding" as a vital dimension in the development of imaginatively fluent literacy.

Sean McLaughlin has been teaching in the Abbotsford School District for seven years. Currently, he teaches at the middle school level in the social studies/humanities department, and is a team leader for literacy in the school. He is also a graduate student at Simon Fraser University, specializing in Imaginative Education with an emphasis in Gendered Studies.

Giuliano Minichiello is a Professor of Pedagogy at the University of Salerno and Director of the Department of Education's Science. Since 1992 he has taught Experimental Pedagogy and the Methodology of Educational Research, and since 2001, Didactics, at the University Institute "Suor Orsola Benincasa." He is coordinator at the Department of Educational Science for research on "Educational aspects of e-learning," "Deep learning," and "Meaningful variables in the learning process: motivation and didactics as mediators."

Kiyotaka Miyazaki is Professor of Cognitive Psychology in the Faculty of Human Sciences, Waseda University. He investigates teaching-learning process from the standpoint of a cultural-historical view on cognition. His particular interest is art and drama education in elementary schools and kindergarten, and he focuses on how children and adults produce artworks collaboratively.

Kanwal Neel is a Faculty Associate at Simon Fraser University working with pre-service teachers on secondment from the Richmond School District. He is an author, software developer, textbook reviewer, and host of the award winning television series *Math Shop*. Past president of BC Association of Mathematics Teachers, he has been a recipient of numerous awards including the PM's Award for teaching excellence in Science, Technology, and Mathematics.

Stefan Popenici is Learning and Teaching Designer at Manukau Institute of Technology, New Zealand. He has been employed in educational institutions in the European Union, Philippines, Canada, was a visiting research professor at The Catholic University of America, and worked as advisor to the Minister of Education and Research in Romania on educational policies and research. He holds a PhD in Education Sciences from Bucharest University and was recently a Postdoctoral Fellow at the Faculty of Education at Simon Fraser University

Dr. Qing-yu Pan received his BA, MA, and PhD in Pedagogy at Shandong Normal University, Jinan, Shandong Province, PR China. He is now a Professor in the College of Liberal Arts at Shandong Normal University. His interests include Philosophy, Psychology, and Educational Theory. He is interested also in Imaginative Education and Chinese Language Education. He currently holds research grants from the Chinese Ministry of Education.

Yakir Shoshani completed his BSc and MSc in theoretical physics at the Hebrew University, and his PhD in theoretical nuclear physics at Tel Aviv University in 1975. Since then he has been a faculty member of several universities and colleges in Israel and abroad. He has been the vice president and head of the research department at the Shenkar College of Engineering and Design in Israel in which he is a faculty member today. His research interests include Sound and Vibrations, a priori theory, and lately–the essence and origins of creativity.

Colin Sommerville has a M.A. from Simon Fraser University in Sociocultural Theory. He has a strong interest in Vygotskian educational psychology and its application in fostering authentic learning in the classroom. He is currently focusing on Developmental Instruction as a tool for guiding effective curriculum and instruction at various levels at the secondary school level.

Tim Waddington is a practicing classroom teacher in the public system, specializing in History and the Humanities. He is also a PhD candidate in the Philosophy of Education at SFU and has spent two years developing curriculum for IERG in connection with their Masters of Education Program. His philosophic interests include Nietzschean studies, existentialism, and hermeneutics.